Evesham Inns and Signs

Collected Articles
of T.J.S. Baylis

Copyright

Acknowledgements

I must, in the first instance, thank the *Evesham Journal* and its editor for granting permission to re-publish these articles. After the original closing article (15th March 1957), the *Journal* editor commented:

> Mr Baylis's work has informed and entertained those who know the Evesham inns. Not least important, however, it has enriched the *Journal* files, which remain the chief source of local information and which are open, with the Editor's approval, by appointment for use by *bona fide* students.

The *Journal* remains the chief source of local information on Evesham and the Vale. The article also noted that:

> Mr Baylis has made considerable use of the unpublished work of the late E.A.B. Barnard, whose notebooks, which were bequeathed to the town, are kept at the Evesham Public Library, and are also available to students with the approval of the Public Librarian.

In my own turn I would like to thank Evesham Public Library for their help, and to recommend their excellent local collection (including the Barnard collection). I would like to thank James Mason for proof-reading the original manuscript, and David Snowden and Gordon Alcock for their help and support.

Publisher

Vale of Evesham Historical Society
The Almonry Heritage Centre
Abbey Gate
Evesham
Worcestershire
WR11 4BG
United Kingdom
www.vehs.org.uk

December 2008
ISBN 978-0-9558487-2-8

Introduction by the Mayor

Having been in the pub game for some 30 years I was absolutely thrilled to be asked to write an intro into what is a fascinating subject.

I first encountered T.J.S. Baylis whilst manager of the Bear in Port Street. His knowledge of pub signs and their history was very profound. This was in 1985 and the pub was undergoing a facelift. I thought that a pub sign would make it even more prominent. We trawled through many books but found nothing that would be suitable. When I took over at the Angel Vaults the pub sign was very dirty and virtually unrecognisable. Many times I have been asked "Why George and the Dragon on your pub sign?" Of course it is not George but the Archangel Michael.

Pub signs have been in use for many hundreds of years starting with probably the first sign being a sheaf of barley suspended on a stake, and called 'The Ale Stake', through to the likes of the 'Slug and Lettuce' and other such names. The pub sign is not only an indication of an inn but also they are frequently used as direction posts.

I am sure that you will enjoy the contents of this book and maybe think to yourselves will the 'Pig and Parrot' be around as long as the 'Red Horse'…

Enjoy

Alan Booth

Town Mayor

Foreword (by the editor)

In the 1950s T.J.S. Baylis wrote a series of articles for the *Evesham Journal* on Evesham inns and signs. I first came across an (incomplete) sets of these articles in a couple of scrapbooks in the Barnard Collection of Evesham Public Library. I found them fascinating; full of insight and local knowledge, not only about inns and signs but more generally about local characters, places, and events. It seemed a great shame that they had not previously been collected together and brought before a wider audience.

The current book does not distinguish between obsolete and present inn signs, as did the original series of articles, but instead lumps them all together. The section *Appendix A: Summary of Articles* shows the original sequence of articles, and indicates how they relate to the various sections of this book. A series of indexes and tables have been added to help readers pin down interesting details.

Tom Baylis was a native of Evesham, a former town councillor, a founder member and former chairman of the Vale of Evesham Historical Society, and one of the founder members of the Almonry Museum. During the Second World War he served in the RAF which took him to some fifteen different countries. After the war he became a teacher at Evesham County Primary School, and later became headmaster of Areley Kings, near Stourport, where he remained until retiring at the age of sixty in 1977. He wrote a number of books, including a history of Stourport and a picture postcard record of 'Old Evesham'. From 1971 he was a member of the Stourport French twinning society, and later was involved with Evesham's twinning activities, being a member of the party that travelled to America in July 1988 to seal a friendship link with Evesham Township, New Jersey, USA.

His realisation that the English inn was unique prompted him to begin special studies throughout the country, as he explained in an article (dated 17th April 1975) prompted by the possibility of the re-opening of the Crown in Bridge Street (which had closed on 18th October 1973):

> Now perhaps I should explain that after a certain age I became more interested in pints in pubs than in pictures in palaces. Next, having spent more years than I could reasonably afford in defence of the realm and in the service of the other Crown, I came home from Cairo wholly convinced that in the sizeable portion of the globe I had trotted, sailed and flown over there was nothing; nil; nought; zero – an absolute absence of anything elsewhere comparable with number 1: The British Pub, and number 2: Real British Ale. Doctor Samuel Johnson had it just about right when he remarked: 'There is no private house in which people can enjoy themselves so well as at a capital tavern.'

> He might even have put it rather more pungently if he'd had three years in the Far and Middle East to improve his palate for ale.

> Put numbers one and two together and the combination is par excellence. So I decided to try and make myself an expert on the true history and social value of English inns, or at least on Evesham inns.

Superficially at first, depending on human memories and recollections of the past, then to published local history in books and newspapers, to council minute books, and police records, to the assize papers and the resources of the county archives, then to private deeds and household records, wherever and whoever would assist my self-imposed task. Deeper and deeper I burrowed into the cobwebs of the past until I could, in cellar or dusty attic placed at my disposal by some helpful but puzzled burgess, close the portcullis to the present and join in the ebb and flow of the affairs of Evesham people long ago – my own ancestors, perhaps. Hours, days, weeks, months, years. And not a minute wasted, in my opinion.

Five years of seeking, sifting and recording passed quickly enough before I gained an opportunity through the columns of the *Evesham Journal* to share my hobby with a wider public. By this time I had 27 existing inns and 67 obsolete signs to write about, ranging from the last of the tiddleywinks; a pokey little one-roomed beer-house opened about 1870 as the American Tavern by Alfred George in Cowl Street, to the rambling mansion on Merstow Green where George Hawkins, Steward of the Leet of Evesham for the Hoby family, died in 1584 at the Sign of the Goat and sometimes called the Signe of the Beare in Evesham.

My first article was published on February 14, 1954, and was concluded on March 15, 1957, with the Vauxhall and Woolpack, the 80th in the series.

In 1977 the brewers Bass, Mitchells and Butlers awarded him a special 'licence' for free beer at the Maiden's Head (recorded in the *Journal* on 3rd March 1977) in recognition for his work in researching and writing a history of the inn. He died in February 1990, aged 73, after a long illness.

Although Tom Baylis wrote the articles some fifty years ago, I have not attempted to update them, as they provide interesting insights into the world of the 1950s as well as a detailed history of Evesham's inns. I have, however, added footnotes, indexes and tables, then rounded the book off with a brief review of those intervening fifty years.

Stan Brotherton

Bengeworth
December 2008

Contents

List of illustrations

Foreword: Evesham Inns and Signs

In a rapidly changing world, the lasting things are the thing that matter. Of this kind, in England, are her inns, which have now served the people for over a thousand years, and never better than now. It is so in many ancient towns, but notably in Evesham, where we have inns whose faces and signs, though familiar since childhood, often hide romantic pasts, possess stories more interesting than the ordinary observer can perceive, and sometimes hold keys to the character of the town itself as well as its history.

An extensive study of the inns of Evesham from the earliest times has been undertaken by Mr T.J.S. Baylis, a native of Evesham and a member of the Vale of Evesham Historical Society. He has compiled a series of articles in which he sets down the results of his research, and these have been published regularly in the *Evesham Journal*.

Early articles deal with the inns of England and Evesham in general against the background of their historical development; then the author explores the remarkable histories of particular Evesham inns in greater detail, describing many of the landlords and their customers, noting happy and sad events, remarking instances of fame and notoriety, prosperity and otherwise; there is also a catalogue of all the inns the town is known to have ever possessed, whether they exist now or not, together with all the information that the latest research has elicited.

Setting the Scene

The Last of the Four Angels

In Evesham today [1954], there are 27 licensed houses, each of which displays a name or sign. Over the centuries, more than thrice that number of inn signs have appeared at one time or another in the streets of the town. Many of these old inns and alehouses still stand, though the premises fulfil other functions and in some cases are altered beyond recognition.

Some former inns have been swept away completely in the cause of progress. The Fleece in Bridge Street was one of these, having been demolished in 1918 to make way for the present entrance to the lower Abbey Park. The aptly named Bridge Inn at the foot of Bridge Street and the Angel in Waterside disappeared when the Workman bridge was built in 1856. Though so many inns have gone and their signs are no longer landmarks to the inhabitants of the towns, they have collectively made a contribution to the history of Evesham which befits their antiquity: the inn has not been called "the second oldest institution in the parish" for nothing.

What is an inn, and how did the inns of Evesham come to be what they are today? The old Saxon word 'inn' has a warm, welcoming sound. The dictionary defines it as "a public house for the lodging and entertainment of travellers." Foreign travellers have remarked upon the hospitality of English inns throughout the centuries, while we Englishmen regard them as part of our national heritage.

Nowadays, however, the average 'inn' is not really an inn at all but an alehouse having a licence to sell ale, wines and spirits. The words inn and hotel are synonymous and imply that accommodation for travellers is available as well as the usual licensed refreshments. In the old days, a 'comehouse' or inn offered lodging and refreshment to its guests; an alehouse sold ale; a tavern sold wine. There is still, in licensing law, an important distinction between an innkeeper and a licensed victualler.[1]

We owe our first taverns and inns to the Roman occupation of these islands, which began in AD43 and lasted for 350 years. They were post houses built for the rest and refreshment of the travellers on the great Roman roads and were called 'ansæ', from the pitcher handle (ansa) which hung at the doorway as a sign of their business. In the towns, the 'tabernæ' (taverns) sold wine and displayed the symbols of Bacchus, the wine god, usually a bunch of evergreen leaves; this practice gave rise to the proverb 'Vino vendibile suspense hedera non opus est' ('Good wine needs no bush') and thus the Bush became the common sign of the tavern.

By the Middle Ages, ale was the national beverage and was universally provided at meals; it could be obtained at roadside houses which displayed the sign of the

---

[1] This distinction ceased in law on the passing of the 1964 Licensing Act. SBB

evergreen bush attached to a projecting pole. As recently as 1870, during local fairs in Staffordshire, unlicensed cottages had a bush hung over the doorway as a hint that beer might be obtained within.

Evesham was granted the privileges of a market town by Edward the Confessor in 1055. the market, under the control of the Abbot of Evesham through the bailiffs he appointed annually, must have attracted many 'foreigners' (as all traders other than burgesses were described) thus creating a demand for accommodation when the fairs and markets were in progress. Houses near the Market Place would be well situated for such business, and it is likely that ale poles were erected in the vicinity.

1: Obverse of Conventual Seal and the Abbot's Chair
Images from E.A.B. Barnard's Notes and Queries Abbot's Chair now in the Almonry.

The Norman conquest, eleven years later, did not disturb the Abbey of Evesham in its jurisdiction over the people of the town, and the monks remained responsible for the conduct of the trade. Trade had to be carried on publicly and sales could only be made in an established market place at fixed prices. The sale of ale and victuals was free from the market tolls to which all other goods were subjected. Every market place had a public balance or scales, known as the King's Beam, maintained by the townsfolk. Customers were protected from dishonest victuallers by the Assize of Bread and Ale, and the Assize of Weights and Measures. In 1236, the liberties of Evesham were suspended because false measures had been used when Henry III was visiting the town; later, on the submission of the Abbot and monks, they were restored.

To ensure that wholesome ale at fair prices was available to the public, ale conners were appointed by the steward of the town, a custom still observed at Alcester. At Worcester, in Edward IV's reign, two "sadde and discreete persons" were delegated to taste the brew; they had to take an oath suggestive of a pleasing if solemn duty:

> You shall resort to every brewer's house within this city, and taste their ale, whether it be good and wholesome for a man's body and whether they make it from time to time according to prices fixed; so help you God.

The Middle Ages brought a period of great religious activity to England. The Crusades stimulated pilgrimages throughout Europe; countless pilgrims visited the shrine of St Thomas à Becket after his murder in 1170. The Church facilitated the passage of these devout wayfarers by establishing pilgrim hostels along the most frequented routes; after the Reformation, many of these developed into regular inns.

On 4th August 1265, was fought the Battle of Evesham, the final encounter of the Barons' War. At the end of the day, the corpse of Simon de Montfort, the protagonist of Parliament, lay mutilated at the spot since called Battlewell, on Greenhill. An authority, nearly contemporary, states that in the place where he was killed there was then a fountain whose waters restored the sick. The remains of de Montfort were interred before the high altar of Evesham Abbey, in the presence (according to Matthew of Paris) of Henry III himself. National veneration for de Montfort did not cease with his burial; the English elevated him to the degree of saint and martyr, though he remained uncanonized by the Pope: his tomb became a shrine to which the diseased, sick and enfeebled flocked from all quarters; over 200 apparently miraculous cures were recorded.

The hostilarius[2] of Evesham Abbey doubtless found great difficulty in providing lodgings for all the pilgrims who flocked to the martyr's shrine, and the wayfarers were probably forced to seek shelter in the humbler dwellings outside the great wall built by Abbot Reginald over 100 years before[3]. The inns of the town, welcoming the influx of strangers on their pious errands, attracted their custom by hanging familiar religious emblems from the ale poles over their doors. Of these signs, the Cross Keys (St Peter's keys, still the emblem of the Pope), the Anchor (emblem of St Clement) and the ubiquitous Angel remain today.

The sign of the Angel is one of the most common and widespread in the country; it comes close to that of the Crown in popularity. Documentary evidence shows that no less than four Angel inns or taverns have flourished at one time or another in Evesham. One existed at 27, Bridge Street until the middle of the 18th century. Three other Angels clustered together near the bridge at the foot of Port Street till less than 100 years ago. Today, the Angel Vaults at 11, Port Street, remains, a token of the indelible influence of Evesham Abbey upon the town that grew up around it.

---

[2] An office of the Abbey responsible for looking after pilgrims and other visitors (that is, providing them with food, shelter and care). SBB

[3] Abbot Reginald (1130 to 1149) built a strong wall separating the abbey and cemetery from the town, to protect them in the civil war of King Stephen's reign. He also intended to build a moat, but abandoned the idea for fear the place would thereby be made so strong that the king would use it as a fortress. William of 'Chiritone' (1317 to 1344) also fortified the abbey with a stone wall, with two contiguous gates towards the gardens with a chamber over them, the remains of which can still be seen down Boat Lane. SBB

The Vicar v. Mr Strayne

Several Evesham inns display heraldic devices on their signs and in two cases this indicates a direct association with the Middle Ages. In that period, the nobility sometimes allowed their country residences to be used as hostelries by pilgrims and wayfarers when they were themselves away at court or in the King's service. When the large retinue of the King or of a powerful noble journeyed from place to place, the gentry were accommodated at night within the castle walls, while the humbler retainers sought shelter in the village inns. Such inns adopted for their signs the badges of the noble families they served.

The ability to read was a rare accomplishment in the Middle Ages, but those who could not read the written word soon learned to understand the familiar heraldic charges. Although ignorant of the mysteries of heraldic terminology, the wayfarer soon recognized the lion gules or lion azure, called in the vernacular the red lion and blue lion respectively.

In Evesham, the sign of the Bear in Port Street was the badge of the Beauchamps, earls of Warwick, who held lands in Bengeworth in Norman times. The Talbot, in the same street, recalls the old English hunting dog, which was the main charge on the armorial bearings of the Courteen family, lords of the manor of Bengeworth during the 17th century.

The Swan, now in Port Street but formerly in High Street, is a very popular heraldic sign derived from royal armorial bearings; it was favourite device of Henry IV (1399-1413). The White Hart and the Red Lion, both now obsolete signs, were the badges of Richard II (1377-1399) and John of Gaunt, his uncle, respectively. The Green Dragon was one of the supporters of the royal arms of the Tudors.

Where the landed gentry have been connected with a locality for a long period, one of the inns usually bears the coat of arms of the family on its signboard. In Evesham, the Northwick Arms Hotel in Waterside is the only inn to observe this custom at present. The Northwick family (of Blockley) formerly owned considerable land and property in Bengeworth, including the Northwick Arms inn. They severed their connection with the hotel in 1902. The custom of using a family's coat of arms, though widespread, is comparatively recent in origin, dating from the end of the 18th century; the Northwick Arms formerly bore the simpler sign of the Red Lyon. Landlords had to be more definite in an age when few people could read.

The Tudor sovereigns took much trouble about ale. Under Henry VII in 1495, the first licensing law was passed. It empowered any two justices of the peace to:

> ...reject and put away common ale selling in towns and places where they should think convenient, and to take sureties of keepers of ale houses in their good behaving.

The spendthrift Henry VIII zealously regulated the price and quality of ale, without regard for the rising cost of barley or the depreciation in value of the coinage, for which he was mainly responsible, and debased the currency to pay his most pressing debts.

When prices rose in consequence of his chicanery, he seized the funds of the craft guilds, which were the fore-runners of the modern trade unions and benefit societies. Then, to abate his tremendous debts, appropriated the possessions of the smaller monasteries on trumpery charges in 1536. Three years later, Thomas Cromwell, Lord Privy Seal, suppressed the great religious foundations on his behalf.

Evesham Abbey suffered the fate of the others despite the earnest entreaties of its 55th abbot, Clement Lichfield, who wrote to the Lord Privy Seal on at least two occasions presenting dissuasive arguments which it was hoped might influence his Lordship's decision and cause him to abandon his intention as regards Evesham Abbey. One missive, addressed to "The right honorable Sir Thomas Crumwell, knight, Lord Privy Seal, and Vice regent of the Church of England..." after citing in detail the geographical advantages of the Abbey's location, continues in these terms:

> And there is no such Monastery to all intent within the compass of 12 miles of the same. Furthermore, humbly advertising your Lordship that the said towne of Evesham is well inhabited, and likewise well repaired at the onely cost and charge of the said Monasterye, wherein there is few Inns and not able to receive and lodge all such noblemen as shall repair and resort to the same, nor have any good provision for such purposes without the said Monasterye; And that within the same towne and countrye nigh adjoining to the same be divers and many pore, needy, lame and impotent people, which daily have succor and relief of the said Monasterye...

But Cromwell was not moved from his master's purpose, and the work of destruction went forward.

The year 1552, the fifth of Edward VI's short reign, produced legislation against "hurts and troubles" caused by "disorders as are had and used in common alehouses and other houses called tippling houses." It ordained that justices of the peace could abolish alehouses at their discretion and that no tippling house be kept without a licence. In Worcestershire, the alehouse keeper had to find two percent to stand surety for him as well as a recognisance of £10 from his own pocket. The terms of the recognisance stated:

> He shall sell ale, and not suffer any unlawful games, tables, dice or any other game forbidden by the laws, nor lodge any suspected person or persons nor nay strangers above one day and one night.

It is perhaps not surprising that by the end of the century one of the commonest subjects of complaint by the Government in London, the justices, the constables and bailiffs was the growing number of unlicensed alehouses which appeared to flourish despite legislation.

That Evesham was not entirely free from the "hurts and troubles" envisaged in the "Tippling Houses" Act of 1552 is reflected in two cases which reached the Quarter

Sessions in Worcester. In 1599 one John Chaundler, of Evesham, was presented before the justices for keeping unlawful games in his house, such as fighting, cards, tables and the like and for selling unlawful measures of ale and victuals.

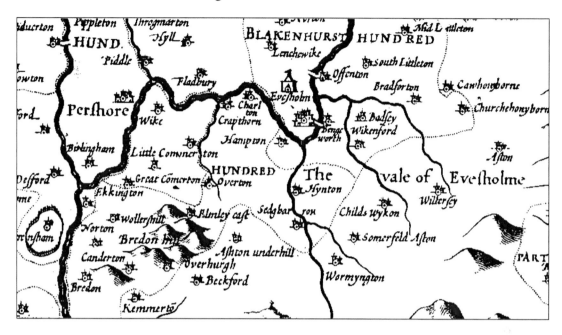

2: Map of the Vale of Evesham (John Speed, 1610)

Three years later, charges concerning the behaviour of Henry Strayne, "a common barrator, drunkard and railer against the bailiffs and other officers of the town," were signed by "Lewis Baylie, Minister of God's Word" and thirteen others, as well as the bailiffs and constables of the town. Unfortunately, no record remains of what action, if any, was taken by the justices against the recalcitrant burgesses.

During the reign of Elizabeth I it was the constant complaint of the Brewers' Company, in London, that materials for brewing were too costly and retail prices consequently fixed too low. Furthermore, they were faced with fresh competition in the shape of spirits and brandy, which Camden, the historian, describes as being introduced here by English troops who had served in the Netherlands.

Elizabeth, like her subjects, usually drank ale for breakfast; she also supplemented her income by exercising a form of monopoly on the sale and export of ale to the Continent: famous throughout Europe, English beer had been exported from very early times. As far back as the 12th century, Thomas à Becket took two wagons laden with good English in iron-bound casks across the Channel as a present to his French hosts "who admired that kind of drink." Edward VI had regulated the export of beer by enacting that no container larger than a barrel was to be used for export purposes. He also insisted that every merchant who exported ale should give a guarantee that he would import sufficient suitable timber as to be the equivalent of that which left the country in the form of barrels.

Brewing in the Mortuary

Evesham benefited early from the political changes wrought by the accession of James VI of Scotland to the English throne as James I, in 1603. From the dissolution of the monasteries (1539), the town had been governed by officers appointed by the Hoby family, who had been granted the Abbey lands and privileges.

Through the influence of Doctor Lewis Baylie, vicar of All Saints' and chaplain to James I's eldest son, Prince Henry, Evesham and Bengeworth were incorporated as a borough in a charter granted in 1604. A fresh charter, by which the office of mayor of Evesham was created, was granted in 1605:

> ...at the humble petition and request of our most dear and well beloved first born son the Lord Prince Henry, being the first petition which he hath made to us in our kingdom of England.

Although suspended for two comparatively short periods in the reigns of Charles II and James II and finally restored in 1688, the charter of 1605 remains in use[4], with only slight changes.

Supervision of the markets and fairs was one of the major tasks undertaken by the newly created mayor and Common Council. The antiquary Leland, who passed through England about 1546, described the Market Place as being "fayre and large," while the markets held there were "very celebrate." Markets were held on Mondays and Fridays, and fairs of two days duration thrice a year. The first fair began on the Monday of the second week after Easter; the second, on the first Monday after Pentecost; and the third on the feast of St Silvanus (10th September). Thus, for over a hundred days every year, the inns of Evesham had to be ready to provide food, drink and lodging for the merchants and country folk who attended the markets.

The price of bread and ale had now become the direct concern of the Council, as may be seen from an order dated 7th October 1611, in the Corporation Minute Book:

> Itt is ordered and inacted by the Maior, Aldermen and Burgesses whose names are subscribed that Mr William Robbins, being one of the Common Council of this Burrough, and John Ree, one of the Constables of this Borrough, being no victuallers, shall for this yeare now nexte ensuing during the Maioralltie of Mr Edward Bowland now Maior of this Burrough have the assessing, rating and setting of prices and assizes of victualls within this Burrough and the said parties were sworn the day and year above wrytten before the said Maior and the rest whose names are subscribed.

---

[4] In 1974 the borough of Evesham became part of Wychavon District Council, and the original Charter became redundant. SBB

Earlier in the same year, the mayor and Corporation had found it expedient to place on record their determination to deal firmly with the ale sellers in the town. Their resolution is a lengthy, and rather pompous declaration, dated 4th January 1611:

> … It is inacted… that foreasmuch as it is thought to be very fitt and convenient for ye publique weale and comfitt of this burrow for the educaytinge up of Comon Burgesses with ye same and suppresinge of mean Tipplinge and blind ale houses which assume libertye to themselves to brew contrarye to lawe and order whereby not only is fuel therebye raysed in pryse and brought into great scarcitye… and that also ye poore of this burrow are not sufficiently served with beer and drinke at such reasonable rates and prices as by the law of this kingdom they ought to be… be it therefore for redress thereof enacted ordered and constituted… that no victualler or alehouse keeper in this Burrow shall brew anye beare or ale within their severall houses or elsewhere within the said burrow with intent to retayle the same within this burrow but shall take and receive the same and such beere and ale as they and every of them shall retayle in their said houses of the Common Brewer or Brewers of this Burrow and for that purpose assigned and appointed whereof Mr Philip Parsons, one of the said Common Council to be one… upon the pain of forfeiting to the use of this Borough toties quoties (as often as) every person shall offend to the contraye thereof ten shillings, one half whereof to the use of this Borough, the other moyetye to him that shall inform.

It may not be without significance that the same Mr Philip Parsons had in 1608 paid the Council £45 and an annual rent of £2 for the lease of premises known as the Charnel House.

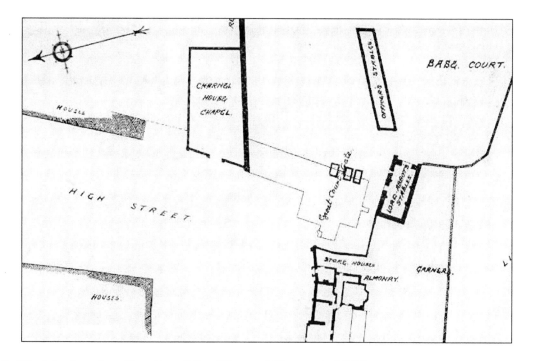

3: Sketch showing the site of the Charnel House (c.1540)
Sketch from E.J. Rudge's A Short Account of the History and Antiquities of Evesham (1820) based on the excavations of the Abbey site.

Presumably he used these buildings to carry on his business of brewing "always excepting the rooms and places most convenient for the placing of dead bodies" as the terms of his lease clearly stated. Quite obviously, the appointment of a Medical Officer for Health was not the concern of the Council in those days.

James I, despite his benefactions to Evesham, was never a popular king and his implicit belief in the doctrine of Divine Right helped to destroy the old harmony between the monarch and the people. An example of his paradoxical legislation was seen in 1606 when he introduced the first act for repressing drunkenness in England, an act which has since multiplied itself into a mass of legislation appertaining to the licensed trade. At the time, it was not well received either by the brewsters or the people, who had been used to pursuing their own easy going ways under the Tudors and their predecessors.

Especially bitter were the complaints against the monopoly for licensing inns and regulating alehouses which James put into the hands of a few personal friends. The chief monopolists, Sir Giles Mompesson and Sir Francis Mitchell, used their patents so selfishly that drunkenness and disorder were encouraged. Public ire was roused; the House of Commons eventually acted; James was forced to revoke the patent; and the two leading monopolists were impeached, fined and condemned to the Tower.

The king's personal conduct was quite astonishing, in view of his edict of 1606. In July of that year, he was visited in London by his brother-in-law, Christian IV of Denmark. Sir John Harrington, who had been noted at the court of Elizabeth for his Rabelaisian wit and had strongly supported James's claim to the English throne, describes how the two kings began "bousing and carousing" so merrily when they met that the whole court followed suit.

> I came here for a day or two before the Danish king [wrote Sir John] and from the day he did come till this hour, I have been well-nigh overwhelmed with carousal and sports of all kinds. I think the Dane has strangely wrought on our English nobles; for those whom I could never get to taste good liquor now follow the fashion and wallow in beastly delights. The ladies abandon their society and are seen to roll about in intoxication…

Perhaps James's escape on the previous 5th November was the excuse for the uproarious reunion party.

The Dolphin – A Loyal Snoek[5]

The principal inns of Evesham in the first half of the seventeenth century were the Crown and the White Hart in Bridge Street, the George and the Swan in High Street, the Round House in the Market Place and the Unicorn in Port Street. The signs of the Woolpack and the Golden Fleece evinced the importance of the wool trade to the borough.

Less prominent inns of the period were the Trumpet, the Leaden Post and the Maiden's Head. The middle years of the century brought a time of political and religious turmoil creating many changes in Church and State. Inns and alehouses, being places of public resort, were particularly susceptible to the vicissitudes of these troublous times.

In the first quarter of the century 'mine host' was still able to greet his guests in traditional style. A graphic picture of the hospitable welcome accorded to the traveller has been left by Fynes Moryson in his *Itinerary* (1617). He describes how a servant runs from the inn yard to take the traveller's horse, walking the beast till he is cold before putting him to bait. Meanwhile another servant ushers the wayfarer to a private room and lights the fire, while a third "puls of his bootes and makes them cleane." Almost at once, the host and hostess appear, to inquire whether the traveller will dine with them or at the common table with fellow guests. In this case his meal will cost 6d. or 4d. but, if he so chooses, he may eat privately in his own chamber where:

> …he commands what meate he will, according to his appetite, and as much as he thinks fitt for him and his company, yea the kitchen is open to him, to command the meate to be dressed as he best likes.

In the course of his repast he is honoured once more by the presence of the innkeeper and his lady, who offer him music which he may freely take or refuse as he pleases and "if he be solitarie, the musitians will give him good daye with musicke in the morning."

> The worlde affords not suche innes as England hath [Moryson asserts] either for good and cheape entertainment after the guest's owne pleasure, or for humble attendance upon passengers; yea, even in very poor villages…

Since Evesham was a corporate borough of growing importance by this time, we trust the inns upheld this reputation. Contemporary documents preserved in the county archives show that in Evesham and the Vale, the proper charge for a gentleman lodging at an inn was 2s. a day and 8d. for his servant. The innkeeper was allowed to charge 6d. a night for the traveller's horse and would supply a peck of oats for a similar sum. It was a pity that such a happy state of affairs was to be disturbed.

---

[5] A type of fish (Thyristes atun) of the family Gempylidae. SBB

As the Civil War approached, inn signs began to acquire political significance. The Puritan element in the country had increased in numbers and influence. Many Puritans now disapproved of the old religious inn signs which to them "smelled of Popery." The sign of the Salutation[6], probably the most popular of these, suffered most; its illustration of the Holy Virgin receiving the salute of the Angel Gabriel often became the Soldier and Citizen, who were depicted bowing to each other. Sometimes a compromise was effected by blotting out one of the figures, thus making the sign of the Angel, even more commonplace than hitherto, as seems to be the case in Evesham, where four Angels survived.

When Charles I was executed (1649) one royalist taverner in London boldly advertised his opinion of the deed by changing the sign of his alehouse to the Mourning Crown. He was quickly forced to take it down. But, being a resourceful type of fellow as well as a poet of some repute, he immediately replaced his forbidden sign with his own portrait and the following caption:

> *There is many a head hangs for a sign:*
> *Then, gentle reader, why not mine?*

In the course of his Midland campaigns, Charles I rested in Evesham from 4th-13th July 1644, following a skirmish with General Waller at Cropredy Bridge, near Banbury. A signboard with an inscription commemorating the visit hangs from an upper storey of the house where he lodged, now Nos.57 and 58, Bridge Street. The king was entertained by descendants (called Martin) of Anthony Langstone, former owner of the mansion, who had been M.P. for Evesham from 1625 to 1628. Presumably, the family fell from grace following the defeat and death of their royal guest. Alfred W. Brown in his *Evesham Friends in the Olden Time* (1885) says the premises were afterwards known as the Dolphin Inn.

The sign of the Dolphin is fairly common in the south of England (there is one at Bishampton at present) and it is the badge of the Watermen's Company. Alternatively, it is known to have represented an anglicized version of the French word *Dauphin*, or crown prince. For most of the Commonwealth period the future King – Charles II – was exiled in France. Did the sign of the Dolphin in Bridge Street represent a silent gesture of loyalty on the part of Evesham sympathisers towards the exiled heir to the throne?

The Martin family certainly remained prominent in borough affairs despite any loss in fortunes and the latter were more than adequately restored by the three Martin brothers, who set up as bankers under the sign of the Grasshopper in Lombard Street, in the City of London, in 1703; but that is another story.

---

[6] Nearly all important monastic hostelries were given the Sign of the Salutation, which arguably was the most popular inn sign that ever existed. The origin of this sign is almost certainly Luke, Chapter I, verses 26 to 50, in particular verses 28 to 30 (*King James Version*). SBB

After the Civil War, the victorious Puritans laid a heavy hand upon the social life of the nation. All places of entertainment suffered severe restrictions. Innkeepers, taverners and ale sellers became the whipping boys of the legislators.

An innkeeper, victualler or alehouse keeper who lodged or entertained any wagoner, carrier, butcher, higgler, drover or their servants on a Sunday could be fined 10s. By the same act, any person over 14 who patronised a tavern, tobacco house or beer shop for tippling, or who sent out for wine, ale or strong waters on the Lord's Day, suffered the same penalty upon conviction. All forms of dancing, singing and the playing of musical instruments were strictly forbidden, while all persons seen "vainly and prophanely walking" on the Lord's Day were also liable to be fined 10s.

It was during the Commonwealth (1649-1660) that William Woodward, then landlord of the Unicorn in Port Street, was ordered by the common council of Evesham to pay 1s. 8d. to "the use of the poor of that parish". Another Bengeworth innkeeper, Edward Pittway, who had been an officer in Cromwell's army, was mayor of Evesham in 1648. He later became a prominent friend of George Fox, founder of the Society of Friends.

From 1648 to 1672 it was permissible for tradesmen to coin their own halfpence and farthings for the convenience of trade. The shortage of small change was due to the disturbance caused by the Civil War when the minting of fresh coinage was conducted in a haphazard fashion by both sides in the struggle. Eleven Evesham tradesmen are known to have issued their own token coins in the mid 17th century.

One of these tokens was issued by Edward Pitway from his inn the Red Lyon in Waterside. It bears in the centre of the obverse, a red lion rampant, the royal crest of Scotland; the reverse side reads simply "E.F.P." The royal device used by Pittway was almost certainly a compliment to James I (and VI of Scotland) when adopted as an inn sign. The coin is ⅝ inch in diameter and was probably worth a farthing.

In 1653, Matthew Michell, of Evesham, issued his trade token bearing the grocer's arms in the centre; it seems unlikely that he too was an innkeeper since arms did not become popular as inn signs until a century later. His trade, however, serves to remind us of Chesterton's lines:

> *God made the wicked Grocer*
> *For a mystery and a sign,*
> *That men might shun the awful shop*
> *And go to inns to dine.*

And Wine for His Worship

By a fortunate coincidence Evesham has two inn signs very close to each other which recall the Restoration of Charles II: No. 1, Vine Street, now known as the King Charles Bar and, a few yards away at No. 5, the sign of the Royal Oak.

The Royal Oak as a sign has enjoyed widespread popularity since the Restoration in 1660. But it is regrettable that the present signboard at the Oak no longer portrays the noble Boscobel tree which hid Charles as he fled from his Puritan pursuers after the Battle of Worcester (3rd September 1651). Until a few years ago, the inn was graced by a sign which depicted the crown in the midst of an oak tree, with Evesham bell tower in the distant background. Designed by Mr Hubert Williams and illustrated in *The Times* on 24th June 1939, when it was new, it was a most felicitous signboard, especially as a portrait of the Merry Monarch himself hung outside No. 1, Vine Street, a few doors away.

This happy situation no longer exists. The present sign at the Oak – a ship in sail – apparently reminded Charles II of the bitter years spent in exile following his flight from Brighton to the Continent, for he has retreated to the back of his inn. The King's portrait now gazes disconsolately towards another sign at No. 72, Bewdley Street – hoping, it seems, that St George will eventually dispose of the Dragon and gallop to the rescue.

Perhaps Flowers and Sons Ltd and Charles Edwards Ltd might be persuaded to undertake another restoration before Jim Huband loses his sovereign as well as Aubrey, who knows the whole story.

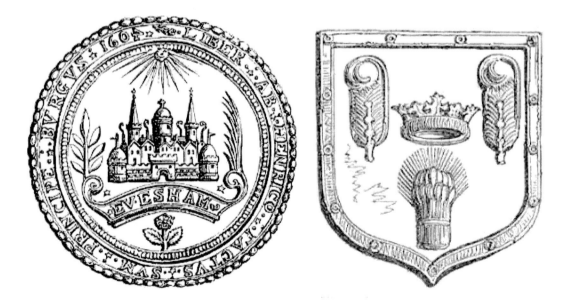

4: Seal and Arms of the Borough of Evesham

Thomas Yarnold was mayor of Evesham in 1660 when Parliament ordered the King's birthday, 29th May, to be "forever kept as a day of thanksgiving for our redemption from tyranny and the King's return to his Government." Ninety years afterwards, despite changes in the dynasty, the loyal burgesses of Evesham still honoured Restoration Day in traditional style.

The Borough Accounts for 1750 show that Thomas Hull, then mayor, spent 16s. on punch and wine, 5s. 7½d. on ale, 3s. 6d. on candles and pipes and 10s. on tobacco for the celebration. The proceedings were enlivened by the bell-ringers (who received 6s.) and the mayor surely added zest to the evening when he "gave to ye fireworks, 2s. 6d." In the years between, Evesham innkeepers and taverners, freed now from the restrictions imposed by Cromwell, played an increasing role in the life of the town.

The introduction of the stage coach on main roads in 1657 heralded a great improvement in the facility of travel. Modern methods of road-making were unknown then: in dry weather the tracks were inches deep in choking dust; when wet they were often quagmires into which coach wheels sank to the axles despite the strivings of six or eight horses. Moreover, the countryside was without hedges and it was very easy to get lost, especially at night. Francis Evans, secretary to the Bishop of Worcester, in his diary (kept from 1699 to 1706) wrote:

> The stage coach held five or six passengers, for nobody could go on top because of the swinging of the coach. Between London and Worcester one had to spend two nights.

Yet, despite their manifold discomforts, the new coach services were patronised by the public and continued to prosper. The larger inns on the coach routes readily adapted themselves to the revolution in road travel and flourished on the influx of new custom.

In Evesham, the George, the Crown and the White Hart soon gained pride of place as coaching inns and held it until the turnpike road on the south bank of the Avon was constructed about 1760. This alteration was effected principally by Mr William Penny, a member of the Corporation and of the Turnpike Trust, and proprietor of the Unicorn Inn, a posting house in Port Street.

But the presence of highwaymen and cut-purses in the countryside increased the natural hazards of travel. Sometimes the owners of small wayside inns were in league with these rogues, but the innkeepers of good repute, like Anthony Brooke of the Crown, had no truck with them.

Anthony Brooke is spoken of, though not by name, in the reminiscences of the highwayman 'Captain' Thomas Dangerfield. The 'Captain' relates how he started on one of his enterprises from London on 2nd December 1684, and, on Wednesday, 17th December:

> …came to Easam, and there not being pleased with the man at the Crowne, I went to the Angell at Parshore.

It seems that he roamed the highways around 'Easam' all the next day, to little purpose, carefully avoiding the town and returning to Pershore at night. Doubtless the disobliging behaviour of mine host Brooke towards Dangerfield was designed to be of service to his guests and neighbours.

Anthony Brooke was succeeded at the Crown by Rowland Broadstock, who had previously kept the George in High Street. Like his predecessor, Broadstock enjoyed the privileges accorded a freeman of the borough. He was a churchwarden and held a number of public offices before he became a member of the Council in 1694 and was elected mayor the following year. His mayoral account presented in December 1696, gives a glimpse of how local government functioned in those days.

On 2nd December 1695, Evesham went to the poll for two M.P.s. "Watching and warding at the election" cost the Council £2 6s. 6d., but a feast (discreetly given at the Crown) in honour of the new members cost £18 15s. 10d.

Account Day and several other occasions when the Council called "for ale at their meetings" cost them £2 4s. 6d. in all. "Coles, candells and fires for ye gaolers" throughout the year cost only £3 5s. The two final items in Mr Broadstock's account for 1696 stand together in silent condemnation of the mayor and the Corporation:

> *For keeping ye present mayor's feast at Mr Broadstock's for two days, £22 6s. 2d.*
> *For repairing ye Markitt Place, 2s. 6d.*

Some idea of the extent of these civic junketings may be obtained by studying further transactions with the landlord of the Crown a few years later. On 19th March 1703, he undertook to provide 30 persons with ordinaries (dinners) at 1s. 6d. a head, and 8d. for servants. The Corporation Minute Book notes:

> Mr Rowland Broadstock now present undertakes to make the same entertainment as above and to provide a hogshead of best fine ale at 2s. 10d. and tobacco pipes and the best tobacco at 2s. ye pound.

We can only conclude that the Council had a taste for something stronger than ale on the feast days.

A hint is contained in this extract from an account presented by Thomas Yarnold, the retiring mayor in 1702 – a son of the mayor who had proclaimed the Restoration of Charles II in Evesham Market Place forty-two years earlier. "Queene Anne being newly crowned," he records his expenses:

> *For wine at the proclaiming of the Queen, £1 14s. 11d.*
> *For ye sessions feast, £9 10s. 2d.*
> *Pd at ye Coronation of ye Queene for wine, £2 2s. 8d.*
> *Thanksgiving for the success of Her Majesty's Armies in the last year, £2 18s. 6d.*

Where the Council Adjourned

By the end of the eighteenth century, the men of Evesham obviously found that their business could be transacted more easily in one of the 'locals' than in the town hall or church vestry. They apparently agreed with Dr Johnson's remark:

> There is no private house in which people can enjoy themselves so well as at a capital tavern.

In 1793, for instance, a special vestry meeting was held to consider the letting of some church property. The vestry sat for a time in All Saints' Church, then adjourned to the Farriers' Arms in Vine Street, where the business was rapidly brought to a satisfactory conclusion. For some twenty-five years afterwards it remained a custom to end the vestry meetings in a nearby hostelry, even the important Easter vestry at which churchwardens were elected and the parish accounts presented.

From such accounts we learn that peals rang out from the bell tower in 1727 "when ye King (George II) landed from Germany" and later in the same year "ten quarts of ale were drunk at ye setting of ye tree." The inn which supplied the ale may be with us yet but it is hardly possible that the historic tree has survived.

"Gave ye men that whit washed ye Church in ale 4s." is an entry that speaks for itself, though somewhat ambiguously. In 1728 the parish "treated one Clergyman with wine" at a cost of 4s. 6d. It would be interesting to know what vintage the reverend gentleman drank, for we learn that the price of wines in the mid 18th century from an account rendered by Mr William Cox, landlord of the White Hart, to the churchwardens in 1755: port was a shilling a pint, canary 1s. 2d., and sack 3s. a bottle.

An item of £1 7s. 6d. for the Visitation Feast accorded to the Bishop of Worcester on one of his triennial visits, did not meet with parish approval in 1732. At the time, the vestry was £17 13s. in debt, so they decided unanimously "that there shall be no more Visitacon dinners nor noe moneys spent on that account that hath been formerly used at Visitacon" and further "there shall be but 5d. spent at any vestry or public meeting…." How well the latter part of the resolution was kept may be assessed by an entry about a vestry meeting in 1752 when "wine, punch, syddere and ale" were dispensed at a cost to the parish of 17s. 6d.

The Right Reverend Father in God, William, Lord Bishop of Worcester (Dr Lloyd) was honoured on 2nd September 1702, with the freedom of the borough. Dr Lloyd (1627-1717) was bishop in turn of St Asaph, Lichfield, Coventry, and finally Worcester. He ruled Worcester diocese from 1699 until his death in 1717 when he was buried in Fladbury Church. His massive monument is to the left of the altar. He is best remembered as one of the Seven Bishops whose sensational acquittal by a jury on charges of treason (refusing to publish the Declaration of Indulgence) was among the immediate causes of James II's downfall in 1688. When Dr Lloyd came to Evesham, the Council paid "to Mr Broadstock at the Crowne for wine to entertain the Bishop £1 2s." – an item, no doubt, of which the vestry was thankful to be relieved.

On 16th August 1705, Joseph Sargeant, the mayor, invited "the Common Council, the Clergy of the Towne, the wives of them all, and the widows of any as have been of ye Common Council" to a feast at the Crown, "it being the day of the Election of the next Maior." It was stipulated that the meals of the councillors' wives must be "payd for by their husbands," but "if any venison is sent, the Maior pay the fee and for two pastyes out of the Common Stock." It must have been a memorable feast, one of many which took heavy toll of the Common Stock.

A little retrenchment was attempted in 1715 (possibly because of the uncertainty created by the first Jacobite rising) when a condition of the feast was "that the Maior doo not exceed half a hogshead of ale and twelve quarts of wine," and (significantly) "that the ordinaryes be collected before the guests rise from the table."

Joseph Sargeant was Maior again in 1729 when the following suspicious items appeared in the borough accounts: "Payd John Koush for wine £3 14s. 7d,. Payd Mr Ashmore for wine £7 7s., Payd Mr Penny for wine £7 7s." It is regrettable that sense of duty had sunk so low among certain councillors about this time that they were once induced to waive the customary fees for admitting a freeman in consideration of "four dozen of wine" delivered to the Council Chamber. But on 4th June 1736, the Corporation (probably forewarned of impending legislation) gathered together the remaining shreds of their dignity and determined to eliminate the slackness which had permeated their administration. This was their first resolution:

> The expenses of chamber meetings held for this Borough in ale and other liquors, pipes and tobacco, have of late been very extravagant and are found by experience to tend very much to the impoverishment of this Body as well as to obstruct the carrying on of the necessary business of such meetings. Ordered, that after Michaelmas next there shall be no liquor of any sort drunk in the chamber itself whilst business is doing, and if any member shall be minded to have occasion to drink during the time of such business he shall call and pay for the same at his own expense, and whatever liquor shall be drunk in the chamber either before or after business the same shall be borne and paid at equal expense of the members present.

Five more laudable resolutions followed, placing the onus of any overspending fairly and squarely upon the mayor. An ominous weakening in determination can be detected in the seventh resolution:

> The mayor of the Borough for the time being shall be at libertye to treat the Body at Xmas, Easter and Whitsuntide, or let it alone as he pleaseth.

But, after further deliberation, this entry was struck out and it was agreed instead:

> That after the expenses of the above are paid all the rest of the money arising by rents, revenues and profits of this Burough shall be appropriated first for the payment of the Corporation's debts and afterwards for raising in fund whereby to support the dignity of the Corporation in its antient rights and privileges.

Evesham Town Council had anticipated by three months the Gin Act of 1736 (9 Geo. II cap. 23), the preamble of which recited:

> The drinking of spirituous liquors or strong waters is become very common, especially among the people of lower or inferior rank, the constant and excessive use whereof tends greatly to the destruction of their health, rendering them unfit for useful labour and business...

Evidently, the gentlemen of the Common Council thought the time had come to put their own house in order and set a better example to those unfortunates "of lower or inferior rank."

Presumably the councillors of 1736 and their successors found much truth in the adage "It's easier said than done" for, by 1774, they were content to follow the example of the Company of Mercers and the seven other merchant companies of the borough who met in the town hall and then regularly adjourned proceedings to an inn of their choice. The Butchers' Arms was most favoured by the Corporation. Many will well remember this inn under its later sign, The King's Head. The site is now occupied by the premises of Timothy Whites and Taylors Ltd, the chemists, where mine host Watkyn Griffiths dispenses draughts that would hardly suit the palates of the 18th century worthies who conned the landlord's brew in the 'good old days'.

The epitaph to this period in the history of Evesham inns and innkeepers was appropriately written about 1794 by the scholarly William Tindal, M.A. (*History and Antiquities of the Abbey and Borough of Evesham*, page 232). Recording the sepulchral inscriptions from All Saints' Church, he wrote:

> There is however one inscription, just at the entrance of this church, which it would have been an injustice to have omitted. It begins with the remarkable sentence, 'He lies an unprofitable servant'. This modesty and humility excited some curiosity. On enquiry it was found that the person buried here, one 'Samuel Morris, who died June 6, 1745, aged seventy four' was a liquor merchant in this town and a great consumer of his own stock-in-trade. No day, it is said, ever passed without his setting the laudable example to his customers of swallowing near two quarts of spirituous liquors, and this without much apparent intoxication. That he should have lived to such an advanced age would seem incredible, unless it be supposed that he began this practice at a late period of his life.

After the Gin Act of 1736, perhaps?

Inspector Arton Reports...

> Whereas, notwithstanding, God Himself has commanded, and the Laws of our Country have enforced the due observation of the LORD'S DAY, commonly called SUNDAY, yet divers Persons within this Borough, do presume to profane it in the most notorious manner, by the exercise of their Trades and worldly business. To prevent such impious and illegal practices for the future, WE, the Magistrates, Clergy and Principal Inhabitants of the said Borough, do strictly charge and command, all Persons within the said Borough, to refrain from the exercise of their Trades and Callings on the LORD'S DAY, on pain of incurring the Forfeitures and Penalties ordained by the Statutes of this Realm for such Offences.... And we forbid and prohibit, all Persons keeping Public Houses, from selling Wine, Ale, Beer, or other liquors, or receiving, or permitting Guests, to be, or remain, in their Houses in the time of Divine service on the LORD'S DAY, as they will be answerable for the Consequences...

Evesham Corporation, with this bye-law in 1803, anticipated by nearly half a century the national legislation as to the Sunday opening hours of public houses. And the power of the justices was strengthened further by the Evesham Improvement Act, 1824, which enacted that –

> ...if any victualler, alehouse keeper or other person selling spirituous or other liquors, beer or cyder, shall entertain or harbour in his or her house or outhouse any watchman or night patrol during any of the hours or times appointed for his attendance on duty...

– he should be fined up to £2 for each offence proved.

When parochial constables who kept watch and ward in Evesham were replaced (under the Municipal Reform Act, 1835) by a regular, salaried police force consisting of an inspector, a sergeant and five constables, one of the rules laid down by the mayor and Watch Committee (who controlled the new police force) stated that a:

> ...constable will pay particular attention to all public houses in his beat, but shall not enter such houses except in cases of disturbance or in the execution of his duty.

The attempts of Inspector William Arton, of Vine Street, and his Duty Men to enforce the local licensing regulations provide an enlightening and often amusing commentary upon the contumacious spirit displayed by some of our ancestors. Some details may be gleaned from the Police Duty Book kept by Inspector Arton from July 1837, to November 1838.

On Sunday morning, 13th May 1838, the inspector reported, seven men were drinking in an alehouse in Cowl Street when No. 4 Duty Man, passing on his beat, informed the landlord that he was not permitted to draw ale before 1 pm, whereupon the latter bluntly "desired the officer to tell me, the inspector, that he would draw beer until 10 in defiance of me or anyone else."

When the same constable reported another alehouse for a similar offence later the same day the landlord returned the still more independent reply that "he did not care a ----- ----- for the magistrates or me either."

With these two rebuffs still fresh in his mind, the inspector dealt tactfully with the next Sabbath disturbance, which happened in June. At 1:45 in the afternoon, he reported "about 40 men and women paraded the streets Singing and creating a Disturbance, and had been 'Tea' Drinking at the Golden Hart."

Evesham continued to return two members to Parliament throughout the first half of the 19th century and consequently became a lively centre of political activity whenever a general election was imminent. Although the borough had a population of almost 4,000, hardly a tenth of these were qualified to vote and half the names on the electoral roll were those of non-resident freemen.

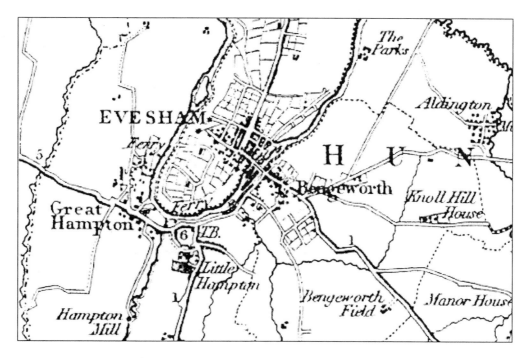

5: Map of Evesham (Christopher Greenwood, 1822)

Accordingly, as George May, the Evesham historian, who saw several Evesham elections, has described, the election agents imported voters wholesale by stage coach, omnibus and post-chaise from London and other distant places when polling time came:

> Inns and places of refreshment open spontaneously at the approach of the welcome visitors; they feast upon the best; appear when wanted at the poll, remain perhaps to witness the result and receive in person a liberal remuneration for their expenses; moreover, without either candidate being presumed to know or feel that any portion of this profuse expenditure is actually furnished by himself.

It is not surprising therefore that petitions against the return of certain M.P.s on accusations of bribery, etc., were presented at Westminster in 1807, 1818, 1830, and 1838. The names of Evesham inns appear frequently in the minutes of evidence upon the hearing of these petitions. The Crown, White Hart, Star, Swan, Bell, Nelson, Fleece, William, Staff and Bear, Rose and Crown, Green Dragon and Butchers' Arms, prominent in the notorious 'Snuff Box Episode' of 1837, are all mentioned.

Occasionally the innkeepers themselves were summoned to Westminster to give evidence before the select committees. The landlord of the Swan, Bengeworth, a particularly ardent worker in the interests of the Blue party, appeared with almost unfailing regularity at the hearings. It is interesting that the Rt Hon Sir Robert Peel, Bt, was chairman of the committee hearing the Evesham election petition of 1838. Ten years earlier he had inaugurated the Metropolitan Police Force, the first 'Bobbies' or 'Peelers'.

The Evesham election preceding the 1838 petition gave Inspector Arton and his men an anxious and busy time. The clouds of party strife had begun to gather on 14th July 1837, when Arton reported that he "cleared several public houses at 12:25 in the morning." Political excitement was soon running high, polling was for two members to represent the borough in Victoria's first Parliament and, on Monday, 17th July, Arton noted a "serious disturbance in Bengeworth, at 1:45 in the morning." The remainder of that week passed calmly enough but, on the next Monday, which was the eve of the poll, the storm broke.

At 7 pm there was a disturbance outside an inn in High Street during which the inspector and a constable suffered assault and battery. Arton described how one assailant "renched or cut my staff from my rist," while half a dozen people were "fighting and creating a disturbance and resisting the officers." Two more constables, trying to help their comrades, were also assaulted; and the last constable to answer the alarm sounded by the inspector's rattle was "assaulted, kicked and beaten."

Evesham blood was up and, realising that his efforts were ineffective, Arton prudently withdrew his force to their headquarters in the town hall. And "the men went out no more that might by order of the mayor." The sun rose next day on the hustings erected in front of the King's Head and the Star. That night there was "nothing to report" in the Police Duty Book. The election had an unfortunate sequel for the constable who had been kicked and beaten in the riot. Some days later he appeared for duty "very drunk" and was sent home. On the following Friday his senior officer refused to pay him for the time lost, whereupon he went home again and, returning, "brought in his clothes" (resigned from the force). His name was John Iorns.

In September, Arton was forced to report No. 4 Duty Man as "being in liquor and off his duty" and very soon afterwards he was called out "to clear the Fox," a tavern in Bridge Street; he was assaulted there but the assailant escaped, though not before the inspector had secured a portion of his clothing.

On a Sunday in October, a constable reported that several men were playing cards in one of the alehouses until 3:15 am and that one of them "lost a pig and moneys." The pig must have been an unusual stake even in those spirited days.

In Praise of Evesham Pubs

That signs is a language Philosophers boast,
Compressed in a little they often speak most.
With the signs of the Zodiac I don't mean to tease ye
But a plain song of signs and I hope it will please ye.

No word need be said in praise or renown
For there's always good living then under the CROWN.
Like good faithful subjects, the Crown then support
And drink bumpers of ale, rum, brandy and port.

NORTHWICK ARMS is a sign where travellers will find
Good dinners, kind landlord and plenty of wine,
Where the gentry oft meet and in full bumpers toast
Church, King and the good Constitution we boast.

A fleece it will keep out the wind and the storm.
This FLEECE has a fire that will keep you all warm
But the outside being warm, why, it is not enough
But to warm the inside he's some downright good stuff.

This FOX is unlike the fox in the fable:
If here you will call, you may drink while you're able;
When you've tippled enough and incline for a walk,
The next house you'll find is the bold DUKE OF YORK.

WHITE HARTs in each gentleman's park do abound
But true GOLDEN HEARTs are scarce to be found;
But the signs are kept each by a hearty good fellow,
So drink off their ale and you'll quickly get mellow.

Volunteers we all know protect our dear land:
To this VOLUNTEER I pray lend a hand.
That hero Lord Nelson must not be forgot:
At the NELSON then drink praise in a pot.

To a plough then we owe all the bread that we eat:
Were it not for a plough we could not get wheat:
To the PLOUGH then stick close and often come here;
By the help of a plough, barley makes us good beer.

ROYAL OAK is renowned, for it sheltered a king;
When snug in this Oak you may laugh, drink and sing;
And once in a week if you call and not glutton
They'll ask you to sup off a good leg of mutton.

To visit an angel we must all think right;
This town has three ANGELs you might call at each night;
And if the good sign should not comfort bestow
Sure comfort you'll find in the cellars below.

To the LAMB, my good friends, I'll have you repair.
Good liquors, kind treatment, you'll surely get there,
And travellers, weary, benighted and dark.
At the LAMB in the High Street we'll soon find an Ark.

To a HORSE AND JOCKEY this town's given birth
Though most horses and jockeys are found on the turf;
But if to this Jockey you choose to resort
No jockeying you'll find, only pay for your quart.

There's the LION of England we must not forget:
The support of our arms which was never beat yet.
The next comes the trumpet to call each to arms
But call at this TRUMPET and you're free from alarms.

KING'S HEAD is a sign which will please young and old
Whether painted on wood or stamped on fine gold,
So of the King's picture, my wish is, d'ye see,
May you all have a plenty and a few left for me.

Ye friends then of Stephens I pray you now wag on
And quickly you'll call at the famous GREEN DRAGON.
You won't be locked up if you call at the KEYS;
At the GEORGE AND THE DRAGON you may sit at your ease.

Wool makes us a cover to keep warm the back.
If you'd keep warm the stomach call at the WOOLPACK;
When there I've drunk freely, it's true what I tell.
My clapper runs freely when at the BLUE BELL.

At the ROSE AND CROWN I'm at home to a hair;
Good treatment you'll find at the STAFF AND THE BEAR.
At Smith's I cast ANCHOR, and I'm free from alarms
When I throw myself safe in the FARRIERS' ARMS.

RED HORSE is a sign I know nought what to say
For a red horse I ne'er saw, by night or by day;
But for my part I wish it, I cannot say less,
May her endeavours to please be crowned with success.

A SWAN of the water we all know is fond
And if in its place, it should be in a pond;
But instead of clear water, if you wish to regale,
A tap there you'll find of most excellent ale.

Good friends, for the favour you've done me this night,
Accept my best thanks for you've made my heart light;
May this town then long flourish, its riches increase
And its townsmen live happy together in peace.

This ballad in praise of Evesham pubs and publicans was composed and sung by Mr Sharpe of the Evesham Theatre, and was published about 1810 by John Agg, printer, of Bridge Street, whose firm ultimately became The Journal Press.

Mr Sharpe was a star entertainer at the Old Drury Lane Theatre which, it seems, was a converted barn situated somewhere between Bewdley Lane and Merstow Green[7]. The theatre flourished in the first quarter of the 19th century but little is heard of it afterwards.

When a census of population was taken in 1841, Evesham had four inns and posting houses, twenty-eight public houses and taverns, and ten retailers of beer – forty-two licensed houses to cater for 4,245 persons, 1,979 males and 2,266 females.[8] One inn, tavern or beerhouse for every hundred persons in the borough seems to indicate, in these sober days, a more than adequate provision for refreshment. It may be that the fabulously hot summers and the fabulously cold winters (no longer experienced, of course) bred a different kind of native in those days. Certain it is, that the opening hours of the public house remain very long; from six in the morning until eleven or twelve at night was commonplace until the Defence of the Realm Act was passed in 1915.

Do innkeepers still take a sly peep at the portraits of habitual drunkards on their Black List before they draw some people's pints? They *should*, under a proviso in the Licensing Act, 1902. Under this Act, the police are required to supply all publicans with photographs of habitual inebriates together with lists of their favourite haunts.

Statutory registration of clubs became compulsory under the same Act but it was not until 1908 that children were excluded from public bars during opening hours.

Many licensed houses in Evesham and elsewhere were closed when the Licensing Consolidation Act became law in 1910, and a further measure, the Licensing Act,

---

[7] Edwin Powell, writing in 1845, notes that Cross Keys Lane (which we now know as Swan Lane) was also called Drury Lane. SBB

[8] One hundred people per licence was the norm in the Victorian period. SBB

1921, set the pattern for modern legislation relating to inns, public houses and the increasing numbers of licensed clubs.

The next section provides a complete and classified list of all Evesham inn signs so far catalogued from documentary evidence. This list precedes an alphabetically arranged series of pen pictures of former Evesham inns, beginning with the American Tavern, the first of the obsolete signs.

The Inns in Evesham

A Catalogue of Inns

Like the latest posters, inn signs aimed at attracting attention and custom; and frequently they were designed to appeal to the particular section of the community from whom mine host hoped to derive the most favour. It is not surprising, then, that in Evesham the Ewe and Lamb overlooked the sheep market when this was held in High Street; or that the Butchers' Arms originally opened its doors upon the town shambles. The Jolly Gardeners, the Sawyers and the Coach Makers' Arms had signboards in the same category. Today, the sign of the Railway Hotel still greets the gaze of travellers arriving at Evesham station.

In Evesham, as might be expected in a town with ecclesiastical origins, a substantial number of bygone inn signs recalled the religious influence prevalent before the Reformation. But the largest group of these obsolete signs, as befits a district now famous for market gardening, related significantly to agriculture.

The background to the history of Evesham inns is complete: now for the particular inns themselves. Here is a classified list of signs, past and present, with locations indicated where these are known.

The italic numerals in brackets which follow some of the inn signs in the list below mark signs referring to the same premises; for example, there is a *(1)* after Maiden's Head, Plough and Harrow and Plough because the inn at 26, Vine Street has, at various times, been known by all these names. Where one of these numerals is found, it is necessary to look through the remainder of the list to find it repeated with other names for the same inn.

Obsolete Signs (in 1955)

Type	Name	Location	Ref.
Agricultural	Black Horse	Bengeworth	
	Dun Cow	3, Cowl Street	2
	Ewe and Lamb	71 High Street	
	Fleece	Bridge Street	
	Goat	Merstow Green	
	Horseshoe	Bengeworth	
	Jolly Gardeners	16, Bewdley Street	
	Nag's Head	Vine Street	
	Plough and Harrow	26 Vine Street	1
	Vine	54, Port Street	
	White Horse	Market Place	
Commemorative	Admiral Nelson	Port Street	
	American Tavern	15 Cowl Street	
	King of Prussia	Greenhill	
	Volunteer	56, High Street	
Countryside	Black Dog	16, High Street	3
	Elm	Bengeworth	
	Fox	39 or 40, Bridge Street	
	Hare and Hounds	3, Cowl Street	2
	Pheasant	Bridge Street	
Descriptive	Bridge Foot	34, Bridge Street	
	Bug and Louse	Rynal Street	
	Guild Hall	Vine Street	12
	Leaden Post	16, High Street	3
	New Inn	Elm Road	4
	Quart Pot	Elm Road	4
	Pure Drop	Cowl Street	
	Round House	2, Bridge Street	
Ecclesiastical	Bell	43, High Street	
	Eight Bells	Bewdley Street	
	Five Bells	Bengeworth	
	Golden Cross	14, Market Place	5
	New Anchor	1, Brick-kiln Street	
	Old Angel	2, Port Street	

Type	Name	Location	Ref.
	Three Crowns	Bridge Street	
Heraldic or Emblematic	Black Bear	43, Port Street	6
	Blue Boar	Bewdley Street	
	Boot	Bengeworth	7
	Dolphin	58-59, Bridge Street	
	Evesham Arms	Hampton	
	Maiden's Head	26, Vine Street	1
	Red Lion	6, Market Place	
	Red Lyon	15, Waterside	8
	Staff and Bear	43, Port Street	6
	Star and Garter	15, Vine Street	
	Swanhouse	79, High Street	9
	Unicorn	27, Port Street	
	White Hart	19, Bridge Street	
Patriotic	George	48, High Street	
	King's Arms	Bengeworth	
	King's Head	60, High Street	
	Prince of Wales	Bridge Street	
	William	Location undiscovered	
Trade and Craft	Brewers' Arms	26, High Street	10
	Butchers' Arms	8, Market Place	
	Coach Makers' Arms	Market Place	
	Farriers' Arms	1, Vine Street	12
	Hop Pole	Bridge Street	
	Horse and Groom	24, Vine Street	11
	Horse and Jockey	24, Vine Street	11
	The Sawyers	14, Market Place	5
	Shoe and Boot	Bengeworth	7
	Three Tuns	26, High Street	10
Unclassified	Cockatoo	29, Greenhill	
	Shoulder of Mutton	Location undiscovered	
	Why Not?	Cowl Street	

N.B. This list does not include inns which are known to have existed in High Street, Swan Lane, The Leys, and elsewhere, for which no signs have yet been discovered.

Existing signs (in 1955)

Type	Name	Location	Ref.
Agricultural	Cyder Mill	Hampton	
	Gardeners' Arms	Littleworth Street	
	Plough	Vine Street	1
	Red Horse	Vine Street	
	Woolpack	Port Street	
Commemorative	Vauxhall	Merstow Green	
Descriptive	Railway	High Street	
Ecclesiastical	Old Anchor	Bewdley Street	
	Angel Vaults	Port Street	
	Cross Keys	High Street	
Heraldic or Emblematic	Bear	Port Street	6
	Falcon	Vine Street	
	Golden Hart	Cowl Street	
	Green Dragon	Oat Street	
	Northwick Arms	Waterside	8
	Oddfellows' Arms	Briar-close	
	Star	High Street	9
	Swan	Port Street	
	Talbot	Port Street	13
Patriotic	Crown	Bridge Street	
	Crown	Avonside	
	Duke of York	Bridge Street	
	George and Dragon	Bewdley Street	
	King Charles II	Vine Street	12
	Rose and Crown	High Street	
	Royal Oak	Vine Street	
Military	Trumpet[9]	Merstow Green	

---

[9] TJSB argues – in the article on the *Trumpet* – that the name is probably ecclesiastical in origin. SBB

American Tavern

The American Tavern had the distinction of being the last beerhouse, as opposed to the fully licensed tavern, to be opened in Evesham. It was at 15, Cowl Street, and existed as a public house from about 1870 until 1910. It was the last of the tiddleywinks.

In 1830, the Duke of Wellington's Beer House Act threw open the beer trade to almost anyone who chose to start a pot house, permitting the general sale of beer to the working classes[10]. Twenty-four thousand excise licences were bought in the first three months of the new Act. Three years later, the national consumption of beer and spirits had risen so much that another bill was introduced by a worried government.

The Beerhouse Act, 1834, drew a distinction between the excise licences for consumption of beer "on" or "off" the premises by reducing the fee for the latter to a guinea and increasing that of the former to three guineas; moreover, an 'on' licence was only granted upon production to the Excise of a certificate of good character signed by six ratepayers. The result was that while the granting of a full publican's licence was a matter for the magistrates, the beerhouse stayed outside their control.

So the position remained until 1869, when the Wine and Beerhouse Act transferred the issue of beerhouse licences to the justices. The Bench, however, had no power to close the existing tiddleywinks, as they were known locally, until the Licensing Consolidation Act, 1910[11], and up to that year they were required to issue a licence for any established beerhouse. Many of the original tiddleywinks closed down before 1910 through lack of trade, while a few such as the Vauxhall, the Oddfellows' Arms and the Gardeners' Arms, became fully licensed. They remain so.

The American Tavern derived its name from its first landlord, Alfred George, who opened it as a tiddleywink soon after his return from the U.S.A. towards 1870. He was succeeded as landlord by F. Nash (1894), Thomas R. Attwood (1897), C.H. Bell (1900), William Aldridge (1903), and finally Arthur Elvins (1906).

Mr Elvins became landlord when he returned from South Africa, where he had fought in the Boer War and worked on railway engines. In the tap room he is reported to have seen a gipsy woman sold by her husband for a pint of cider – a fateful incident reminiscent of Thomas Hardy; and the story may not be as fanciful as it seems, since that particular area of the town was still known as 'The Four Corners of Hell' – a name it had acquired in the mid 19th century[12].

---

[10] The Duke of Wellington's Act allowed only beer to be sold in a beerhouse. SBB

[11] This Act maintained the distinction between public houses and beerhouses. SBB

[12] The junction of Cowl Street, Oat Street, Chapel Street, and Mill Bank was known, for obvious reasons, as the Four Corners. The corner of Mill Bank and Chapel Street was demolished after the Second World War and the road re-modelled. The corner of Chapel Street and Oat Street was

When Mr Elvins left, in 1910, he took over the licence of the Mother Huff Cap at Great Alne, Alcester, where he remained, a popular and widely known personality, until his death on Christmas Eve, 1953. He had the unusual experience of being landlord of two public houses with unique signs; for, despite diligent research over the past three years, I have been unable to discover a house anywhere else named Mother Huff Cap or American Tavern.

Ten years after it had ceased to be a tiddleywink, the American Tavern was offered for sale at the King's Head. The house (said the particulars) contained two sitting rooms, with seating and shelves, kitchen with cupboards, pantry and five bedrooms, and a large stone paved cellar or storeroom. There was a lock-up double-door side entrance to the partly covered carriageway, with a four-stall stable with loft over and a large yard with open shed and brewing furnaces. Gas and water was laid on. The premises were suitable for a market gardener, tradesman or storage room; and vacant possession would be given.

On 1st November 1920, it was sold for £750. For many years afterwards it was the trade premises of the blacksmiths, Messrs E.T. Davies and Son. Three years ago it was vacated again. The old beerhouse is now used as a store by Coulters Garage (Evesham) Ltd, though it still fits is former description and the brew house still stands – a pathetic memorial to the last tiddleywink.

Angel

Angel in Port Street

The Angel (later called the New Angel), kept by Mrs Edith Maries at 11, Port Street, is the last of four hostelries bearing the same sign which have stood during the past two-hundred years within a stone's throw of Evesham Bridge, the traditional gateway to the town. Yet another inn of the same name existed not far away in Port Street on a site which I have not been able to ascertain.

No other inn sign has ever been so popular in Evesham, which, by tradition, owes its foundation to a supernatural visitation of the Blessed Virgin to Eoves[13], a humble swineherd employed by the Bishop of Worcester, St Egwin, in 710. It is, therefore, most fitting that her sign, that of the Salutation, should become most favoured in the community which gathered beneath the walls of the abbey erected here in her name.

---

demolished in 1965 to help create a large public car park. The corner of Oat Street and Cowl Street was demolished to create a small private car park for the Green Dragon. SBB

[13] It is a common and long-standing error that Evesham is named after the swineherd 'Eoves'. O.G. Knapp comprehensively discussed the issue in the *Evesham Journal* (3rd April 1920), concluding: "We may therefore take it as certain that the real name of the Swineherd was not Eoves, Eofes, or even Eofa, but Eof... The form Eoves, though current for many centuries, is a mere blunder." SBB

The original signs of the Salutation frequently depicted the Virgin receiving a scroll or parchment from the hand of the Angel Gabriel, with the words *Ave Maria, gratia plena: Dominus tecum* inscribed thereon. When, after the Reformation, Our Lady was blotted from the signboards at the behest of the new order, the angel remained.

6: Angel Inn, Castle Street (c.1900 and c.1920)
This inn, later known as the New Angel, is now called Angel Vaults. In the earlier photograph the sign of the Unicorn can just be seen.

Angel in Bridge Street

The earliest documentary evidence concerning this popular inn sign emanates from the deeds relating to 27, Bridge Street, a property now owned by Mr A. Hodgetts, the cycle agent. Acting upon observations made by the research group of the Vale of Evesham Historical Society when pursuing other inquiries some two years ago, I deduced that the cellars of the building had certain interesting features worthy of further investigation. By the courtesy and ready assistance of Mr Hodgetts, I was enabled to examine the oldest deeds of the premises with the following gratifying results.

By an indenture dated 19th June 1732, the sixth year of George II, and a conveyance of the following day, we learn that "all that messuage and tenement in the parish of All Saints, Evesham, in or near a certaine street commonly called Bridge Street and commonly known by the Signe of the Angell" was "granted, bargained and sold" by Robert Phipps, a blacksmith, to Henry Stone, an innholder, for five shillings and one "peppercorn to be paid at the Feast of St Michael the Archangel annually." By 1769, the description of the "Signe of the Angell" was no longer in use and presumably the house had then ceased to be an inn. The bargain price of 5 shillings may be regarded as a nominal sum not representing the true value of the property; this deal probably formed part of a larger transaction of exchange between the parties concerned.

Angel in Waterside

About 100 yards away, just across the Avon, stood the second Angel Inn. It occupies a site almost exactly where the traffic island stands today in the centre of the road junction between Port Street, Waterside and the Workman Bridge. This Angel was one of an extensive range of buildings which had to be razed in 1856 in order that the Workman Bridge scheme might be completed satisfactorily.

The 'island' property consisted of an extensive 'port' and wharf having a double entrance gate facing Messrs Burlingham's wharf on one side, flanked by a shop and a dwelling house; while round the corner in Waterside was the Old Angel Inn and another gateway giving access to the wharf. The gateways were there for the convenience of carts drawing loads of bark, straw, hay, lime, coal, etc., to and from the town weighing machine, then located on the Waterside wharf. The inn, perforce, must have been almost opposite Messrs Harrison's Seed Shop, then a private residence, with only a narrow causeway separating the two premises. The access to Port Street or the bridge with this constricted approach must have presented considerable difficulty, perhaps danger, to the fast coaches staging at the Northwick Arms and Woolpack and to any other vehicular traffic using the Hampton turnpike. The riverside road itself became impassable when the floods were out.

On the Bengeworth side of the old bridge was a commodious basin or port for unloading boats and barges, for the river flowed in two channels below the bridge, one close to the present A44 road and the other alongside Mr S.J. Grove's Tea Gardens. Just below the bridge, a large osier-covered[14] eyot formed an island blocking more than half of the present watercourse and stretching as far downstream as Battleton Bridge, where a small public wharf still exists (between the bridge and the western extremity of the Workman Gardens).

Soon after the Workman Bridge had been completed in 1856, the obstructive eyot was removed from the centre of the river, the stream was canalised in its present course and the Workman Gardens were laid out on the spoil heaps which had been dumped in the old east channel of the Avon. Later on, in the 1870s, an ornate drinking fountain, cum direction post, cum lamp standard, presented by Colonel Bourne – erstwhile member for the borough – was erected at the junction of Waterside with Port Street. It was removed in June 1927. All the foregoing is so very difficult to visualise in 1956 that I feel bound to justify my assertions with the following details culled from an auction bill advertising a sale which took place on Thursday, 10th June

---

[14] Osier is any kind of willow used in basket-making. SBB.

1830, at the Woolpack Inn, when the estate of the late George Day, of Prospect House, was disposed of. Lot No. 4 appears as:

> ...a leasehold coal yard and wharf and warehouses, stables, counting house, weighing machine and other appurtenances thereto, now occupied by Mr William Milton on the south side of Evesham Bridge... also that well-frequented Inn with appurtenances called the Angel, in the occupation of Mr John Mills.

Mr John Mills, who succeeded Richard Millington, landlord in 1820, carried on his business as ironmonger and innkeeper until the reconstruction of the old bridge began at the end of 1855 with the demolition of the Bridge Inn on the west bank of the river. Thomas Cull, who had kept the Bridge Inn for a good many years, moved across the doomed structure to the Old Angel where he presided for the last few months of its existence before being ousted again, this time to the Talbot, where he remained until he retired.

While these sweeping changes were taking place in 1856, their instigator, Henry Workman, presented the weighing machine from the Angel wharf to the Bridge Trustees, who caused it to be re-erected in Vine Street outside the town hall. The profits accruing from the useful machine were applied, by common consent, to the cost of repairing, painting and cleansing the newly-erected bridge. The old weighing machine continued to operate outside the Fire Station for seventy more years until, by a curious chance, it was irreparably damaged by the weight of a lorry laden with aggregate for the new ferro-concrete bridge in the course of construction further downstream in January 1927.

Angel in Bengeworth

Lewis's 1820 *Directory of Worcestershire* indicates that three Angel inns existed in Bengeworth at that time. One of these was kept by Richard Millington; another is shown as belonging to John Skey. This was, in all probability, the inn referred to in corporation records dated 10th October 1809, indicating that the sessions adjourned from the guildhall (now town hall) to the house of James Cull, known by the name or sign of the Angel. No reason is ascribed for this apparently odd procedure on the part of the justices who, having reassembled in the parlour of this small Bengeworth inn, went on to appoint surveyors of the highways for the ensuing year. John Proctor and Ebenezer Pearce were made responsible for the road in All Saints' parish, Thomas Hughes and Charles Yarding in St Lawrence's and Dr Thomas Beale Cooper and John Acton in St Peter's. Three years later a similar meeting was held at the Angel, then described as the house of James Guion.

James Cull later became landlord of the Plough and Harrow (now Maiden's Head) in Vine Street; James Guion opened a little alehouse called the White Hart in Cowl Street. From 1820 to 1842 John Skey kept this Angel inn but it does not appear in Slater's *Directory of Worcestershire* for 1850 and must be presumed to have closed in the interim period. Nothing is known of its probable location.

Angel in Port Street

The most important Angel inn in the town was at the junction of Port Street with Waterside: now the premises of R.F. Cassidy Ltd, jewellers. In 1820 a coach left the Angel every afternoon at three for London and for Worcester every morning at 7:30. In a land tax redemption certificate of 1806, it is described as a public house leased by Anthony Roper and occupied by Richard Matthews.

7: Angel Inn, Port Street (1900) (during the 'New Century Flood')

A bill of sale dated 1827 described it as "lifehold premises held on lease under the Right Honourable Lord Northwick." The sale took place at the Northwick Arms, when the particulars noted that it was a well-established inn with stabling for twenty horses and was occupied by a yearly tenant, Robert Vince. According to a note on the bill, "Young Matthews" bought the inn for £305 and paid £45 deposit.

Mr Matthews was the first Evesham innkeeper to avail himself of the services of Evesham police force, which was constituted in February 1836. On 23rd February, Inspector Arton wrote in his book:

> ½ past 10. Boswell reported that he was called by Mr Matthews, Old Angel, Bengeworth, to take Mr T. home. The landlord stated that he had had him

locked up ever since nine in the morning, that C. and B. came in, that T. said that he durst not go home or he should be murdered.

One cannot help wondering what Mr T. had done to upset Messrs C. and B. but whatever it was he seems to have chosen his voluntary prison with an eye to his own comfort, at least.

No. 2, Port Street, was described as the Old Angel in 1836, a name which it shared with its neighbour in Waterside until the latter was demolished in 1856: it must have been confusing to have two inns of the same name cheek by jowl. Landlords following Richard Matthews (1806) were Charles Booth (1809), Mary Walker Booth, possibly his widow (1820), Margaret Walker (1835), and Robert Vince (1836). William Matthews, who bought the lease in 1836, was the proprietor for another twenty years or more. In 1863, Mrs Prudence Mills became the third woman to hold the licence. Ten years later, Thomas Callow moved from the Blue Anchor in Brick-kiln Street and, at the Old Angel, continued in business as a market gardener and fruit salesman until he retired in 1897 to Fairfield Cottages at Little Hampton. He died, aged 90, in 1919.

His successor was William Walter-Candy, still well-remembered for his good manners and keen wit. Invariably dressed in tweeds, breeches and stockings and a deer-stalker hat, and with his liver-coloured spaniel at his heels, he looked more like a farmer than an innkeeper; and there was nothing he enjoyed so well as a day's shooting. But he could be found in his bar, which, incidentally, had stained glass windows set in leaded lights, at 6 o'clock every week-day morning prepared to serve rum and hot coffee to his clients on their way to work. At 10 am he was relieved by two barmaids, who remained on duty until the doors were closed at 11 pm, then cleaned and polished the rooms ready for morning before retiring for the night – no light task by modern standards.

Uncle Bill, as he was affectionately known to his regulars, was a familiar figure in Evesham before the first World War, as he took his daily stroll through the town with his waistcoat pockets well filled with silver threepenny pieces. In winter, when bad weather held up work on the land and created unemployment among the labouring gardeners, Uncle Bill had a practice of visiting the town hall corner where the men congregated; and, after a few observations on the state of the weather, he would slip a coin from his waistcoat pocket into the palms of the hard-up individuals, with the admonition that is should not be spent at the Old Angel. This was his way of ensuring that the men would patronise his public house when they were in funds but would not bother him for 'tick' when the reverse was the case.

Uncle Bill Candy was most reluctant to give credit and would do his best to avoid having to do so. Once, however, he found himself being asked for 'tick' by a regular customer who became financially embarrassed during the course of a convivial evening. Rather than break his own rule, but having great sympathy for his client, Uncle Bill offered the man a pint of cider free for every pint of water he was prepared to drink. Nothing loth, the little man accepted the bargain with gusto, and downed three pints of cider, sandwiched between three pints of water, before leaving for home – in a hurry. A veil is drawn over what happened on the way.

Bear

As the Angel symbolised the clerical power wielded by the abbots of Evesham, so the Bear represents a secular power, the Beauchamps of Elmley Castle, earls of Warwick. The origin of their badge – the bear and ragged staff, now familiar as the county emblem of Warwickshire – is part of the legendary history of ancient Britain. While in the service of King Arthur and the Knights of the Round Table, Arthgal, first Earl of Warwick, earned the cognomen of 'the bear' by strangling one such beast with his bare hands; Morvidius, another ancestor of the Beauchamps, slew a giant by clubbing him with a freshly plucked sapling tree – hence the ragged staff.

8: Bear Inn, Port Street (1865 and 2003)
Picture on the left is a detail from an illustration in Shawcross' and Barnard's Bengeworth (1927).

It is almost certain that this was the Bear adopted for the inn sign in Port Street, since the noble family of Warwick held land in Bengeworth from the Conquest until the end of the thirteenth century. In the reign of Stephen (1135-1154), William de Beauchamp built a castle near the bridge on the Bengeworth bank of the Avon. But, for despoiling the property of Evesham Abbey, he was excommunicated by Abbot William de Andeville, who, according to records, also razed the castle walls and consecrated a burial ground on the site[15].

A century later, the Beauchamps – now in the manor of Bengeworth – were challenged by Walter Cantilupe, Bishop of Worcester, to show why they had removed

---

[15] The purpose of consecrating the ground was to prevent the Beauchamps from building any new structure on the site. SBB

Bengeworth from the jurisdiction of the Hundred of Oswaldslow to the Court Baron of Elmley without the bishop's consent. The baron was excommunicated but the quarrel dragged on and was not settled until the end of the thirteenth century when the Beauchamps sold the Manor of Bengeworth to Abbot William de Whitchurch of Evesham, who was no friend of the bishop. By this act the Warwick family terminated their connection as landowners with Bengeworth and Evesham.

There have been a surprising number of variations in the wording on the inn sign since it was described in a Relief Account Book for St Peter's parish in 1724 as "the Bare." Mr Sharp, in his 'Song of Signs', published at the end of the eighteenth century speaks of the "good treatment you'll find at the Staff and the Bear." In 1820, when Stephen Walker, one of the "Pump Keepers for the Upper Circuit Pump in Bengeworth" was landlord, the inn was described in Bentley's *Directory* as the Black Bear. By 1835, when Margaret Walker was the hostess, and in election petitions just prior to that time, it was called the Bear and Ragged Staff. Between 1840 and 1850, while William Hughes kept the inn, it passed simply as the Bear; but in police records for 1859 it was noted as the Old Bear Inn. Under the next landlord, John Darby, it became the Bear inn once again until it attained hotel status at the turn of the century.

An amusing incident took place at the inn soon after the establishment of the first Evesham police force early in 1836; it reflects some of the difficulties encountered by administrators of the law in those robust days. A constable, a Bengeworth man bearing a Bengeworth name, was reported by one of his colleagues for being found asleep on the steps of Mr Henry Workman's house in Bengeworth at about 1:30 am. The next day, Inspector William Arton found him in the parlour of the Bear and Ragged Staff and there reminded him not only of the rules and regulations laid down by the Watch Committee but also of a similar incident earlier that month when the constable had been relieved of his lamp by the inspector while asleep on another step. He advised the man that "he would do better if he drank no more beer" but, alas, in defiance of his superior officer, the wayward constable "drank beer from out of the Cup which two Fishermen were drinking from" and said he intended to go on doing so when and where he pleased. At the official inquiry which followed, he was suspended from duty for a fortnight, but the Watch Committee need not have bothered – for their erstwhile limb of the law had "resigned."

Port Street, particularly in the immediate aspect of the Bear Hotel, had a much different aspect in those days. The construction of Burford Road in 1898 turned the Bear, then occupied by W. Bailey, who was also in business as a saddler, into a corner house and enforced its reconstruction.

The next tenant of the reconstructed premises was Mr William Cooke, who moved from the Jolly Gardeners in 1904 and began to brew on a much larger scale in buildings now used as a garage at the rear of the inn. Soon after the beginning of the first World War, Mr Cooke retired from innkeeping and sold the Bear to Mr Harry Byrd, who continued to brew there, in conjunction with his Vine Brewery just across the road, until 1919, when Hunt, Edmunds and Co. Ltd, of Banbury, the present owners, acquired the inn. Since then, the licensees have been: F.J. Clarke (1920), A.P. Edwards (1925), Miss Syms (1930), Mrs A.M. Phillips (1933), and from 1935 to the present day, Mr A.A. Milward.

Bell

Bell in High Street

Evesham had two inns bearing the sign of the Bell. One still flourishes, as the Talbot, in Bengeworth; the site of the other, which stood at 43, High Street, is now occupied by Walker's Ltd, the grocers.

Bell in Port Street

"The oldest inn in Bengeworth," wrote the Rev. J.P. Shawcross (*Bengeworth*, 1927), "is the Talbot Inn, formerly known as the Bell. It is mentioned (the only case of its kind) in the Register: 'Item, 29th daie of November, John houlle bell in was buried 1573'."

It stands in the centre of the village to the north of the old churchyard, and would be the nearest inn to the belfry, hence its name. Originally it consisted of four or five rooms, was built of brick and timber beams and had a back-yard enclosed by a high wall.

> Outside this wall was the village pump, which faced Church Street. The Bell was the scene of may social and cheerful meetings. Here the ringers assembled after ringing merry peals at Christmas, Easter, Restoration Day (29th May), Gunpowder Plot and New Year's Day, and on royal birthdays, national festivities, weddings and other occasions, including the meets of the hounds. In the parish accounts appear sums given to the ringers on some of these occasions.

The sign of the Bell is one of the earliest and most popular of English inn signs and one authority asserts that there are 483 Bells in England excluding those with additional names such as Blue, Five, Ring o' Bells, Bell and Crown, etc. The sound of bells, of course, had a deeper significance in the Middle Ages than at present, especially in a town like Evesham, which lay beneath the walls of a great abbey, where bells were rung at regular intervals throughout the day, marking the various hours of the Divine Office.

An entry in All Saints' parish register dated 5th April 1681, shows that the importance of bells did not cease with the disappearance of the Abbey. The vestry ordered "that if for the yeare following the bell-ringers doe at any time neglect to ring the great bell either morning or evening according to the custom of the town, then for such neglect which the churchwardens know or have due notice of from any of the parishioners, they shall detayne four pence from the bell-ringers out of the quarterly wages."

George May (*Descriptive History of Evesham*, 1845) comments on bell-ringing traditions during his lifetime:

A custom somewhat peculiar and observed beyond memory till within the last two or three years was that of rising the tenor bell, which hangs in the bell tower, at 4 o'clock in the mornings of Monday, Thursday and Saturday, throughout the year. Why these mornings should be preferred and why the early hour, especially in winter, it is difficult to say.

But surely this was the market bell, outliving its usefulness. Its original purpose, now no longer significant, was to mark Prime, the early morning part of the Divine Office, at which hour trade began in the Market Place. A conveniently situated church bell saved the expense of setting up a market bell. Thus the Abbey bells served a dual purpose.

Black Dog

Situated where Nos. 16 and 17, High Street now stand, the sign of the Black Dog was a favourite among innkeepers in the 18th century. The reference was probably to the old English terrier dog, an extremely popular breed among the sporting fraternity of the period, but which has now become extinct. The inn had the curious name of the Ledden Post in the previous century, a sign to which no reference is made in Larwood and Hotten's *History of Signboards* (1866) or the recently revised version of the same reference book by W.E. Tate.

The earliest information about the premises which became an inn is contained in an indenture date 16th January, 38 Elizabeth (1596), where the property is described as then being "between the tenement of Arthur Marshall on the north part and that of Joseph Wynoll on the south part." The parties to the deed were Thomas Teckeridge, of Evesham, gentleman, and Thomas Higgs, of Evesham, yeoman. The house was then in the occupation of a Thomas Nash, presumably as his private residence. Thomas Seasom, Henry Foster, John Stoneman, senior, and John Smythe witnessed the deed, probably in the porch of the parish church, St Lawrence's, on a Sunday afternoon, a common time and place for property transactions at that period.

No other documents exist concerning the ownership of the messuage for almost a century afterwards, during which lapse of time the premises had become the Ledden Post, an inn kept by Thomas Bouts, cordwainer, and Sarah, his wife, who had leased the property from James Michell (landlord of the George Inn) and Sarah, his wife, on 21st January 1688. Ordnance survey maps of the borough as recent as 1888 show that a public pump existed on what is now the asphalt parking space in front of the modern buildings on the site. It is likely that the inn derived its name from this pump, the "ledden post" probably being the outside casing of lead surrounding the pump as protection against the weather.[16]

---

[16] An answer to query 671 on public pumps, in 'Notes and Queries' column 327 from the Evesham Journal (7/12/1912), and column 333 from the Evesham Journal (18/1/1913), mentions a pump at High-street, opposite No.17. SBB

The first reference to the sign actually occurs three years previously in the third volume of Corporation Minutes 1684-1758 under the heading "An account of chief rents due and payable every halfe yeare to the mayor and Common Council of this Burrough from persons inhabiting the houses" for the year 1685. "In St Laurence Parish," appears the entry, "Thomas Bouts for the Ledden Post 4s."

Thomas Bouts, the innkeeper, had been appointed surveyor of the highways in St Laurence Parish in 1660 and again in 1667, he served as a churchwarden in 1669 and was admitted as a freeman of the borough (probably as a reward for public service) on 15th July 1684. It appears that he died soon afterwards, for on 29th July 1688, a fresh lease was negotiated between the owners and his son, also Thomas Bouts. The son apparently had other interests, for he gave up the tenancy of the inn on 11th September 1690, when the premises were leased by James Michell and Margaret, his (second?) wife to Joseph Slatter, a glazier.

A.W. Brown's book *Evesham Friends in the Olden Times*, the source of much fascinating information about the Quaker community in Evesham during the 17th and 18th centuries, mentions another member of the Bouts family. The very fact that Humphrey's relative (probably his brother) was an innkeeper could easily have been the reason for his disgrace in the eyes of his fellow Quakers and his condemnation by them as a "Disorderly Walker."

Whether Thomas was involved or not, the fact remains that Humphrey Bouts failed to observe the homely and practical counsel of his mentors "that all Friends that do profess the truth beware and absteine from unnecessary frequenting alehouses, keeping idle company, misspending their precious time," etc. Consequently Humphrey Bouts was arraigned by the monthly meeting of Friends and called upon to confess his misdemeanours and promise to make amends, which he did in writing, thus:

> ffreinds: - I lett in a careles speritt, that have brought agreate dishonor to ye truth, for drinkeing more bare than was fitt for mee to drinke that speritt drawed mee into many wordes, and then lightnes gotte up not having regarde to the Lord as I ought to have done I gave way to yt speritt and joined wth it. It drawed mee into great Anger against my wife; I stroked her wt the backe of my hand, and other ill behavours, and all was, out of God's truth... And in a senseable feeeling of ye judgements of the Lord I am constrained to give forth this paper to clare God's everlasteing truth, be yt owneds Gods judgements will finde mercy... My deare love have been ofte times in mee towards all friends in ye truth. This written by mee, Humphrey Bouts. Given forth ye 21st of ye 5th month, 1672.

The repentant Humphrey apparently found the "careles speritt" stronger than he had anticipated for he disappointed the hopes of the more sober members of the Quaker congregation. The Society, meeting "in Bengeworte upon ye 6th day of ye 7th month in ye yeare 1672, ye following paper was gave forth" concerning their "black sheep":

> Wee whose names are hereunder written in ye behalfe of ye body of friends who are scornefully called Quakers have taken into consideration ye sad estate

and condition of Humphry Bouts who have walked disorderly in drunkenes and other bad carriage and behaviour wherin God's truth have suffered much by him. Although we have had a Godly care of him, and have severall times tenderly admonishte him... yt he might owne his Condemnation for his unrighteouse actions; wch seemingly he did by giving forth a paper againste him self confesseing to his disorderly walking... But notwithstanding wee do not find by sad exsperiance yt still he goes on his wickedness and ungodly actions breakeing forth into sad effects to ye grieving of ye hearts of ye righteouse... wee utterly deny his actions and hereafter do deny him to be a member amoungst us excepte he return to the Lord through harty repentance.

Henry Gibbs, Thomas Cartwright, James Wall ye older, Joshua ffrensham, Steven Pittway, Will. Collins, David Walker, John Clements, Tho. Darke, John Woodward.

Unfortunately we shall never know if Humphrey Bouts ever regained and followed the strict path of moral rectitude which has always been the criterion of Quakerism, and which was particularly so in the 17th century, or whether he continued (as must be feared) to "walk disorderly" for the remainder of his days.

John Slatter continued to trade under the sign of the Ledden Post established by the Bouts family as is shown in an indenture quinque partite dated 18th March 1692, in which James Michell, mercer, and Margaret, his wife, together with twelve other persons in the neighbourhood were concerned. The transaction included "The Leaden Post now in the occupation of John Slatter" and property in Cole Street[17] "purchased by Richard Oldacres from William Martin."

Then, in 1702, in a deed between "Joseph Slatter and William Etheridge, of Alderminster, yeoman, and Bridget, his wife," it appears that the sign of the Leaden Post had ceased to exist as such, and that the premises were then known "by the name of the sign of the Black Dogg, late in the possession of Thomas Hazard."

At this time, John Roberts inhabited the house on the north side and Samuel Whitford senior still occupied the house on the south side, as he had in 1688. One of the witnesses to this deed was Robert Cookes, who had built Dresden House a few years before and, incidentally, was the owner of the Black Horse Inn, Port Street – the next on our list.

By 1747, the Black Dog formed part of the estate left by Thomas Etherington, a carpenter, and his wife Elizabeth, to their two sons William and Thomas. The last deed of interest was dated 11th May 1777, when John Ash, of Pershore, doctor of law,

---

[17] Now known as Cowl Street. The earliest reference is from Abbot Randulf's Institutes (variously dated from 1202 to 1223) which mentions Colestrete as well as Bruggestrete, Brutstrete, Magnus Vicus and Merstow. The name 'Colestrete' probably originally signified 'street where coal was sold'. Certainly Kenneth Cameron in *English Place Names* (London: B.T. Batsford, 1996, reprinted 2001), p.224, cites "Cowl Street (Evesham) 'coal'" as an example of a name derived from local trade. Please note the mention of 'cole' and 'candells' in the corporation account book from 1696 (page 16). SBB

and sole executor of Elizabeth Millington, widow, of Pershore, sold the property to John Hughes, of Evesham, gardener, son of Richard Hughes. This deed refers to "a certain building formerly used as, and then called, a meeting house."

It seems that the meeting house referred to was a barn at the rear of the house (now No. 17, High Street) which had been converted into a place of worship by a congregation of Presbyterians (Protestant Dissenters). The trustees of the body purchased the freehold of the meeting house in 1701. In 1730, the premises at the rear of the Black Dog were conveyed to a new set of trustees headed by the Rev. Francis Blackmore, who held the trust in its original terms "for the use of the congregation of Protestant Dissenters assembling for Divine Worship." These trustees eventually sold the premises in 1738, after purchasing a site in Oat Street where they erected the building now familiar as the Unitarian Meeting House.

Black Horse

In Bengeworth records of the 18th century, the sign of the Black Horse appears twice.

The first reference is found in the will of Robert Cookes, Gent., made on 20th March 1741, some six years before he died and was buried in All Saints' Church. His will relates mainly to his well-known property, Dresden House in High Street, then occupied by his son-in-law, William Baylies, Doctor of Physic, later to become Physician to Frederick the Great of Prussia. His other properties in the town included "a messuage in Bengeworth, near the Bridge-foot, there, formerly an inn and called or known by the name of the Black Horse."

The Black Horse Inn reappears in the Bengeworth Overseers' Accounts as one of the inns where the parish relief was distributed to the needy in 1793. The last reference to "the Black Horse Inn, Bengeworth," is found in the Phillips Collection (Birmingham Reference Library) dated 13th September 1809.

The sign of the Black Horse has no heraldic significance but it was probably related to the "strong black horses" from the surrounding countryside which made the four fairs held annually in Evesham "particularly famous" according to William Tindal (*History of Evesham*, 1794, p.213).

An earlier and rather striking observation on the same subject came from the pen of Thomas Habingdon, who toured the country early in the 17th century writing his famous *Survey of Worcestershire* after being confined within the county bounds for the rest of his life for his minor part in the Gunpowder Plot.

Of Evesham, he noted:

> These fayres of Evesham with that Vale doe soe exceed for strong and able horses as they are often preferred from Cart and plow to the Court and the tylt, and which is most laudable, to serve in the warres.

Blue Bell

Blue Bell in High Street

Known as the Blue Bell because of its association with the Tory Party, the Bell Inn at 43, High Street, was a popular hostelry early in the 19th century, its heyday. But it was there in 1751, when Mrs Watson was hostess to the company of Mercers holding their annual meeting and feast there.

It was a popular venue for auction sales and it appears to have been favoured by the travelling companies of actors as theatrical lodgings during the 1800-1850 period.

The first meeting of the Evesham Tories in the General Election of 1820 (following the death of George III) was held at the Bell, when a committee for Sir Charles Cockerell was formed by Edward Savage, the mayor, Thomas Beale Cooper, William Preedy, and Messrs Day, Barnes, Soley, Edge, Roper, Taylor, Proctor, Brown, Murrell, Izod, Whitford, Humphries, Moulting, Atkins, Rodd, Benton and Robert Preedy. Those appointed as canvassers were Joseph Davies, Robert Stratton, Josuah Matthews, Thomas Smith, Joseph Millington and Henry Whitford (landlord of the Lamb in High Street).

Sir Charles invited his friends to supper at the Bell, ostensibly to celebrate "the anniversary of the Determination of House of Commons establishing their exclusive Rights as Freemen and Burgesses to return members of Parliament for the Borough of Evesham"; while the Nelson Inn in Bengeworth and the Rose and Crown in Evesham were to be "open with ale and pipes tomorrow evening for Sir Charles's friends."

In the event, though following militant endeavours by both Tory and Whig interests, a contest was not necessary; two members, one from each party, were returned and sat together until the next election.

All this time, John Moulting was landlord of the Bell. He was succeeded by Edward Sears (1835), Josiah Wheatley (1837), and Benjamin Luxton (1842), who moved to the Cross Keys when the Bell closed its doors for the last time as an inn, about 1850.

The Bell figures several times in the early Police Records of the borough. Josiah Wheatley, in 1837, charged a Worcester man with wilfully breaking one pane of glass and a looking glass at the Bell and the accused (who "had been committed on several occasions") was jailed for a month. Two years later a Lincolnshire man was fined 5s. for being drunk and creating a disturbance there. In 1840, G.S., of no address, was committed for trial at Worcestershire Quarter Sessions for stealing a quantity of Wheatley's working tools.

It seems that Josiah Wheatley owned the property, as some considerable time afterwards his descendant, Mr Arthur Wheatley, opened the premises as a boot and shoe shop, thus becoming the forerunner of the firm of the same name and trade, with shops at present in High Street and Bridge Street. The old Bell was finally demolished in 1903.

Blue Bell in Cowl Street

The sign of the Blue Bell did not at once disappear from Evesham when the High Street inn ceased to exist as such. It was adopted by a small beerhouse in Cowl Street, kept by Isaac Baylis, lingering there till the turn of the century, when lack of trade and changes in the licensing laws deal the final blows that ensured its demise.

Blue Boar

This was the sign of an alehouse in Bewdley Street. The location is uncertain, but hearsay evidence leads me to believe that it hung near the present entrance to Borthwick Terrace, possibly at No. 52, Bewdley Street. A derelict malt house still stands next to this house, on the west side of the passage entrance to Borthwick Terrace – formerly known as Borthwick Street.

The sign of the Blue Boar is heraldic in origin, deriving from a cognisance used by Richard, Duke of York, father of Edward IV, who had "a blewe Boar with his tuskis and cleis and his membres of gold."

In the middle of the 19th century when the Blue Boar was a flourishing alehouse in Bewdley Street the adjective 'blue' was a word with great political meaning in Evesham. It seems more than likely that the alehouse was the rendezvous of the strong Tory or Blue faction that undoubtedly existed among the independent market gardeners who monopolised Bewdley Street in those days. The steadfast loyalty of these Tory partisans may best be illustrated by their support at the General Election of 1841 for Peter Borthwick, the Tory candidate after whom Borthwick Terrace is named. Mr Borthwick neither canvassed personally nor appeared at the election – he was in fact in Paris at the time – but his adherents in Evesham saw to it that he was well and truly elected and this assuaged their disappointment of four years earlier when the same candidate was elected, then lost his seat when charges of bribery were substantiated[18].

Bridge Inn

The Bridge Inn stood almost exactly upon the site of Mr Newman's wool shop at 34, Bridge Street. An illustration in May's *History of Evesham* (1845) shows it as a gabled building having a rather prominent exposed chimney stack on the east front and a range of low outbuildings between the house and the river. The earliest evidence of its existence appears in 1772, when the company of Mercers met there, but it is likely that an inn had stood close to the river crossing from earliest times. About a hundred years ago a most interesting Evesham character lived there.

---

[18] The story of this incident is told under the sign of the Butchers' Arms. SBB

Born in Cheltenham on 16th April 1824, a member of old Evesham families on both sides, Thomas Cull lost his mother when he was still a child and at quite a tender age got employment on Pickford's fly-boats which, before the advent of railways, did a substantial carrying trade on the Avon and other waterways. When he came of age, he inherited a house in High Street which had belonged to his mother; this he sold and, with the proceeds, set up in the carrying trade on his own account, bringing coal to Evesham by boat. At first the venture did not prosper, nobody would buy his coal, and about a hundred tons of it accumulated on his wharf. But then he had a stroke of luck.

A sixteen-week frost set in. Other stocks were rapidly exhausted. No more could be got, as the river was frozen. Mr Cull was therefore able to sell his coal at any price he cared to ask of it. Becoming prosperous, he developed an extensive trade and he also went into the hay and straw business, sending his trows up to Birmingham and the Black Country, via Stratford, laden with hay and straw, and bringing them back full of coal. He and his wife (formerly a Miss Beale, of Alderminster) now left their cottage in Abbey Gardens (since demolished) and took the old Bridge Inn, or 'Bridge-foot' as it was commonly called then. His coal wharf was where the Methodist Church now is; the river bank was much lower than it is now, and afforded no difficulty in unloading the cargoes. He used to supply coal to the old Evesham Gas Company (established 1835) as well as to private consumers.

9: Bridge Inn, Bridge Street (1845)
Detail from illustration in George May's History of Evesham (1845). The building on the right of the picture is the Bridge Inn.

The bargees in those days were a roughish lot of men, much given to alcoholic refreshment, with the result that Mr Cull sometimes had difficulty in getting his barges home. Fortunately he was as tough as any; and when he found a barge that was overdue, after riding up the river bank in search, he would tackle the bargemen, give them a sound thrashing and see the coal safely to his wharf. It must perhaps be explained that the fly-boats had to be bow-hauled, by the men, on the Avon, but on the Stratford-to-Birmingham Canal they were drawn by horses.

At one time a good deal of Mr Cull's coal was unloaded at the Battleton Bridge wharf (now derelict) where, by some means or other, Dr Beale Cooper, who lived at the Mansion House, managed to levy a wharfage of twopence a ton. But the wharf was eventually declared free, as the result of a lawsuit, and it presumably remains so to this day.

Before the old Evesham bridge was demolished in 1856, a temporary wooden causeway was thrown across the river from Mr Cull's wharf to Burlingham's wharf on the Bengeworth side, so that road traffic could be accommodated while the Workman Bridge was being built. Work began with the demolition of the Bridge Inn, so Mr Cull moved across the river to the Old Angel, an inn which occupied the site of the present traffic island at the junction of Port Street and Waterside; and he then had this coal wharf where the Workman Gardens now are. To complete the bridge scheme the Old Angel was also pulled down, after a time, then Mr Cull took the Talbot, in Port Street, where he stayed for several years, still carrying on his hay and straw business.

In 1860, when his wife died, he quitted the Talbot and had a cottage at the bottom of the Leys. Then he bought some gardening land and a row of cottages at Owlett's End from a Winchcombe draper, Mr Grizzell; he moved into one of the cottages and lived there as a market gardener until he died, on 2nd August 1915, aged 92; he lived to be the oldest man in the town.

After the opening of the railways the carrying trade on the Avon decayed rapidly but Mr Cull was not ruined. He supplied large quantities of straw and fodder to the Midland Railway Company, who sometimes paid him as much as £200 to £300 a month – a substantial sum when gold was the common currency.

The coal business established by Mr Cull so many years ago is still carried on in the town. He sold it to Mr Hollies, from whom it was acquired by Mr Joseph Bailey (another nonagenarian). Mr Bailey continued it, in conjunction with a timber business he owned in Sawmills Lane and eventually his son, Mr Ansell Bailey, of Cheltenham Road, took over the coal business and continued with it until a few years ago. When he retired he disposed of it to Mr G.V. Kyte, of Cambria Road, who still has it.

Thomas Cull was a remarkable man in several ways. Although not a qualified veterinary surgeon he knew a good deal about animals, especially horses, and many local people had more faith in his advice than in the vet's. He had a regular 'surgery' on his premises and was said to have effected some quite startling cures. Innkeeper, coal merchant, barge master, corn merchant, market gardener and vet. Yet he lived to be ninety two, and never had a day's illness in his life!

Bug and Louse

The Bug and Louse, kept by Thomas Day in the middle years of the nineteenth century, was a small alehouse in Rynal Street. It was probably the black and white cottage that is there now, standing immediately to the north of the 'Journal Press' buildings on the western side of the street, though there is no direct evidence of this.

Following the custom of most Evesham publicans of his time, Thomas Day had two occupations; hence his name appears twice in Slater's *Directory* for 1850 – as a wheelwright and as a retailer of beer.

The late E.A.B. Barnard, writing in 1915, listed this sign as the Rag and Louse; but careful inquiries lead me to believe Bug and Louse to be more correct. During the course of these inquiries, a resident who was born in Rynal Street assured me that in his youth the slang name for the street was 'Bug Alley.' Like old soldiers, perhaps, the names of inns never die: they only fade away…..

Butchers' Arms

The sign of the Butchers' Arms graced two licensed houses in Evesham. It first appeared early in the eighteenth century on premises close to the town shambles in High Street, where it flourished until 1808, when it was discarded by James New, the landlord, in favour of the King's Head, a sign which itself became obsolete in 1938, when Timothy Whites and Taylors Ltd, the chemists, bought the redundant inn and built their shop there.

Butchers' Arms in High Street

Sir Thomas Bigge, of Lenchwick Manor, was one of the first seven aldermen appointed under the Charter of 1604 by virtue of which he was also returned to represent the borough in parliament that same year, with Sir Philip Keighley, and continued in office until his death in 1614. In his will he showed his regard for the borough:

> Whereas my desire is to confer some benefit upon the poor inhabitants of Evesham and Bengeworth and also to express my love in the best measure to the whole incorporation of Evesham, I have thought it a work very necessary and behooful for the said borough to have a Butcher Row or Shambles, for strange butchers to stand in; I do hereby will and bequeath for and towards the building of the same Shambles twenty three trees and twenty marks (£13 6s. 8d.) in money to be assigned out and bestowed by my executors; and my will is that the rents of the said Shambles shall be yearly paid and distributed amongst the poor inhabitants of Evesham, two thirds to the poor of Evesham and a third part to the poor of Bengeworth.

And yet inasmuch that some inhabitants of Evesham before whose doors the same butchers do now stand may receive prejudice by the erection of the said Shambles therefore my will and desire is that the incorporation shall satisfy and give contentment to all parties grieved.

The Shambles were duly erected in the south-east quarter of High Street within six months of Bigge's death and I have no doubt but that the sign of the Butchers' Arms was hoisted opposite very shortly afterwards. There the Shambles remained until 1795 when, having fallen into a state of gross disrepair, they were demolished by the municipality. It is of interest to observe that the picturesque Tudor building in which Mr Harry Hughes now trades as a butcher stands very close to the site of the Jacobean "Butcher Row." Tradition, it seems, dies hard in Evesham.

The Welsborne family, who held the Butchers' Arms for about a century, figure prominently in the life and affairs of the borough. Charles Welsborne was mayor of Evesham in 1751 and again when he died on 7th February 1767. His son Charles also became mayor, in 1779, after moving across High Street to become landlord of the George Inn.

A good deal of borough business was settled under the hospitable roof of the Butchers' Arms. The Company of Mercers met there in 1739 and 1745, while on 4th November 1747, the Glovers' Company spent 2s. 6d. "at the butchers arms" and a further sum on 20th November "at Charles Wellsborne on ye Mayer on ye Master etc being sworn."

On 30th August 1774, a meeting of the Common Council was held in the town hall for the purposes of electing twenty-seven candidates as freemen of the borough "by right of their being sons of freemen." The business concluded with the resolution: "We hereby adjourn the above meeting till four o'clock this afternoon to be held at the Sign of the Butchers' Arms within the said Borough." The adjourned meeting was duly held and several more freemen were elected during the course of it. It should perhaps be noted that each newly-elected freeman contributed three guineas to the "common stock." On 29th August 1775, a similar meeting "adjourned to the Butchers' Arms at five o'clock in the afternoon to be there dissolved."

The churchwardens also regarded the Butchers' Arms as a suitable venue for the annual ceremony of balancing the parish accounts; thus in May, 1793, the sum of 5s. 3d. was expended there "at the settling of the book." Charles Welsborne, senior, was a churchwarden at St Lawrence's in 1755 and his son Charles also served in the same capacity. His name appeared with those of three co-wardens on the brass minute dial, nine inches in diameter, which was affixed to the bell tower clock by William Worton, of Birmingham, in 1775. The dial was removed when a new clock face was erected in 1876, and hung in the vestry of All Saints' for many years afterwards.

When the Inclosure Commissioners visited this district in 1765 a notice was put up in the porch of the parish church of Norton and Lenchwick announcing their first meeting which was to be held "on June 10, 1765, at the house of Charles Wellsbourne, the Butchers' Arms, Evesham."

Butchers' Arms in the Market Place

Soon after 1820 the old sign was revived by James Russ, very appropriately a butcher, who had his shop in the building now known as the Walker Hall. In those days, Evesham Post Office[19] was the site of two Georgian houses, and it was on the one nearer to his shop that landlord Russ resuscitated the sign of the Butchers' Arms. Mr A.T. Colson's frontispiece to May's *History of Evesham* depicts the butcher's shop and the adjoining inn as they appeared about 1845.

10: Butcher's Arms, Market Place (1845)
*Detail from A.T. Colson's frontispiece to George May's History of Evesham (1845).
The Butcher's Arms was in the left-hand side of the imposing Georgian building to the
right of the Walker Hall (the site of James Russ's butchers shop).*

Mr Russ evidently had a keen eye for business, for at Easter, 1822, when the usual vestry meeting had been held at All Saints', he submitted his account "for expenses of the meeting," from which it appears that more than £2 was spent on "Eating, Liquors, etc." These items and the proximity of the hostelry seem to have given every satisfaction to the parochial body, for thereafter it became a popular proposition that parish meetings "be adjourned to the Butchers' Arms."

That James Russ was not a man to be trifled with is evident from the number of times he appeared as a successful prosecutor before the Evesham magistrates in cases of drunkenness and fighting on his premises. On one such occasion he accused his

---

[19] The site in Market Place most recently occupied by the shop 'Home Style'. SBB

servant, J.C., of being drunk and neglecting his employment, with the result that the man was sent to a month's hard labour.

In March 1838, the Butchers' Arms figured prominently in evidence given by local residents before a select committee of the House of Commons, under the chairmanship of Sir Robert Peel, to which had been submitted an election petition by Robert Salmon and others, accusing the two Tory M.P.s, the Hon. George Rushout and Peter Borthwick, of bribery and corruption before the election held at Evesham on 24th July 1837.

With less than 500 voters entitled to return two members for the borough, the competition among the principals and their agents for the avowed support of each individual voter was understandably keen, especially as the issue was frequently decided by a majority of ten votes or less. Each voter had two votes, and all kinds of questionable tactics were employed to enlist his support as a "plumper," that is, to give both his votes to one candidate.

Treats of ale at various public houses in the town for weeks on end before the election were a common feature of the election campaigns. Concerning the election of 1818, George May notes:

> The amount of money expended upon this deplorable contest, from its commencement to the close of the subsequent petition, was, upon the most moderate estimate, twenty thousand pounds! Of this amount, the expenses for cramming and swilling electors must of itself have formed a weighty item in the sum.

Everything points to the conclusion that the 1837 election could not have been much less expensive to the candidates.

Minutes of evidence (ordered by the House of Commons to be printed, 8th June 1818) show that the main barbs in the attack upon the two Tory M.P.s were directed against Peter Borthwick. Consequently, the case against the Hon. George Rushout was abandoned at an early stage in the proceedings. The major charge against Borthwick accused him of bribing a voter by making a present of an engraved silver snuff box following a treat of ale held at the Butchers' Arms a week before the election in 1837.

Briefly, the story goes that in 1836, after voting as a plumper for Borthwick at a previous election, Ebenezer Pearce, a retired schoolmaster resident in Bengeworth, when in the company of a Tory agent, expressed admiration for Borthwick's crest and motto, as displayed upon the latter's carriage. Pearce said he would like a snuff box with the arms of Borthwick engraved upon it. His wishes were communicated through Charles Best (an attorney and Borthwick's agent) to Borthwick himself, who ordered the box in London.

The year following, as the election approached, Pearce was canvassed by Borthwick to become a plumper on his behalf. Pearce declined to promise either of his votes to Borthwick, he said, until the Whig candidate, Lord Marcus Hill, be safely elected.

About a fortnight before the election was due, Pearce attended a treat of ale given by Borthwick at the Butchers' Arms for his prospective supporters. During the course of the treat, Borthwick informed Pearce that a snuff box had been waiting for him in Evesham for six or seven months. A few days later, his chief agent, Charles Best, delivered the snuff box personally to Pearce with the instruction to "put it aside until the election is over."

After the snuff box had been accepted by Pearce, he was canvassed several times by Borthwick but, as the evidence shows, he remained obdurate and flatly declined to promise his first or second vote unless he saw Lord Marcus Hill safe. This must have come as a severe setback to Borthwick after his persistent efforts to influence Pearce. Realising that his former confidence had been misplaced, he then sought means of retrieving the situation for, in the event, Pearce never appeared at the hustings on 24th July 1838, to vote for either party.

What happened? The answer is contained, appropriately enough, in the notorious silver snuff box itself, now in the possession of Mr L.C. Cox, of Evesham. Beautifully chased and ornamented, with the initials *E.P.* inside a shield on the exterior, the inside of the lid is engraved with Peter Borthwick's crest – a blackamoor's head in profile coupled proper – and beneath this, the inscription:

EBENEZER PEARCE
Ex dono Amici Sui,
Qui conducit

The wording is ambiguous. But it has been taken to mean "The gift of a friend of his who corrupts or hires." It could equally mean "The gift of a friend of his who leads on." But it is a small parchment inside the box which completes the history of the political intrigue hatched at the Butchers' Arms:

> This is the notorious Snuff Box, the giving of which, during the Election of 1837, was declared by the Committee, presided over by Sir Robert Peel, as an act of Bribery on the part of Peter Borthwick, and to have vitiated his Seat for Evesham, which was transferred to Lord Marcus Hill, and retained by him for fifteen years. This result led to a bloodless Duel between Mr P.B. and Mr Geo. Rushout, his colleague. It appeared that at a previous Election some token of regard had been promised but never given to the Voter Ebenezer Pearce, who had been a warm partizan of Mr P.B. but, as in an intermediate Contest between Lord Marcus and Mr Rushout, he had voted for the former, it was feared that the Vote might be in jeopardy, and the Snuff Box was thereupon despatched from London and delivered to the Voter. This was subsequently disclosed by the Voter – *indignant as having been made drunk, carried off to Liverpool and so prevented from keeping his word to Lord Marcus.* The words inscribed within the box, 'Amici Sui. Qui conducit' (*conducere* – to corrupt) have been much commented on. Twenty years after the event, the Box had been presented this day to Lord Marcus Hill by Mr Oswald Cheek of Evesham, his most efficient Conducting Agent. 18th March 1858.

Cider Mill

Now that the Oddfellows' Arms is no longer a free house, the distinction of being the last independent publican in Evesham passes to Mr Samuel Pritchard, of the Cider Mill, Hampton. Octogenarian though he is, Mr Pritchard is still actively interested in the busy inn which he now manages with the help of his sons, Walter and Eric, and his daughter, Miss Dorothy Pritchard.

11: Cider Mill, Hampton (2003)

Mr Pritchard came from Charlton in February 1912, to live at the Cider Mill, which had formerly been kept by Mr William Poole and before that by Messrs George Grove and William White as an off-licence house. In 1928, just a century after the first justices' licence had been granted to the house, Mr Pritchard made a successful application for an 'on' licence.

According to a *Journal* report of the proceedings in court at the time, Mr Pritchard's application was supported by Mr David Gisbourne, who said he lived next door to Mr Pritchard and honestly believed an 'on' licence was needed because people were continually called at his house to borrow bottles. Questioned whether there would be jubilation in the village (Hampton did not become part of the borough until 1933) if the licence were granted, Mr Pritchard replied: "Yes, they would put the flag out."

Mr Alfred Hicken, who had been a licensee of the Swan in Bengeworth, also applied for a licence at the same sessions to convert Nos. 40-42, Pershore Road into The Falcon Hotel and Hydro, but his application was turned down.

Immediately after the extension of his licence, Mr Pritchard carried out extensive improvements at his premises. The building which actually housed the cider *mill* was converted into a club room and billiard room and has since proved a great asset to the inn and the parish generally.

The cider store at the rear of the inn must be unique among out-buildings in Evesham. It was constructed by German prisoners during the 1914-18 war, under the supervision of Mr Sidney Davis and Mr Pritchard himself. It consists of a timber-framed building with wattle walls and thatched roof but the unusual feature is that the walls are filled with gorse, cut at Hinton Roughs, none of which has been replaced since it was first put there thirty years ago – and the building was accepted for insurance against fire. I have not heard of any building similarly constructed anywhere in the district.

Since it became a fully licensed house, The Mill has become a recognised social centre in the parish of Hampton. The home of crack teams in the Air Gun and Darts Leagues, the Hampton Angling Club, the British Legion and other societies, it continues in fact to fulfil the best traditions of the village inn (including the annual cider-making) and will remain, I am assured by Mr Sam Pritchard himself, a free house as long as he has any control over its destiny.

Coach Makers' Arms

The Coach Makers' Arms in the Market Place appeared twice in the almanacks of the time: Slater's *Directory*, 1850, showed the landlord as Thomas Williams; and the inn was mentioned in Kelly's *Directory*, 1854. The sign does not seem to have existed before 1850 or after 1875.

In the course of its comparatively brief existence it served as headquarters for two of the carriers who operated from the town, and it probably derived its curious name from its proximity to a building now known as the Walker Hall, which was then used as a branch establishment by Whitgrove, the coachbuilder, of The Butts, Worcester.

Local coachmakers and wheelwrights, of which there were seven, did a flourishing business in supplying the requirements of carriers by land in the fifties. Names like Ashley and Gilbert have been associated with the trades almost to the present day.

A hundred years ago 75 carriers were established in Evesham but the business was soon to suffer a set-back from competition by the newly arrived Oxford, Worcester and Wolverhampton Railway, which was appropriately nicknamed the "Oh! Worse and Worse!" – as it certainly was from the carriers' point of view.

Kelly's *Directory of Worcestershire*, 1854, indicated that 32 carriers quartered at the King's Head, 24 at the Royal Oak, 6 at the Red Lion, 3 at the Bridge Inn, 2 at each of the Butchers' Arms, Plough, Woolpack and Coach Makers' Arms, while the remaining two wagons started from the railway station.

Evesham, with a population of between 4,000 and 5,000, was already firmly on the path to becoming the thriving market town it is today. This comment appeared in Kelly's 1854 edition:

> The staple branch of industry is market gardening, for which Evesham has long been famous, supplying the larger towns, Tewkesbury, Cheltenham, Birmingham, Dudley and even London with fruit and vegetables. There is much business in seeds and some in hops. There are maltings, a tannery, parchment and glue works. Eight yearly fairs are held in High Street and the Market Place.

The sign of the Coach Makers' Arms belongs to that period when a spate of 'arms' swept the signboards of English inns. A few, like the familiar Masons' Arms (Pebworth) and Blacksmiths' Arms (North Littleton) could, with toleration, be allied with the crests and devices of the ancient guilds and merchant companies which had been widely adopted as tavern signs in antiquity. But the mid nineteenth century produced such heraldic anomalies as the Chaffcutters' Arms, the Hot Pressers' Arms, the Puddlers' Arms and – in one noteworthy case – the Engine and Tender Arms: all of them plainly nonsensical. The last words on this topic are borrowed from the signboard of a modern pub at Peckham. It rejoices in the astounding name of the Gold-Diggers' Arms.

Cockatoo

The Cockatoo existed for about ten years and it was on Greenhill. The story goes that early in the nineteenth century an Evesham man colloquially known as "Old Nobbs" emigrated to a tropical paradise where, settling down, he prospered. In due course he sent for his family, and his sons joined him. Eventually, however, one of them returned to his native town and, with funds provided by "Old Nobbs", built the house which is now 29, Greenhill. This was Joseph Nobbs, described by Bentley's *Directory*, 1840, as a retailer of beer, for he opened his new house as an alehouse under the sign of the Cockatoo.

Young Nobbs chose his site with a very shrewd eye on its business possibilities. It will readily be appreciated that it was the first place of refreshment which the dusty pedestrian encountered as he approached Evesham from the northward; conversely, it was the last opportunity for him to have "one for the road" if he was outward bound.

Horse-drawn vehicles coming from Worcester and Alcester had been halted at the toll gate near Blayney's Lane, so that a few more minutes spent at the Cockatoo to wash the irritating particles from the driver's throat were of little account. And every decent horseman leaving the town behind was bound to rest his nag, and refresh himself, when he reached the crest of Greenhill.

Drovers, passing to and from with the animals bought and sold at Evesham's fairs and markets, had the best excuse of any for patronising the Cockatoo, as their beasts clustered at the pool opposite, setting an example that could hardly be ignored.

Joseph's skill was worthy of his enterprising father and, though he never again appears in local history, it is pleasant to speculate on his subsequent fortunes. With such unbounded opportunity for selling beer, he probably made a lot of money, grew rapidly wealthy and retired from business at an early age to become what, in fact, he was already – "one of the nobs" – for the Cockatoo was no more by 1850.

Cross Keys

> Cross Keys Commercial Inn, High Street, Evesham. Thomas Partington respectfully returns thanks to his friends and the public generally for the support he has received since taking the above and trust that by combining good accommodation with moderate charges to merit and receive a continuance of the same; he also takes the opportunity to invite the special attention of commercial men and others to the first class stabling, loose boxes, etc., largely erected by him, which are equal to any in the county. Flys and dog-carts for hire.

Thus, in 1863, the landlord of the Cross Keys advertised his house at the junction of High Street and Swan Lane in the columns of the *Evesham Journal*. In those days, all the cattle and vegetables markets were held on the site of the present omnibus station and it seems that Mr Partington adopted the right policy in seeking the patronage of the commercial men for in May, 1871, he was able to purchase the inn himself for £950 at a public auction. During Mr Partington's sojourn at the inn an omnibus left daily for Alcester.

The next major alterations to the inn took place in the summer of 1938 when it was revealed as almost entirely a half-timbered building beneath the Georgian shell of slate and stucco. One of the more striking features was the discovery of a steeply pitched Tudor-style gabled roof intact beneath the existing slate structure. Much of the timber salvaged from the old inn was purchased by Mr Thomas Hyde, well known as people's warden at Hampton church for many years past, who later discovered a faded document tucked away in a crevice in one of the ancient beams.

Through the good offices of Mr K. Gill Smith, now president of the Vale of Evesham Historical Society, and the late E.A.B. Barnard, F.S.A., the document eventually found its way to the records office at Guildhall in the City of London where, expertly cleaned, repaired and backed with gossamer transparent silk and now entirely legible, it is valued as the only plague certificate relating to the Great Plague of 1665 in the possession of the City authorities.

The document certifies that Mary Walker, servant to George Bostock, of the parish of St Andrew Undershaft in the ward of Lime Street in London, is free from plague; and it is dated 5th July 1665. A week later than this, according to Samuel Pepys, "above 700 died of the plague this week…"

Between 1653 and 1765 it was the custom for the churchwardens of All Saints', Evesham, to enter into agreements with various local tradesmen to do certain maintenances to the church fabric and its surrounds for a term of twenty years. In 1712 John Whitford "att the Cross Keys, plaisterer, agreed to do all the work relating to his trades for twenty years" at a cost of forty shillings a year. By 1717 he had not been paid for his work on the church and, together with another creditor, Richard Worrell, was elected churchwarden for the ensuing year. Three years later the Evesham Company of Glovers spent "7 shillings for a rump of beef and a shoulder of mutton at the Cross Keys and 5s. in ale at the same time."

12: Cross Keys, High Street (c.1890 and 2003)
The old Cross Keys building was demolished in 1938. In the 1840s Swan Lane was known as Cross Keys Lane. The symbol on the corner of the new building is the only remaining indication of its history as an inn.

On 16th November 1820, the Cross Keys was the scene of a public dinner (tickets 3s.) organised by the Whig faction in Evesham and district to celebrate the failure of "the bill of pains and penalties" against Queen Caroline in the House of Lords six days previously. The bill, by which George IV sought to dissolve his marriage with Caroline on the ground of her misconduct, created a furore throughout the country. Public feeling rose high that so bad a husband as George should complain of his wife's conduct. Brougham, the most prominent Whig lawyer, became the Queen's legal champion and so strong was the feeling engendered that the government ministers dropped their bill after it had passed a third reading in the Lords by a majority of only nine.

In Evesham, Edward Savage, the mayor, refused to sponsor an address of congratulation to Her Majesty or convene a meeting for the purpose of so doing, or to allow the town hall to be used for such a meeting. But his political adversaries were not to be denied the privilege of signifying their approval and in consequence a notice appeared informing inhabitants of the borough that "an address now lies for signature at Mr Kinsey's late house in Bridge Street."

The dinner at the Cross Keys was duly held under the presidency of Charles Edward Hanford, of Wollashill; the town was illuminated and a subscription list was opened by Mr Nathaniel Hartland, of Hartland's Bank, by which 1,200 needy families in the town were supplied with bread and meat. Readers may well wonder how Evesham came to be 'lit up' in those days when gas and electricity still lay in the future. Loads of clay were dumped in the streets for the free use of householders in manufacturing balls of the material with candle sockets; these were stuck in the doors of their residences and lighted candles at dusk completed the 'illuminations'.

Between 1820 and 1840 William Trotman was landlord. He was a fervent freemason and the Masonic Lodge of Mercy and Truth met there in 1824, 1826 and 1827. A Lodge of Instruction operated there in 1824 and 1825. At this time also the Cross Keys was the excise office for the town, Thomas Kitchner (1835) and James Aveline (1840) being the officers concerned.

Susannah Trotman was the licensee in 1842, Benjamin Luxton in 1850, Mark Hughes in 1854 and Thomas Partington in 1862. Later landlords included W. Firth (1894); J.L. Wood (1898); U.C. Meadows (1913); T. Orton (1915); W.J. Doyle (1917); W.C. Doyle (1920); and S. Stanbra who kept the 'Keys' from 1935 until Mr Hector Morris moved there from the Plough in 1951.

The inn used to display a pair of gold-painted iron keys, "the keys of heaven and hell," as the arms of the Papal See, the emblem of St Peter and his successors, are so often described.

Crown

Crown in Bridge Street

> Ordered that an Ordinarye at 1s. 6d. be provided at the Crowne in Evesham at the next Easter Sessions for 30 persons and 8d. ordinary for servants for 2 days, viz Tuesday and Wednesday in Low Sunday week. And that a hogshead of ale be provided also for the said entertainment. And if any of it be left it is to be disposed of by Mr Maior for the use of the Corporation. Mr Rowland Broadstock now present undertakes to make the same entertainment as above and to find and provide a hogshead of best fine ale at 2s. 10d. and Tobacco pipes and the best tobacco at 2s. ye pound.

This entry in the Evesham Town Council minute book dated 19th March 1703, is typical of the many private and civic functions held under the hospitable roof of the Crown during the eighteenth century. The Crown became a most popular venue for the feasts of the various companies of mercers, fellmongers, ironmongers and innholders trading in the town as well as the borough election feasts held annually in

December, which often cost very substantial sums of money. More typical of the general trade of the inn is a bill head dated 1715 which reads:

> Paid to Mr Broadstock at the Crown, Evesham, ye ordinaryes of Mr Gardner, Mr Walker, Mr Andrews, Will Hendy and myself, 15s. 6d., three horses there 6d., maid 6d., ostler 2d.

It is of interest to trace the fortunes of landlord Rowland Broadstock at this period. He seems to have followed Anthony Brooke as landlord of the Crown at the close of the seventeenth century. Previously, he had succeeded his father, also Rowland Broadstock, as landlord of the prosperous George in High Street. He had been admitted a freeman of the borough on 7th October 1681, and probably became a member of the company of innholders at the same time. In 1683 and 1684 he was a churchwarden at St Lawrence's; he was overseer of the highways in that parish in 1682 and 1697 and coroner for the town in 1692. He became a member of the corporation in 1694 and mayor in 1695-6.

For the next ten years he played a prominent part in the life of the town, in his new role of mine host of the Crown, but by 1707 his signature in the minute books of the corporation was becoming shaky and he signed for the last time in 1711.

13: Crown Hotel, Bridge Street (c.1845)
Picture from George May's History of Evesham (1845).

Financial difficulties appear to have brought about his decline, as may be inferred from a letter now in the records of Martin's bank (which was established by an Evesham family early in the eighteenth century); it reads:

Sir, - I told you that in one year's time probable I might assist you be ye time is not expired nor do I reckon wt I said incumbent on me. I am, yours T.M. (Thomas Martin). Mr Rowland Broadstock, Postmaster, Evesham.

In 1719, Henry Higgins, master of John Deacle's school, died and the corporation were asked to recommend two persons to Mr John Deacle, executor of the founder, for the vacancy. They submitted the names of Mr John Whittingham, of Elmley Castle, and Mr Rowland Broadstock; and the choice fell on the former. The once prosperous publican probably needed the salary very badly by that time for when he died some ten years later his widow was voted the sum of one sovereign as a gift from the council and she also received from Lady Tracy's Charity a half-crown for coals every Christmas until her death.

Rowland Broadstock had a son, John Broadstock, who was educated at Queen's College, Oxford, where he matriculated as the son of "Rowland Broadstock, of Evesham, plebeian" in 1701 at the age of 19. He took his degree, B.A., in 1705 and apparently returned to his native Evesham as stipendiary curate of Bengeworth, leaving again in 1712. It would be interesting to know whether the cost of educating his son had any bearing upon the father's financial plight.

Broadstock's successor at the Crown was short-lived; his over-grown tombstone may be found in All Saints' churchyard, close to the south wall of the chancel: "John Welsh, inn keeper of the Crown inn in this town," died 23rd July 1724, aged 39.

A discovery which created a stir in the town concerned the next keeper of the Crown. The event is recorded in a letter to Mr John Rudge, of London, from his agent in Evesham, Mr Robert Cookes, dated 13th July 1726:

About a weeke agoe John Collet, thinkeing he coulde find some pipes of leade, began diggin about two or three yards from the churchyard and carried it to All Saints' porch, about 14 yards, in which space he tooke up above 500 weight of lead pipe; where it was dry 'twas almost mouldered to dust; where wettish 'twas fresh and good....

The whole lies about four feete deepe. And it is probable that pipe spreads in several branches from Hampson's house to Mr Harvey's garden, where the Abbey Church stood; every little matter runns people's imaginacons high. Now they fancy there were at the dissolucon of the Abbey (when everybody runn away with what they could get) many other valuable thinges hid in the ground. Ashmore at the Crowne talkes of diggin the Cross churchyard[20] and doubts not, if noe other valuable goods, at least to find a great many valuable stones that were foundacons of a great many buildings belonging to the old Abbey Church. And perhaps Mr Harvey and some other of your tenants may have the same thoughts.

---

[20] Now known as Upper Abbey Park. TJSB

It must be presumed that Ashmore and his neighbours were restrained by their landlord from raiding the supposed El Dorado, since Mr Edward Rudge undertook an excavation of the Abbey site between 1811 and 1834, and published his findings in book form in 1820. A piece of the lead pipe in question is now in the possession of Mr W.A. Cox, of Abbey Gate (formerly Mr Harvey's house); and it has been promised to the Almonry museum.

As this extract from the *Worcester Postman* of 22nd November 1723, shows, at least one man was content to make the Crown itself his El Dorado.

> Whereas a tall lusty man who owns his name to be Thomas Robinson with Black curled hair, long Visage wearing a white Fustine frock to short for him.... being on 8th November 1723 commited to Evesham Gaol for stealing divers goods out of the Crown inn in Evesham... broke out of the said gaol from Thomas Clemens, keeper thereof, and made his Escape. These are to give notice that if anyone can secure the said Person so as the said Thomas Clemens may have him again he shall have a guinea reward and reasonable charges.

When the company of Mercers held one of their many feasts at the Crown in 1744, Mr William Cox was landlord. In 1751 the landlord was Thomas Hodges who had been previously at the Fleece; in 1761 Mr Hodges paid the recently imposed window tax for 32 lights - £2 11s.; he was also a churchwarden of All Saints' for several years. Towards the end of the eighteenth century, John Headley was the landlord of the Crown when, on 16th May 1791, the following advertisement appeared in *Berrow's Worcester Journal*:

> To be let and entered upon on 10th October next, one of the largest and most convenient and best accustomed Inns in the Kingdom, known by the sign of the Crowne, and situate in the market town of Evesham and the county of Worcester, together with about twenty acres of richer meadow and pasture land into which the inn yard opens; the whole now in the occupation of Mr John Headley, and will be let either from year to year, or on lease, to a substantial tenant. For particulars and terms of holding apply to Messrs Welch and Blaney, Evesham.

John Headley died in 1834, and was buried in the graveyard of the Baptist Chapel in Cowl Street.

The following lampoon dated 25th March 1818, was published as everyone in Evesham knew, by Tom Jarrett, a former landlord of the Crown inn. It concerns the parliamentary election of that year which, despite so much sound and fury against him, was won by the Whig member, the maligned Humphrey Howarth.

> Who did in the year 1801 last past present himself and offer himself as an Upright and Honest Man to represent you in Parliament and solicit your suffrages for the purpose? Humphrey Howarth!
> Who gave Orders for Himself, his agents and Voters to be provided with Breakfasts, Dinners, Teas, Suppers, Wines, Ales, Liquors and other

articles of comfort; House room and Bedding at the time at the Crown Inn in the Burgh of Evesham? Humphrey Howarth!

Who partakes of many Feasts and Entertainments ordered by Humphrey Howarth at that Inn? Who? Why, Humphrey Howarth and his Agents, Voters and Friends.

Who was arrested in London for the House Bill for such treats and entertainments at the Crown Inn in the Burgh of Evesham? H.H.

Did Humphrey Howarth come forward and discharge the Inn Keeper's Bill for his Feasts and Entertainments upon his being arrested? No, he did not!

Was the cause tried? Yes, it was, at Worcester Assizes, 1802.

How did the jury give their verdict? Humphrey Howarth having pleaded the Treating Act to avoid payment a Verdict was found in his favour!

How did the Landlord of the Crown Inn get through his difficulties owing to the conduct of Humphrey Howarth refusing and avoiding payment? He was sadly oppressed and proceeded against by his Wine Merchants, Maltsters, Butchers and Bakers, his landlord, and others and utterly ruined!

And all this was owing to Humphrey Howarth was it? It was.

Is he a conscientious and fit Person to sit in the House of Commons as a Representative for the ancient Burgh of Evesham or any other place whatsoever? No, he is not.

It would be tedious to relate the full details of the part played by the Crown, its landlords and patrons in nineteenth century politics but any reader who would like to learn more on the subject of the 'dirty game' should consult the various election petitions published at the time.

Tom Jarrett was, according to one contemporary account, "a tall, strong man with the air and manners of a duke," who once, for a wager, undertook to take part in a race handicapped by carrying a sack of wheat on his back. He was also renowned for his outspokenness and native wit. One story about him recalls his piebald horse with a white face which he was leading up the main street in Bengeworth one day when he met lawyer Blaney (of Blaney's Lane).

"Why, Jarrett," said Blaney, "your horse is looking very pale this morning!" Jarrett retorted: "You will look pale, too, when your turn comes to wear a halter."

In 1803, Tom Jarrett gave up innkeeping to become an auctioneer and addressed this letter to the public:

Having let the Crown Inn and premises to Mr Lewis Prosser, late of the Star and Garter, Tewkesbury, whose exertions I am persuaded will ever be on the alert to render accommodation comfortable and pleasant to the public; it would be unbecoming the obligations I feel as a duty of gratitude not to acknowledge to my late customers, particular friends and a large proportion of a generous public who have honoured me with their support were I to retire from my position silent and insensible of those tokens of respect which the common example of mankind require me to offer to the world on such an occasion. With a heart full of thanks for all favours I beg leave to distribute them where due, and it is with pleasure I hope ever to keep a grateful record in my memory through life of numerous indulgences I have so liberally experienced at the Crown.

Finding, however, the auctioneering business more congenial to my inclination and wishes than my former avocation, I am determined to pursue that employment with unremitting diligence and assiduity; and wish to avail myself of this opportunity to repeat my earnest solicitations to the public, professional gentlemen, farmers, tradesmen and others, for their kind support in that line of business; in other transactions of which, I shall always endeavour to discharge my duty (according to my best judgement) with the strictest honour and integrity.

Jarrett made a great success of his new business, despite his pleas of "utter ruin."

Up to 1845 the Crown still retained much of the appearance of the coaching inns immortalised in *Pickwick Papers*. A sketch in May's *History of Evesham* (1845 edition) gives a good impression of the appearance of the Crown at the time, with some of the old external timber galleries still remaining. In this drawing, the Crown Vaults (now an off-licence) popularly known as the Hole in the Wall from its unusual access, has a signboard proclaiming it to be the Crown Tap. As such, it would almost certainly be the place of refreshment for coachmen, grooms and servants, while the 'quality' were regaled above, in the main rooms of the inn.

Coaching days and the hazards of travel in the eighteenth century on 'The King's Highway' were recalled for the people of Evesham when the film of that name was made in the district in 1927. Using the Crown as their headquarters, the film company directed by Mr G.A.L. Sinclair-Lewis, O.B.E., of Stoll Pictures, shot scenes in period costume at Wick Manor, the Combertons, Defford, Elmley Castle, Pershore, Campden, the Almonry and the Crown itself, often using local 'extras' to simulate Bow Street runners, ostlers, serving wenches and other Georgian characters.

The coaches and horses stabled at the Crown created much interest. Among the vehicles used was a coach formerly owned by Queen Victoria and a gig at one time the property of the Duke of Connaught. The stars of the film, Matheson Lang and Joan Lockton, made personal appearances at the Clifton (then the Scala) cinema, and for a week the Crown was besieged by fond mothers and daughters anxious to pursue a film career. Mr Sinclair-Lewis wrote to the *Journal* afterwards:

Never before have we found people more helpful or courteous than in Evesham and the surrounding villages.

In Bridge Street, Evesham, the Crown Hotel displays one of the oldest and most popular of all English inn signs. Over 1,000 Crowns, according to Monson Fitzgerald, offer hospitality to travellers throughout the country. On the score of antiquity, a much-quoted anecdote concerns a cockney innkeeper, William Walters, who made a declaration that he would make his son "heir to the Crown" in Cheapside. It was 1467 and unfortunately for William the Wars of the Roses had made Edward IV extremely touchy about puns concerning the succession to the throne; the result was that Walters lost his head for high treason.

Nobody knows exactly when our Evesham Crown was built, but it could not have been long after this incident, for there is evidence of the original building being constructed in the early Tudor style before the dissolution of the Abbey in 1539 and the subsequent sale of the site and lands to Sir Philip Hoby, a Leominster landowner, in 1542.

Among the many interesting antiquities from Evesham Abbey now preserved at Abbey Manor, home of the Rudge family, is a bloodstone depicting in high relief the figure of an angel clad in armour, probably St Michael. This was recovered from the Crown yard over a century ago, and was probably in the first instance a jewel set in the back of an abbatial glove. Extensive improvements to the inn, carried out by Messrs Ushers in 1938-40 revealed a very fine Tudor fireplace which now constitutes a striking feature of the smoke room at the Crown.

Writing in 1820, Edward John Rudge, F.S.A., who, together with his father, was responsible for excavating the site of the Abbey between 1811 and 1834, noted that some parts of the inn were co-eval with the Abbey in structure, particularly the top of the kitchen (now smoke room) chimney, carved in stone, and the remains of ancient doorways and window openings in cellars next to the street (now the off-licence). A quarter of a century later, George May (writing in 1845) made observations concerning the "considerable alteration" then in progress at the Crown:

> ...an ancient hostelry, of which most of the external galleries of communication remain, although the side of its original quadrangle which fronted the street has, at some comparatively recent period, been taken down.

Thus, from its location and architectural associations, it is reasonable to assume that the Crown was one of those early inns which accommodated the pilgrims visiting Evesham Abbey.

The name of the Crown Inn is mentioned in title deeds to Evesham properties as far back as 1598, and is itself included in a marriage settlement made in 1633. The marriage was between William Courteen, the younger, then 24 years of age, and "the lady Katharine, one of the daughters of the Right Honourable John, Earl of Bridgewater, Viscount Brackley and Baron Ellesmere, Knight of the most Honorable Order of the Bath, Lord President of His Majesty's Council established in Wales and one of His Majesty's Privy Council."

In return for "a competent sum of money" settled upon the young couple by the earl as the marriage portion of his daughter, the Courteen family (London merchants who had succeeded the Hobys into the former Abbey possessions) granted the earl specified properties in the county for the Lady Katharine's jointure in case she should happen to outlive her husband. Included were lands at Great Hampton and Bengeworth, together with:

...all that syte of the late dissolved Monastery of Evesham with the rights, members, liberties and appurtenances thereof... all that house and tenement called the Almery House... all that park and enclosed ground called the Parke in Evesham... and all that house, tenement and Inn called or known by the name of the Crowne... which were purchased by Sir William Courteen by indenture dated November 22, 1625.

In 1664, following disastrous merchant ventures in the New World, William Courteen conveyed to Edward Rudge, another London merchant trading with China, some 260 acres of the Evesham Abbey estate, "together with the Crowne Inn, garden and wharf adjoining, the gardens next the churchyard and certain tenements and royalties in the conveyance."

To Thomas Baskerville, son of antiquary Hannibal Baskerville, of Bayworth House, Abingdon, we are indebted for the name of the first innkeeper of the Crown inn on record, in addition to a glimpse of Evesham in 1678. Together with Mr Stevenson, his friend, Baskerville, the younger, travelled widely in England during Charles II's reign and left two manuscript volumes of observations. One of these belongs to the Duke of Portland and is preserved in the library of Welbeck Abbey; the other is in the Harleian MSS. at the British Museum. This is what Thomas Baskerville had to say about Evesham in July 1678:

> The prospect of Evesham offers well at some distance for it hath three pretty handsome churches in it, two of them in one churchyard, and a fair tower built of hewn stone, with six good bells in it, standing alone by itself at some distance from the churches; to go in it here is a stone bridge built over the Avon, full of jack, perch, roach, dace and other kinds. Here are some houses belonging to the town on this side of the bridge. Esom is a mayor town and sends two burgesses to Parliament. The competitors at present for the places were Sir James Rusher (Rushout), Mr Parker, the recorder of the town, and Mr Ridge (Rudge). Here they have great markets for the sale of corn and oats. We lay at the Crown kept by Widow Bayley.

Anthony Brooke is the next landlord of the Crown of whom we have cognisance and he appears to have been an important burgess, a member of the Borough Council and surveyor of the highways in All Saints' parish. On 14th March 1682, the council passed the following resolution:

> This day and yeare aforesaid this chamber in gratitude to Thomas Savage, esquire, of Elmley Castle, one of the aldermen and a Justice of the Peace of the borough, and now High Sheriffe of the County of Worcester, doe hereby order and appoynt that two men in livery according to ye livery of ye next Lent Assizes att Worcester, bee provided att ye charge of this Chamber. And that they doe attend the said High Sheriffe at ye next Lent and Summer Assizes in their said liverys to doe as they ought. And that Anthony Brooke and Nicholas Field, the sergeants-at-mace of this Borough, be the sayde liverye men.

Mr Savage was indeed honoured by an escort in the persons of two such eminent burgesses, for Mr Nicholas Field was the mayor that year, while Mr Anthony Brooke looked after the welfare of the Council men by providing "beer and fire at ye Chamber and at ye Crowne on ye account day..." at reasonable sums to the satisfaction of all concerned – judging from the regular patronage accorded him while he held sway at the Bridge Street hostelry. The Corporation expended £6 19s. on the "liverye according to ye liverye of the sayd High Sheriffe" and a further sum of £1 16s. was spent on two hats. We may well imagine how Messrs Field and Brooke, thus arrayed, made a suitable impression on the dignitaries and plebeians assembled for the Assizes and returned to Evesham fully conversant with the importance of their position in the eyes of their fellow townsmen and willing to dilate upon the responsibilities of their solemn office at length over a quart of spiced ale in the parlour of the Crown.

14: Crown Hotel, Bridge Street (c.1920)

On Sunday morning, 1st April 1928, Mr F.J. Clarke, the proprietor of the Crown in Bridge Street, was startled to hear a "rumbling noise" emanating from the ground immediately in front of the main entrance to the hotel. There were, however, no visible signs of what had occurred and it was not until the employees of Messrs Espley's, who were repairing the yard, had removed a large stone slab near the stone steps, that a well and two passages leading to it were discovered. Mr G.J. Bomford gave it as his opinion that an underground subsidence had taken place when the sides of the well converged, thus causing the roofs of the passages to slip. It was theorised that the passages were used for the conveyance of water from the well to the basement kitchens of the house and that the well and passages were between two and three hundred years old.

In 1930 a carpenter working in the present entrance hall to the hotel disclosed another domestic well with signs of passages leading from the sides. A grill was affixed to the well head and by means of a suspended electric light bulb this interesting ancient feature of the inn was made available for public inspection. In the winter of 1952-53 members of the Vale of Evesham Historical Society explored this 'secret passage' after Mr Tom Zikking, the Bidford-on-Avon water diviner and well sinker, had correctly predicted that it was less than fourteen feet long. The depth of the well was thirty-three feet and it contained six feet of water.

Dolphin

This house
is part of the
mansion of
the Langston family
here
King Charles I
stayed in July
1644

Hanging almost unseen over two shop fronts in Bridge Street, this signboard recalls an eventful month during the Civil War and marks the site of a seventeenth-century inn called the Dolphin.

15: Remains of Langston House, Bridge Street (2003)

Langston House, later to become the Dolphin Inn, comprised the premises now occupied by David Grieg Ltd, and those latterly occupied by Hunter's Tea Stores. The west wall of David Grieg's is the outside main wall of the old mansion whose extent is clearly shown by the overhanging eaves and the projecting bays of the upper storey.

When the prominent gable end was expose during alterations in 1933, an ornamental panel executed in old plaster was discovered; the verges also were decorated. Charles I came to Evesham and lodged there 4th July 1644.

En route from Oxford to Worcester, the king had skirmish with parliamentary troops under the command of General Waller at Cropredy Bridge, near Banbury, only five days previously. Erroneously assuming that Waller had been defeated in the encounter, the king addressed a conciliatory message to Parliament during his brief sojourn in the town:

> To the Lords and Commons of Parliament, C.R.
>
> We are deeply sensible of the miseries and calamities of this our kingdom and of the grievous sufferings of our poor subjects do most earnestly desire that some expedient may be found out which by the blessing of God may prevent the further effusion of blood and restore the nation to peace; from the earnest and constant endeavouring of which, as no discouragement given us on the contrary part shall make us cease, so no success on ours shall ever divert us.
>
> For the effecting whereof, we are most ready and willing to condescend to all that shall be for the good of us and our people; whether by way of confirmation of what we have already granted, or of such further concession as shall be requisite to the giving of a full assurance of the performance of all our most real professions concerning the maintenance of the true reformed protestant religion established in this kingdom, with due regard to the ease of tender consciences, the just privileges of parliament, and the liberty and propriety of the subject, according to the laws of the land: as also by the granting a general pardon without, or with exceptions, as shall be thought fit.
>
> In order to which blessed peace we do desire and propound to the lords and commons of parliament assembled at Westminster, that they appoint such, and so many persons as they shall think fit, sufficient authorised by them, to attend us at our army, upon safe conduct to come and return (which we do hereby grant), and conclude with us how the premises and all other things in question betwixt us and them may be full settled; whereby all unhappy mistakings betwixt us and our people being removed, there may be a present cessation of arms, and as soon as may be a total disbanding of our armies, the subject have his due, and we be restored to our rights.
>
> Wherein if this our offer shall be accepted, there shall be nothing wanting on our part which may make our people secure and happy. Given at our Court at Evesham, the fourth of July, 1644.

The offer was not accepted; it promised too little and was made too late; Parliament returned no answer and the slender hopes of a Treaty of Evesham were shattered. Meanwhile, Waller had moved west from Banbury, captured Sudeley Castle and advanced to Broadway. The king, doubtless cognisant of de Montfort's fatal procrastination in 1265 when similarly deployed, partially destroyed the outer defence works of the town, broke down the bridge and prudently withdrew the whole garrison to Worcester on Thursday, 6th July.

Clarendon, in his *History of the Rebellion*, 1839 (vol. II, p.379) describes the next stage in the campaign:

> Waller with great expedition marched to Evesham, where the evil inhabitants received him willingly; and had, as soon as the king left them, repaired their bridge over the Avon, to facilitate his coming to them; which he could not else so soon have done.

A few days later, Waller left Evesham, with the obvious intention of besieging the king at Worcester. But, by a series of skilful manoeuvres, Charles evaded his pursuers and returned in haste to Evesham, intent upon rejoining his army at Oxford. Evesham, left unguarded by Waller, offered no obstacles to this second incursion by the king's men within a fortnight. But the townsfolk were not to escape retribution for their unseemly alacrity in receiving Cromwell's men. The "evil inhabitants" were directed by Charles to provide him with £200 and one thousand pairs of shoes, which commands "without any long pause" were submitted to and performed he again broke down the bridge and headed for Oxford, on or about 17th July.

In January 1928, when structural alterations were being made in that portion of the old mansion which is now 58, Bridge Street, an interesting relic came to light. A workman discovered behind a wainscot an iron lozenge-shaped pikehead, seven inches long and about an inch and a quarter across its broadest part, with a fragment of wooden shaft left in the socket.

By what accident it was lost we shall never know but it may well be a link with those royal visits to Evesham in 1644. For many years the pikehead was in the possession of the late H.W. Mayer, owner of that part of Langston House for many years. Its present whereabouts are unknown to me, but I hope that a permanent repository for such ancient finds may soon be established at the Almonry, so that the public may be made more aware of Evesham's historic past. Fortunately, the Langston house itself is scheduled as an ancient monument and thus preserved.

The occupants of the house during the Civil War lost none of their zeal for the royalist cause despite the success of Parliament and the subsequent defeat and execution of their royal guest.

Langston House became the Dolphin Inn – bearing a sign which could readily be interpreted as *Dauphin* or Crown Prince by loyal supporters of the future Charles II, exiled in France during the Commonwealth and destined to return in triumph in May, 1660.

Duke of York

Another new sign which calls for favourable comment is that recently erected on the Duke of York inn in Bridge Street. It is an excellent reproduction of the portrait by J. Jackson of Frederick, Duke of York and Albany (1763-1827) aged 59, when he was Commander-in-Chief of the British Army in 1822. The star he wears on his scarlet tunic is that of the Garter.

Prince Frederick spent the whole of his life from the age of 16 in the Army. He commanded in two important military campaigns on the Continent and was for 30 years "the best commander-in-chief the Army has ever had," as one historian put it.

But to posterity he will always be the subject of the jingle[21]:

> *Oh, the brave old Duke of York,*
> *He had ten thousand men;*
> *He marched them up to the top of the hill*
> *And he marched them down again.*
> *And when they were up, they were up,*
> *And when they were down, they were down,*
> *And when they were only half-way up,*
> *They were neither up nor down.*

Curiously enough, the sign depicting the Duke is almost exactly half-way up the hill in Bridge Street, so it seems that our Evesham forbears were not without a sense of humour.

In the background of the sign may be seen the Duke of York's Column in Waterloo Place, SW1, a memorial to which, it is said, every soldier in the British Army subscribed.

One of the unusual sights in modern Evesham is the hatter's sign[22] which lends distinction to the façade of Messrs Harrell and McHugh's shop at 14, Bridge Street. Some of the older generation will remember that the same metal hat hung outside Mr Candle's shop of former years but few, if any, will be aware that it first graced the front of the Duke of York inn over a century ago.

The originator of the sign was Charles Badger, who learned the trade of hat making in Alcester before returning to his native Evesham to begin business on his own account in 1817. At first the hat was embellished with a smart cockade.

---

[21] According to *Brewer's Dictionary of Phrase and Fable*, the rhyme is a derisive commentary on the duke's abortive operations against the French in Flanders (1794). Curiously, the land there is flat, which means the rhyme is hardly accurate. SBB

[22] This hatter's sign can now be seen in the Almonry Museum, Evesham. SBB

In the fifties Charles Badger prospered as innkeeper and hat maker. Following the custom of the time for all articles of wearing apparel and footwear, Mr Badger made his hats to order. It seems that during the annual horse fairs, for which Evesham was famous over three centuries, his customers would buy a suitable pony or colt pelt and deliver it to Mr Badger for manufacture into a beaver hat of the latest style in time for the next fair; generally, the completed hats were sold at a guinea apiece.

Eventually, however, French silk hats were introduced into this country and spoiled the 'quality' trade for the genuine English headgear. But this came about long after Charles Badger had left his hat factory at the Duke of York to concentrate on making hats only at premises in High Street. His son, Thomas, moved the sign to another shop in Bridge Street where, in 1873, he advertised thus:

> Hats and Caps to the most approved shapes always in stock and made to order. Hats cleaned and made fashionable. A select stock of Scarves, Ties, Collars, Braces, Mourning Bands and Hat Guards always on Hand. Established 1817. The only legitimate hatter in the town.

Of Thomas Badger, the late E.A.B. Barnard has written:

> The good old man used to stand outside his shop, always wearing a top hat beneath which obtruded showy curls. I well remember that as boys we used to mutter as we passed 'Old Badger', 'Who's your hatter?' and then – when a safe distance away – a crescendo shout of 'Badger!'.

About twenty years before Charles Badger became landlord of the Duke, the inn was notorious as the resort of the Glover family, the head of which was Frank Glover, a tall, stout man, a cooper by trade. His amusements were "raising the elbow" and fisticuffs – a dangerous combination, as it proved, since he became quarrelsome very quickly and "offered it out" with any opposing party at the smallest provocation. The fighters would adjourn forthwith to the little island in the Avon just opposite the present cricket ground, which was then a kind of no man's land between the parishes of St Lawrence and St Andrew, where the parish constable advisedly saw fit not to venture on occasions such as these.

Bare-knuckle fights in which Glover, his sons or kinsmen were usually the participants, became so frequent here that it soon became the accepted practice to settle arguments in the traditional fashion on Glover's Island – a name the island still bears.

Yet the Glovers did not always oblige authority by fighting out of town. They were not above 'persuading' certain freemen of the borough how to vote at election time – according to which candidate's beer flowed most freely in their direction. Thus, in November, 1837, when an election petition alleging personal bribery was presented in the Commons against one of the candidates, the Duke of York became the scene of a wild fracas in which one combatant "seized the kitchen poker to cut down" the police inspector who was trying to restore order.

The inn was kept by Mrs Hannah Glover who seems to have suffered a good deal at the hands of her rumbustious relatives and their cronies, judging by the number of times she was compelled to seek the aid of the police against them. The catalogue of charges she made ranged from stealing a quart of ale to smashing eight panes of glass, apart from the many simple accusations of being "drunk and creating a disturbance in the Duke of York." Perhaps it all got too much for her in the end for she gave up the inn about 1840 and the fighting Glovers turned their attentions elsewhere.

Hannah Glover was succeeded for very short periods by Joseph Kean and James Cuttridge before Charles Badger opened his hat factory behind the inn. He eventually gave way in 1854 to George Timms whose widow, Mrs Elizabeth Timms, was still in occupation in 1873. J.B. Bayliss was landlord in 1894, Thomas Anthony Major in 1897, Louis Sprosen in 1911 and Robert Fox in 1913. The present licensee is Miss Mary Louise Fox.

During alterations and demolitions at the rear of the inn in 1913, an inscription was found scratched on a window pane: "Mem: Benjamin Cother and Sarah Pierce married August 20th, 1744." A Benjamin Cother was churchwarden at St Peter's, Bengeworth, from 1711 to 1715.

'Pedistrianism' is the curious title of a document I came across recently: it is written on the back of a handbill circulated about 1850 by R. Whitford, druggist, Evesham:

> Alfred Virgin, a man a little below the middle stature and lightly built, undertook on Monday last to walk from Evesham to Stratford-on-Avon and return twice in the day (the distance is little short of 60 miles) and perform the task each successive day for six days. A great deal of excitement prevailed on the road and in the street and crowds awaited his arrival and accompanied him to the Duke of York inn where he halted.

> Purposeless and profitless as the labour appeared to be, he duly performed it without faltering till Saturday when on returning the second time his animal spirits were overpowered by more ardent spirits which brought him down on the road several times between Norton and Evesham. However, by staggering and running he succeeded in reaching the Duke of York before 11 o'clock amid the cheers of the populace.

The sign of the Duke of York is a very unusual one. There is no evidence to show which Duke of York is commemorated though it was probably he who is depicted on the present signboard: Frederick, Duke of York and Albany, second son of George III, born 1763, died 1827. He was commander-in-chief of the army for thirty years and known as the "soldier's friend."

His popularity in Evesham may be judged from the following extract from the parish accounts: January 1827 – Frederick, Duke of York, died and a funeral peal was rung from the bell tower. The singers, ringers and town crier were given 16s. 6d. amongst themselves as Christmas boxes.

Dun Cow

The Dun Cow, originally known by the sign of the Hare and Hounds, was situated at 3, Cowl Street. Samuel Matthews was the host in 1820, when it was called the Dun Cow. The inn sign, very popular in the Midlands, derives from a legend surrounding the heroic Guy of Warwick, and commemorates his slaughter of a spectral dun cow which haunted Dunsmore Heath, near Church Lawford, Warwickshire. These lines from the Huddersford Wiccamical Chaplet describe his feat:

> *By gallant Guy of Warwick slain*
> *Was Colbrand that gigantick Dane.*
> *Nor could this desperate champion daunt*
> *A dun cow bigger than elephant.*
> *But he, to prove his courage sterling,*
> *His whinyard in her blood embrued;*
> *He cut from her enormous side a sirloin*
> *And in his porridge pot her brisket stewed;*
> *Then butchered a wild boar and eat him barbicued.*

It seems tragic that such a vigorous and valiant knight eventually gave up everything for the love of the fair lady Phillis. He forsook the world to become a hermit and died in a cave at Guy's Cliffe, a mile from Warwick. One feels that he might have missed his vocation; like other retired champions, he would have made a noteworthy innkeeper – of the Butchers' Arms.

Eight Bells

Eight Bells was the sign of a tiddleywink in Bewdley Street, situated just below the Anchor towards the turn into Littleworth Street. It was kept between 1830 and 1850 by Charles Brotherton. The sign is a variation of the familiar inn sign, Ring o' Bells, and both indicate the full peal. In this particular instance, however, it seems more likely that the nautical use of the expression was intended since the Anchor was in close attendance. On board ships, where time is indicated by bells struck at half-hourly intervals, eight bells signals the change of the principal watches.

Elm

The Elm, next to the oak, has been the most popular tree appearing on inn signs. The Elm at Bengeworth was presumably a small wayside alehouse used by the cattle drovers on their way in and out of the town on market days. It was situated on the north side of Elm Road, a little below the Offenham turn. Obviously the name was adopted from the venerable elm tree which stood for so many years in the centre of the present road junction, giving the spot the local name of 'the one elm.' The old tree was removed two years ago as a safety measure for traffic. The inn itself is nowhere mentioned in the parish papers relating to Bengeworth. It was closed by 1876.

16: The venerable elm tree at the top of Elm Road

Evesham Arms

The Evesham Arms was a public house at Great Hampton, to which a sole reference has been found. A sale bill gives the following details:

> To be sold by auction by Mr C. Kendrick at the Northwick Arms Inn, Bengeworth, on Monday, 22nd October 1827... Lot 3: A desirable freehold residence at Great Hampton, lately known as the Evesham Arms public house, pleasantly situated between the high road and the river Avon; together with an orchard and close planted with choice and thriving fruit trees, containing in estimation three acres and a half; also a barn, stable, brew house and other outbuildings. The premises are in the occupation of John Salmon as tenant at will, at the yearly rent of £25. They are admirably adapted for the corn or coal trades, or any other business requiring water or water carriage, being close to the turnpike road and bounded by the river. The tenant is under notice to quit...

It seems likely that the Evesham Arms was situated on Church Bank, probably fairly near to the church itself. At least one old house was demolished to make way for Hampton Vicarage in 1886.

Ewe and Lamb

On 4th May 1666, Evesham Town Council passed a resolution "that the Sheep Market be reported and taken to be and shall be in High-Street between the Swan there and the house in the tenure of Mr John Ballard." Today the Swan is called the Star; and John Ballard's house, until recently the Clifton Cafeteria, is 71 High Street.

The order further stated that all persons inhabiting houses between the two corner properties must pay a ley of £5 per annum because of the advantages they derived from the said sheep market, and the rent was to be paid before 1st November of the same year.

But the householders, of whom there were seven, refused to obey, so early in 1667 the mayor, Richard Godard, was deputed to use any lawful method of obtaining payment. For twelve months he tried in vain, the householders remaining stubborn, and on 3rd May 1667, the Council decided to remove the sheep market altogether from High Street.

The new site was to be "the street leading from the New Hall to the Merstow Green on both sides, from the dore of Mr John Harewell to the corner house in possession of William Roberts on one side, and from the Mayden Head Corner to the Church Gate on the other side, and that Mr Maior for the time being provide pennes for the penning of the sheepe." The pig market then held in Vine Street was to be removed to Cowl Street.

Conscious of what they were about to lose, the recalcitrant High Street householders humbly petitioned the Council not to move the market and agreed, one and all, to pay the £5 demanded, by the next November. Their petition was granted and the sheep market remained where it was until almost the end of the last century.

This anecdote from the transactions of Evesham Town Council serves to illustrate why James Ballard's house at 71, High Street, eventually became a flourishing market inn under the sign of the Ewe and Lamb. It was a popular sign in the seventeenth century, especially in Worcestershire. At the Ewe and Lamb in Worcester the apt comment of a traveller in the coaching days is still preserved scratched on a pane of glass:

> *If people suck your ale no more*
> *Than the poor Lamb th'Ewe at the door,*
> *You in some other place may dwell*
> *Or hang yourself for all you'll sell.*

Certainly this might easily have been applied to the Lamb in High Street for the sign succumbed to lack of trade before the coaching days were over in Evesham. Despite its eligible position overlooking the cattle and sheep markets, the inn had closed its doors to the farmers and their men for the last time by 1850 – a sad reflection upon the state of agriculture in the Hungry Forties.

John Mills (1818), Henry Whitford (1820), John Sears (1835), Henry Hodgetts (1840), James Williams (1844), were successive landlords of the Ewe and Lamb. Of these, Messrs Whitford and Hodgetts plied the trade of plasterers as well as victuallers.

In common with the other public houses in the town, the Lamb came within the purview of the newly constituted police force in 1836 and, although Inspector Arton was compelled to record a disturbance there at Christmas, 1838, the landlords of the inn appeared in the magistrates' court more often as accusers than accused. Two of the cases provide an interesting commentary on the penal code in the 'good old days'.

On 18th December 1838, the landlord Henry Hodgetts appeared before the mayor, John New, to prosecute his servant Charles G., who was the scion of a truly pugnacious sire whose name was adopted to describe one of Evesham's topographical features because of his fistic exploits at the spot[23].

The son was accused of stealing four candles, the property of his master at the Lamb, and was committed by the mayor to the sessions at Worcester. His sentence was six months' hard labour and he was to be whipped twice.

In the following November, his father was charged by the landlord, James Williams, with "being drunk and creating a disturbance at the Lamb and with creating a fight in the streets," by no means his first offence. But he was dealt with in a much more humane manner by the magistrates at the town hall – fined five shillings, "to be paid in one week from today."

The Lamb was surprisingly free from troubles, considering its proximity to the Four Corners, a particularly notorious neighbourhood at the time; so much that in 1844 the Watch Committee felt obliged to appoint special constables to patrol with the regular police on Sundays "to prevent the gaming nuisance and obstructions at the Four Corners; Wheatcroft's Corner (the Crown); The Alley; and the Lamb Corner."

Like the Blue Bell, White Hart and other old Evesham inn signs which were adopted by small beerhouses when the fully licensed premises were closed, the Lamb may have had a short period of revival. When the coaches finally ceased to provide a regular service through the town about 1860, one of the old coach drivers, Bobby Kendricks, opened a tiddleywink in the Leys facing the entrance to New Street.

Years ago New Street was commonly known as "Ship's-yud Row". So it seems quite feasible that Kendricks borrowed the sign of the Ewe and Lamb in some form or other and this in turn gave its name to Sheep's-head Row. But I should welcome any fresh evidence from readers on this point, either supporting or disproving my speculation.

---

[23] This is a round-about reference to Frank Glover, after whom Glover's Island is named. SBB

Falcon Hotel

The sign of the Falcon is of comparatively recent origin in Evesham, having been adopted about 1930 by the Cheltenham brewery to name the licensed premises at 2, Vine Street, hitherto styled as Felton's Wine Vaults. The house had traditionally been a wine lodge from the hey-day of the wine trade in the mid eighteenth century, when Anthony Stratton, who was admitted as a freeman of the borough on 17th December 1764, was in business there as a wine merchant and silk thrower.

By 1820 the Vine Street business had passed into the hands of John Atkins, who may have given the present house its characteristic Regency façade. He was probably succeeded by Joseph Joseland (1842) and John Bamford (1850), before the business came into the possession of Edwin Felton in the 1860s. Thereafter, it was carried on in Felton's name for over eighty years.

Some customers of the Falcon may recall Mr J. Bennett, who was landlord of the house when succeeded by Mr Harry Morton in 1930. Mr Morton was very well known and respected in Evesham up to his death at the age of 77 in 1951. Born at Long Marston, he first came to Evesham as coachman to the late Dr Gilpin. He took the licence of the Golden Hart ('Heart' in his day) in 1904 and remained there until 1930 when he removed to the Falcon to complete over 47 years in the licensed trade.

17: Falconry, Vine Street (c.1930 and 2003)
For the last thirty years or so the Falconry has been a restaurant; most recently a Chinese restaurant.

The family of Stratton is commemorated in Evesham by the portrait of Matthias Stratton which hangs in the town hall. He was the son of the Anthony Stratton mentioned above and was himself described as a distiller when admitted to the roll of freemen on 30th August 1774. He carried on his father's business as wine merchant and gin distiller, the gin reputedly being flavoured with the juices of juniper berries collected from the evergreen shrubs which then clothed the slopes of Clark's Hill at Hampton. He was chamberlain of the borough in 1789 and four times mayor, in the years 1790, 1794, 1795 and 1813. During his third mayoralty he was faced with circumstances which called for great tact and personal bravery.

In 1795, there was deep and widespread dissatisfaction with the conduct of the war with France. Grievances connected with the activities of the press gangs, methods of recruiting, the scarcity and dearness of food, etc., gave rise to rioting in Birmingham and other such towns. As winter approached, the alarm spread to country towns and feeling against the Government intensified. Matters came to a climax on 29th October when George III drove through hostile crowds to the state opening of Parliament in Westminster.

The ominous silence of the populace finally gave way to uproar and seditious utterances as the journey proceeded. Eventually, shortly before reaching the Houses of Parliament, the coach had one of its windows broken by a missile, presumed to be from a gun shot. On the return journey, the king again encountered angry demonstrators and he abandoned the state coach at St James's Palace in an attempt to proceed to Buckingham Palace in a less obvious conveyance. But this carriage was also intercepted and attacked by the mob and the king was finally rescued by a strong force of guards from his unhappy situation.

As the representative of civil authority in Evesham, Matthias Stratton was the target of a similarly hostile crowd which assembled before his house in Evesham in that same year. Armed with swords, sticks, stones, and other weapons of aggression to demonstrate their intentions, several hundred people crowded from the Market Place into Vine Street and called for the mayor.

Stratton, bareheaded and unattended, stepped from his doorway and forced a way into the armed throng and demanded to know their intentions. It was to murder, burn, plunder and destroy, they said. Stratton reminded them of the consequences of riotous conduct and how, as chief magistrate it would eventually be his duty to exact the penalties demanded by the law for any such conduct. He must send them to be hanged, transported, imprisoned and flogged if they should later stand before him in the town hall.

He reminded the men of the miseries they would be inflicting upon their families and advised them to disperse, return quietly to their homes and meet him personally at the Crown hotel, on a day he named, to air their grievances, which he undertook to settle to the best of his ability. If that did not suit, he concluded, they had better begin by murdering him on the spot and take the consequences.

Such was the respect for Matthias Stratton among his fellow townsfolk that all agreed to do as he advised, they cheered him and returned home until the appointed day. When that day came the mayor met the agitators over a good dinner at the Crown and their grievances were settled by his peaceful endeavours.

The king heard of the occurrence and immediately sent word by royal courier to Evesham, commanding Stratton to appear at Windsor so that he might be suitably honoured. The mayor, however, declined the invitation, sending back word that he desired no knighthood, having only done his duty as a loyal subject of the crown. Later that year he put his signature to the following document sent from Evesham to London:

> To the King's Most Excellent Majesty.
>
> Most Gracious Sovereign, We, Your Majesty's Most Dutiful and Loyal Subjects, The mayor, Aldermen, Capital Burgesses, Recorder and Chamberlain with other Inhabitants of the said Borough, beg leave to approach Your Majesty with Heartfelt Joy for Your late Escape from the Horrid Attempts of some Diabolical Assassin.
>
> And we also assure Your Majesty of our Steady Fidelity and Loyalty, and our Detestation of such Inhuman and Heinous Designs, with the above Impressions we humbly Implore the Divine Being (who upon all Occasions had Manifested his Protection of this Kingdom, and more especially in the Extraordinary Instance of the Preservation of Your Royal Person) to Continue to Us the great Blessing of Your Majesty's Life, so absolutely necessary to the Welfare of our most Excellent Constitution, and the Happyness of all your subjects.
>
> Given under our Hands at the Guildhall aforesaid the 4th day of December 1795. Matt. Stratton, mayor.

Evesham people will naturally remember when members of the Felton family lived at 2, Vine Street. I personally have vivid recollections of Alderman John Felton who was for so many years of my youth introduced at school functions as "the oldest old boy" (of Prince Henry's Grammar School) and how we cheered when he requested the usual 'half-day'…

More detailed recollections are contained in Mrs Eva Beck's absorbing book, *When I was a Little Girl* (1952), which gives a most graphic account of life in the old house in Vine Street at the turn of the century from which, with grateful acknowledgement, I conclude with this descriptive paragraph:

> Vine Street was a grey, quiet street, except at Fair time when it was too noisy. Uncle's house was very old and grey also. There were three stories and the nurseries were on the top floor. There was no bath room, no water laid on, no gas or main drainage, but in those days this was no novelty, even in large, well-built houses. Every drop of water had to be pumped in the yard and carried in to heat on the fire. For the children's baths it had to be carried up two flights of stairs and then the dirty water carried down again! The earth closet down the yard had to be emptied at regular intervals and the contents carried through the house and emptied into a cart that collected the same load from all the old houses in Vine Street.

Farriers' Arms

On the pewter communion plate displayed in St Lawrence's Church is the inscription 'H.J. Sherriff, William Waring: Churchwardings, 1688'. Now, William Waring was a blacksmith by trade and he kept an inn called 'ffarriers arms' in Vine Street. In the late nineteenth century, the same inn was known as the Guildhall public house. Today, it is called the King Charles Bar at No. 1, Vine Street.

Several years ago, Mr Aubrey Storey, a former landlord of the inn, found a number of parchment deeds on the premises in an excellent state of preservation; the earliest, dated April and July 1724, recorded a transaction between Thomas Waring and Joseph Tovey whereby the inn changed hands for the sum of £395. The same deed made it quite clear that the Farriers' Arms was the second house in Vine Street, the first being occupied by Robert Barton, Esq. This constituted something of a puzzle until I was able to make a thorough examination of the inn which appears, from the street, to be a substantial house in the late Queen Anne style. This is entirely illusory for I am reliably informed that the impressively ornate cornice is a fake, being made of cast iron and not plaster as one might readily suppose. The interior of the house is much older, having considerable stone plaster and timber work above ground and the most extensive range of cellarage in Evesham below ground.

Despite alterations, the premises still show signs of having been two separate houses having a common carriage entrance (where the bar and snug now stand) to the farrier's shop at the rear. Here, the lofts and horse standings, etc., may still be discerned with ease.

The parish registers and other records I have consulted show that a certain James Tovey married Anne, relict of William Waring (the "churchwarden") who died in 1704. Joseph Tovey seems to have been James's son by a previous marriage, for Anne died in 1715, aged 65, and Joseph Tovey, having acquired the Farriers' Arms from Thomas Waring, himself became churchwarden at St Lawrence's from 1725 to 1728.

An indenture dated 2nd November, 1768, lent me by Mr Sam Leech, shows that the inn was leased for one year to Thomas Pimlott "of Bowdon in the county of Chester" by George Kelsall, "a gardiner of Evesham." The inn was then described as "late in the possession of Mary Tovy" and occupied by Nanny Chamberlayne. The last of these old deeds shows John Chamberlayne as the tenant in May, 1766 and John and Benjamin, nephews of Joseph Tovey, as the owners.

On 16th January 1732, the Company of Mercers adjourned their meeting in the town hall to the "sine of the fairyers armes to compleat the residue of theare business" – which may be conjectured. On 11th October 1734, the same gentleman recorded an expenditure "at 4 Quarterly meeting at the ffarriers arms in ale, tobacco, pipes, etc., £1 9s., ale for ye feast £2 10s., for eating £1 17s., to ye Jaylor [for turning a blind eye?] 1 shilling."

In 1793 a special vestry meeting convened to settle the letting of certain church properties also concluded its transactions in the Farriers' Arms and in 1795 the Bengeworth overseers' account carried a reference to the same hospitable house.

From 1820 to 1845 when it was an important terminus for "carriers by land," William Grove, Thomas Millington, his wife and Charles Tomes, were successive landlords. On 2nd September 1831, Tom Jarrett, a former landlord of the Crown, sold the Swan House (now the Star Hotel) by auction at the Farriers' Arms.

In September 1920, No. 1, Vine Street was offered for sale by Mr J.T. Williams as a going concern with "the goodwill of the fully licensed wine and spirit business and retail trade in the shop and bar as carried on by the family for nearly a century." Mr Righton said a nice family trade had always been done there and could easily have been doubled, the wines and spirits were of the highest quality and it was one of the best businesses in the Midlands.

18: King Charles, Vine Street (c.1925 and 2003)

The property was knocked down to Alderman Charles Edwards, of Worcester, at something over £3,000, the auctioneer remarking that it was the worst sale he had had for many years. Charles Edwards (Worcester) Ltd introduced Mr Charles Lucas as manager of the premises in 1923. He eventually adopted the sign of the King Charles, which hangs in the inn yard at present, and remained to become a well-known sporting character in Evesham until his death in 1953.

The King Charles is the headquarters of Evesham Old Contemptibles' Association[24], and one wonders how many of the little army still meet to remember the Kaiser's War on the first Saturday in each month.

---

[24] When Kaiser Wilhelm II considered the size and ability of the British Expeditionary Force (BEF) despatched to France in 1914, apparently he dismissed them as John French's 'contemptible little army'. When this became known to the men of the BEF, they adopted the name for themselves and were afterwards known as the 'Old Contemptibles.' SBB

Five Bells

The following is taken from *Bengeworth* by Shawcross and Barnard:

> The site of this inn is uncertain, but the sign may have been changed to the Swan or the Angel. It is mentioned in the Relief Account Book: '1724. Sept. 7, give the poor peopel when they went of from the fife bells of betty Tailers with there child 4s. 3d.'

and again: 'Paid for the Repairs of the Five Bells house for the use and by consent of the Parish £7 4s.'

Although the sign of the Five Bells is by no means uncommon, the descriptive "betty Tailers" is unique and certainly has some special local significance. The word tailer is a corrupted form of teller, a campanological term denoting a stroke on a bell at a funeral. A multiplicity of bell-ringing practices concerning the death knell existed in the past in various parts of the country, frequently differing from village to village.

A fairly common custom was to toll the passing bell thrice for a man, twice for a woman, and once for a child; but this was varied in some districts in the proportion of three to one: three for a child, six for a woman, nine for a man. The latter gave rise to a curious old expression of contempt at the expense of tailors – "Nine tailors make a man," signifying that a tailor was so much more feeble than anybody else that it would take nine of them to make a man of average stature and strength. Perhaps this stemmed from the fact that the occupation of tailor and the cramped position in which he worked were not conducive to a good physique. Another funerary practice was to ring five tellers on each bell of the ring for a girl and six for a boy, followed by the tolling of the age of the deceased on the great bell. That some similar observance was customary in Bengeworth is established by an entry in the churchwardens' book for the parish dated 26th April 1681, when this resolution was noted:

> Noe person whomsoever shall have the 5th bell to ring out at any Funerall, but the 2nd only; unless they pay twelve pence for every such forth peals to the churchwardens, for and towards the repairing of the Church, who are to give an account thereof to the parish in Easter week before they go out of their office or before their Accounts shall pass. Agreed and subscribed by us who were present at the making of this order. Daniel Hide and John Harris, churchwardens. Tho. Watson, Tho. Willes, Vic. Richard Hide.

This arrangement remained in force for some considerable time afterwards, but in 1709 it was agreed that "John Davis, Clarke, shall have the money which the Great Bell gets for his use."

The Five Bells inn became the subject of a dispute between the parochial officers and a parishioner. A vestry meeting held on Easter Monday, 7th April 1729, when John Whitfield and Anthony New presented their account, revealed expenses of £6 3s. – a deficit of 11s. 10¾d. upon the year. Apparently the deficit caused much concern, for at another meeting three weeks later this solemn declaration was made:

We whose names are hereunto subscribed, churchwardens, overseers and other principal inhabitants of ye parish of Bengeworth, at a parish meeting held this 29th day of Aprill 1729 do desire and employ Mr John Bulleine (an attorney) for us and in our names to cause Mr Silvanus Watson to show his title that he claimeth to ye house formerly called ye Ffive Bells in Bengeworth aforesaid, a house ye rent thereof hath for many years past been applied towards ye repairs of the said parish church. And we doe promise to stand and abide by what charge the said Mr Bulleine shall be at in prosecuting the same. John Whitfield, and Anthony New signum, Peter Penny, Jas. New, Edw. Pratt, Benj. Cartwright, Dennis Barker, Sam Preedy, Ed Waring, Jos. Nicholls.

The outcome of the dispute is unknown, for the vestry records ended ten years later without further references to the matter. Possibly the Five Bells inn had been a favourite resort of the bell-ringers before and after their Sunday exercises in the belfry. With their rendezvous sequestered and no longer functioning in the approved fashion, however, they lost interest in their Sabbath recreation. To make matters worse, a fit of economy seized the vestry in 1762 when, after passing the accounts and seeing the parson out, "itt was then agreed for ye Benefitt of each other than ye churchwardins shall not alow any money to ye Ringers on ye 29th of May (Restoration Day) or ye 5th of November (Gunpowder Plot) for Bell Ringin."

19: Bengeworth Old Church
From E.A.B. Barnard Notes & Queries (vol.I)

Fortunately, loyalty got the better of parsimony in the year of Waterloo, 1815, and the entries "ale for the Ringers for Ringin on 29 May 5s." and "Ale for the Ringers had Nov 5 5s." were duly approved. But by 1898 enthusiasm for campanology had declined in the parish of Bengeworth to such a degree that when the Vicar, Rev. Walmsley Stanley, suggested to the bell ringers that they should ring a peal on Easter Day he was very quickly informed that this was "only done when the hounds met in the parish outside the Talbot"!

Fox

The Fox, sometimes spoken of as the Lower Fox, was a humble inn, which, until it was demolished about ninety years ago, stood on the site now occupied by Mr J.S. Sutton's shop at 39, Bridge Street. A photograph taken about 1860 shows that it formed one of a block of three gabled houses almost opposite the present Duke of York inn. It seems that the whole of the north side of Bridge Street between Mill Street and Cowl Street then consisted of timber-framed houses with plastered exteriors, with the notable exception of a Georgian-style residence, the office of Messrs New, Prance and Garrard, solicitors, which stood where the Worcester Co-operative shops now are, on the Mill Street corner. None of these buildings has survived.

The account books of the Evesham Company of Mercers show that they met there in 1751 when Thomas Roper was landlord and again in 1769 when Robert Beckitt was there. Later licensees were: Walter Dobbins (1820), Joseph Coles (1830), Richard Mayo (1835), Jemima Matthews (1840), and John Turberville (1842).

It is, however, in the early police records that the Fox appears most frequently. Very soon after the Evesham police force was constituted (1836) a certain C.B., known as "Tib," was fined ten shillings for "being drunk and creating a disturbance at the Fox and resisting an officer." The magistrates were the mayor (William Barnes), Thomas Beale Cooper and William Soley.

Two years later, Inspector Arton reported that he had been called out "to clear the Fox." In the course of this operation he was roughly handled by a man who afterwards escaped; but he salved his pride to a certain extent, recording that he "brought part of his clothes to the station." At 12:15 am on Saturday, 27th February 1841, after "a noise and disturbance at the Fox."

His growing exasperation with the turbulent inn was made apparent in his entry for another Saturday night only three weeks later. At 12:45 am (he recorded in his duty book) "the Fox public open and several persons in drinking, the landlord drunk. I went in at half past twelve and requested them to dismiss the company. They did not. The landlord was abusive to Baylis (No. 1 duty man) at half past eleven."

What happened after this incident was not recorded. But the final reappearance of the Fox in the police records was quite out of character with the foregoing incidents. The landlord, John Turberville, accused a man bearing an old Evesham surname (M.H. of Bewdley Street) of purloining two bottles of lemonade. Needless to say, the magistrates in their wisdom discharged the accused at once, no doubt guessing correctly that very few customers at the Fox were sufficiently fond of lemonade to steal it.

Gardeners' Arms

Structurally one of the smallest inns in Evesham today, the Gardeners' Arms has three distinctive features worthy of notice here. First, it is the only public house in the town where the customer must descend a couple of steps from street level on entering. Secondly, it still retains much of its original 'character', which I mean that it can still be visualised as a 'tiddleywink' or dwelling house for the retail of beer, having so far escaped the 'chromium and plush' treatment meted out to a lesser or greater degree to most of its contemporaries. Thirdly, it was the last Evesham inn to brew and sell the home-brewed ale beloved of the past generations of market gardeners and now unfortunately no longer "on tap" anywhere in the town.

20: Gardeners Arms, Littleworth Street (c.1950 and 2003)

A thriving 'outdoor' trade in home-brewed beer was one of the traditions of the house. When Mr Sam Langston sold the inn to Messrs Hitchman and Co., of Chipping Norton, in 1920, one old Evesham resident, recalling the great trade done with the market gardeners, said they used to sell more beer at the Gardeners' Arms between six and nine in the morning that all the rest of the inns in the town. The licence remained in the Langston family for 51 years, the house having been purchased by Mr George Langston in 1869, the year in which his son, Sam, was born.

An earlier tenant was James Brotherton, whose name appears in the old police books for having his beerhouse (in the Littleworth[25]) open before half-past twelve on a Sunday in 1857 – a pretty general complaint in those days.

Mrs Huban was the tenant of the inn until 1934, when Mrs Emily Tooley took over. When she retired, aged 81, in March 1952, she had spent eighteen years at the Gardeners' Arms and a grand total of 41 years as a licensee. Her first licensed house

---

[25] That is, Littleworth Street. The names of the older districts of Evesham – including the Leys, the Bewdley, the Rynal – tend to take the definite article. SBB

was the George and Dragon (now kept by Mr Jim Huband, a descendant of the previous landlady) where she spent 16 years. There followed seven years at the King's Arms, Cleeve Prior. Mrs Tooley remembered the days when she was expected to keep open from 6 am to 11 pm, and how the gardeners' labourers would stop in her house all day long when the weather made work impossible. She said they could afford to with beer and Guinness at 2½d. a pint and a measure of gin for threepence. Later landlords have been Mr R.A. Teague and Mr J. O'Hara.

George

Saint George of England has been depicted on English inn signs since the earliest days. In Church and State the martyr was equally honoured; several religious houses were dedicated in his name before the Conquest and his effigy often appeared on monastic seals, frequently without the traditional dragon. Edward III began many of his statutes, "To the honour of S. Mary the glorious virgin, and St George the martyr." Following the establishment, by the same King, of the Order of the Garter, representations of St George were increasingly adopted as inn signs, mainly because he was the patron saint of soldiers.

The first mention of the George in Evesham is contained in a deed poll, written in Latin and dated Tuesday 8th June 1576 – twelve years before the Armada. The English version is interesting:

> John Hayward of Lyllington, co. Warwick, yeoman, and Anna his wife and daughter heiress of the late Robert Dyngeley of Powick, co. Worcester, gentleman, sell for £90 to John Smythe of Evesham, all that messuage and tenement called Le George situate in the parish of St Lawrence, Evesham, now in the possession of William Haye, and all the tenement in the occupation of Gilbert Norburye next to Le George and two crofts or closes of pasture land in the parish of St Lawrence, of which one is in the possession of William Haye between Le Pott Lane on the east side and a close on the west side of James Michell and the other now in the occupation of Gilbert Norburye lying between Le Comon Backhouse there on the west side and the barn and gardens of William Phelps on the south side and the street called Capon Lane on the north side.

Possession was taken by John Newington and George Hawkins, attorneys, on Sunday 23rd October, 1577, and the premises were delivered the same day to John Smythe, "in the presence of George Hawkins, junior, Thomas Willoughby, John Harward, John Jacksone, Tymothye Smith, Abraham Smith, Robert Wattes, John Brantley, William Reynolds, William Salwey, Wyllyam Brantley, Phyllip Haye, John Smith alias Baker, James Nothinghame and others." The transaction was probably completed in the vestry or porch of St Lawrence's Church when all parties were present for Divine Service.

The unfamiliar names of the highways mentioned in the deed give rise to speculation as to their whereabouts. The George was situated on the west side of High Street near the town hall. The late E.A.B. Barnard established fairly conclusively that Capon- or Caponpot Lane, as it was variously called, corresponded to the present-day Avon Street. Working from this, Le Pott Lane would roughly coincide with Littleworth Street and Le Comon Backhouse with Brick-kiln Street. The common backhouse seems to be a likely enough name for a road designed to serve as a common back way to the substantial properties fronting on High Street – a purpose still evident in the main function of modern Brick-kiln Street.

Against this supposition must be weighed the evidence of George May, the historian, who said that Brick-kiln Street was known as Brittayne Street[26] in 1584, seven years after the transaction mentioned. He also makes the categorical statement that Chapel Street was "the ancient Caponpot Lane leading to Conduit Hill,"[27] but the latter cannot possibly be made to coincide with the location of Capon Lane as given in the deed, since it is in All Saints' parish.

The original function of inns was, of course, that of rest houses for the pilgrims who tramped great distances to visit the shrines of the saints, martyrs and kings. After the dissolution of the religious communities by Henry VIII a great number of the hostels attached to monasteries became licensed houses more as we know them today. Many retained their original names, however, and the George at Evesham may have been a case in point. It constituted extensive premises at 48 and 49, High Street, now in the occupation of W.F. Bailey (Worcester) Ltd. Old photographs show the original building projecting, in part, several feet in the direction of Bridge Street, in front of the present façade, thus almost completely obscuring the entrance into Vine Street from passengers down High Street.

Three massive stone arches were demolished in the main cellar of the building (now an ironmongery store) when the present shop was constructed in 1931. The substantial remnants of a stone doorway may still be seen in the east wall of this cellar. During the reconstruction effected by Mr Harry Averill, the owner in 1931, several interesting fragments of carved oolitic stone were recovered from the walls of the old building. Two pieces, obviously ecclesiastical in origin, were preserved by Mr Averill, who still

---

[26] Brick-kiln Street was certainly known as Britain Street in the 1800s. E.J. Rudge wrote of "Bricken or Briton-street, called formerly Brutstrete or Brutayne-street" (*A Short Account of the History and Antiquities of Evesham* (1820) p.106). Edwin Powell wrote of "Bewdley Street by name, With Britain Street adjoining on to same" (*A Miscellany of Poems* (1845), p.41). The name Brick-kiln Street is quite a recent coinage, and may have been inspired by the six hop kilns apparently built there in the mid eighteenth century. Hops were grown locally (see p.106) and for a long time there was a brewery at the end of the lane (owned variously by Williams, Sladden & Collier, and Rowlands). SBB

[27] The identification of Capon Pot Lane with Chapel Street appears in both of George May's histories: *History of Evesham* (1834), p.136, and *Descriptive History of Evesham* (1845), p.211. The location of Capon Pot Lane is discussed by E.A.B. Barnard, *Notes and Queries* (1911), vol. I, p.155, and he concludes that it's an old name for Avon Street. T.J.S. Baylis here clearly supports this view. The question remains, however, as to why George May (living in Evesham at the time) thought differently, and why he didn't revise his opinion for his 1845 history. Moreover, documents relating to the site of the first Wesleyan Methodist Chapel (c.1808) apparently refer to Capon Lane, which lane is now Chapel Street (which name it has borne from at least 1827). The situation remains unclear. SBB

has them in his garden at Hollywood, Greenhill Park Road. A curious recessed basin remains inset in the stone wall of an adjacent cellar; it bears some resemblance to the stoups for holy water found in some of our ancient parish churches. Still, these discoveries invite the question to what extent was the George associated with the Church before Evesham Abbey was dissolved.

On 31st January 1587, John Smythe, described as a "boocher" in the deed, sold the George to James Michell, an innholder, for £73. The inn was brought by Smythe for £90 in 1576. Michell's will, dated 7th October 1596, established a charity which functioned in his name for over three hundred and fifty years: his heirs held his properties on condition:

> That they yearely and every yeare for ever after my death pay or cause to be payde to the Bayliffe of the Parrishe of Sct Lawrence in Evesham aforesaid and to the Churchwardens of the same parishe for the tyme being the Annuall or yearely some of Forty shillings of lawful mony of Englande to be yssuinge and payde out of the same Messuage and Tenement with th'Appurtenances commonly called the George at twoo terms or seasons in every yeare (that is to say) At some tyme between the Feast of Sct Andrew th Apostle and Sct. Thomas the apostle XXs to be distributed to the poorest people inhabitinge within the said parrishe of Sct Lawrence before the Feast of the byrth of O'r Lord God then next followinge at the discrecon of the sayde Baylifs and Churchwardens for the tyme being And at some tyme between Sonday commonly called Myd lent Sonday and the Fryday commonly called Good fryday next following the other XXs to be distributed as afforesaye before the Feast of Easter the next following.

Writing in 1845 George May said:

> The premises were in 1788 conveyed to Anthony New senior subject to this rent charge; and now constitute tenements severally occupied by Mr Averill and late by Mr R. Cooper. Mr John New, the present proprietor, sends a certain quantity of bread weekly to be distributed at the church, which the churchwardens consider equivalent to the above donation.

In 1916 when Mr John Averill (himself a churchwarden) owned the property, there was a reversion to payment in money: an annual chief rent of £1 12s. The charity continued to be distributed in bread to the poor at St Lawrence's Church on St Thomas's Day and Good Friday every year. It ceased, in common with several others, in 1927.

After the establishment of this particular charity the George remained in the ownership of the Michell family for three more generations: John Mitchell, of Knowlton, in Kent, gentleman (1652), John Mitchell, of the City of London, watch case maker (1686), and by 1698 James Michell (mayor of Evesham, 1680), and Rowland Broadstock (mayor of Evesham, 1695) had taken possession.

In the meantime, the George had achieved the distinction of being the first inn to be mentioned in the Corporation Minute Book, which was begun in 1605. On 5th February 1612, the Common Council resolved:

> No butcher or butchers shall stand in any stall or booth or standing to sell any flesh by retail or otherwise therin upon the west side and north end of the New Hall of this Burrow at, upon or before the several houses of John Nott, called the signe of the George; Alexander Angell; John Ruddy and Richard Lydeat.

The evidence reveals that the Corporation had chosen to deal firmly with the butchers because they were encroaching upon market space traditionally claimed by another of the merchant companies of the newly constituted borough. The Company of Glovers, on 1st June 1613, ordered that sheep fells be sold (among other areas):

> ...from the signe of the George unto the King's Board and so forward toward Bridge Street, unto the corner house wherein Richard Harrod now dwelleth, towards the Market Place where the butchers are accustomed to stand unto the house where Thomas Moring now dwelleth.

According to Dr Prattinton, the famous Worcestershire antiquary, the King's Board – "near eight inches thick" – was situated at the south-west corner of the Round House, just inside the Market Place. On it, fish were exposed for sale and the Town Crier was required to proclaim the varieties on offer. An illustration of the King's Board may be seen in the frontispiece of May's *History of Evesham*, 1845. Fish was sold not very far from the spot until only a few years ago.

21: The King's Board in the Market Place (1845)
Detail from frontispiece of George May History of Evesham (1845).

The George appears again in the Corporation's minutes on 21st January 1676, when it was agreed that:

> Thomas Tysoe shall have a lease for four score and nineteen years (if he shall soe long live) of all that small Leane-to adjoining Jas. Michell's house over against ye George dore att ye yearly rent of one peppercorn. And Mr Cave ye Chamberlayne is ordered to make a lease to this purport and to re-receive 37s. of ye said Tysoe for a ffine.

On 21st December 1688, the Corporation held their customary feast at the George after electing Thomas Yarnold mayor. Jarrett Smith, the retiring mayor, footed a bill of £5 10s. for this.

On 2nd September 1701, Bishop William Lloyd of Worcester was entertained at the George after receiving the freedom of the borough. The innkeeper, Rowland Broadstock, presented a bill for £1 2s for "wine to entertain the Bishop." The chief rents paid to the Council show that at this time the George was the most important inn in the town.

When Broadstock became landlord of the Crown in 1702, he and James Michell sold the George to Francis and Thomas Perkins, watchmakers. William Sambach of Snowshill owned it by 1710 and shortly afterwards it passed to John and Ann Knowles. John died in 1748, his wife ten years later aged 77; both are buried in St Lawrence's churchyard. Ann Knowles, their daughter, who married Thomas Williamson, then controlled the inn until 1774 when Williamson died. Ann lived until 1782 when James Wellsbourne, former landlord of the Butchers' Arms and mayor of Evesham in 1785, took over.

The premises probably ceased to be an inn when they were conveyed to Anthony New, woolstapler, in 1788. It has not been possible to establish the exact date when the George closed but some light is thrown on the subject by documents in the calendar of Mr Bruce Collenette's papers in the Worcestershire County Archives. Among deeds relating to the premises now occupied by Rightons (Evesham) Ltd, is a lease dated 9th March 1792, referring to:

> ...a corner house near certain streets called High Street, Pigmarket and Bewdley and adjoining on the south side a messuage *formerly known as the George Inn* in the parish of St Lawrence.

The last official words upon the defunct inn were written in a deed poll relating to 49, High Street, dated 28th May 1838, which stated "the said premises for many years have ceased to be an inn."

George and Dragon

The patriotic sign of the George and Dragon is an old popular one throughout the country but since it does not appear in the earliest local trade directory (Lewis, 1820) we may assume that it was an early beerhouse that improved its status.

22: George and Dragon, Bewdley Street (2003)

Early innkeepers appear as follows: John Tomkins (1835), Mrs Hunt (1836), Mr Groves (1837), George Brotherton (1840), Henry Boswell (1850), Mrs Luxton (1863), Alfred Haines (fruit salesman and commission agent) (1873), Mrs Sarah Haines (1897), George Mustoe (1901), George Smith (1902), John Camkin (1903), Thomas Nappin (1906), and Mrs Napping (1911 to 1927) who later, as Mrs Tooley, became licensee of the Gardeners' Arms.

Our old stand-by, the Evesham police duty book kept by Inspector Arton, shows that early days at the George and Dragon were very different from what they are now. A month after the police force was constituted in Evesham we find Dutyman Boswell reporting that:

> …he was called by Mrs Hunt, George and Dragon, Bewdley Street, who said she was in danger of her life in her own house." He went in and "charted the peace and all was Quiet for a few minutes, then they commenced Fighting and crying Murder.

He went in again and was violently assaulted by "the party" in attempting to bring "the party" to the station at the town hall. It was no joke being a landlord – or a policeman – in those days.

Henry Boswell attracts our notice for the token he issued during his sojourn at the inn. The obverse shows a pictorial representation of the George and Dragon, as on the present signboard, with the words "By H. Boswell" beneath. The reverse carries the inscription "The Vale of Evesham Bowling Room, 3d."

Henry Boswell was also "mayor of Bewdley Street" from 1847 to 1851. The election of this mayor was apparently regarded as an annual event among the gardeners. It took place on the Wednesday of Whit Week, when they were not busy. Consultation took place in advance among the inhabitants of the Bewdley concerning the qualities of the prospective candidates. When voting had taken place on Whit Wednesday, the 'mayor' was escorted in procession to the George and Dragon, where a celebration took place.

Afterwards, he was mounted on the back or 'craitch' of a market gardener's cart to be drawn in state (or 'a state' perhaps) up and down the street. A wide ditch traversed the carriage-way at the bottom of the street and it was always the object of the voters to upset the 'mayor' into the ditch as the cart was swung round for the return journey to the George and Dragon. Obviously, if the successful candidate had celebrated well but not too wisely, he was likely to lose his balance and tumble into the roadway, whereupon he lost his honourable position and the electors proceeded to select another 'mayor'. This performance was repeated as many times as was necessary to find a suitably qualified gentleman to hold office for the next twelve months. I rather think Mr Boswell was the last holder of the title since the election was discontinued soon after 1850 following a particularly uproarious celebration.[28]

Goat

> I, George Hawkins, sicke in bodye but in good remembraunce, thanks be unto Allmyghty God, doo make this my last Will and Testament in manner and forme following. First, I bequeath my soul unto Allmighty God and to his sweete sonne Jesus Christ my onely Saviour and Redeem'r and to the holy Company of heaven, and my body to be buried (if I dye in Evesham) in the pishe Church of All Sts in Evesham in the Alley next behinde myne owne seate there.

> I will and give to my wife Elizabeth (yf she be so contented) for and in the name and recompense of her Joynture and dowrie during her natural lyfe my house and Tenement with appurtenances wholly wherein I dwell now called the Sign of the Goat and sometime called the sign of the Beare in Evesham and my close to the same belonginge called Merstowe Close nighe Evesham to here own use during her natural life keeping.

---

[28] Uproarious conduct, and its unceremonious outlawing, were common in this period. For example, in 1851 the Cotswold Olympics were banned due to drunkenness and fighting amongst the spectators. The Games were reconstituted in 1956. SBB

Then follow, in this Elizabethan innkeeper's will, references to "tacks and leases of closes in the Merstowe and about Evesham, the home (holm-flat ground near a river) by lytleton meddowe and yard-land in Bengeworth fields and three leaze (pastures) there." He bequeaths the inn and another adjacent close "lyinge in the Merstowe" to his son William, after his mother's decease.

Concerning the fixtures of the inn he devises "that the greate Cisterne stone, the great brewinge leade, the iiij mortleads (malt leads), the furnace and all the glasse and lattys in the windows, all cheynes of iron and iron barrs in the Chimneys, racks and maungers in the stables shall remain as standards in the house for the use of hym or her from tym to tym of their interests."

Thus, in part, on 29th November 1583, did George Hawkins, Steward of the Leet of Evesham, bestow his worldly goods, making his mark at the foot of his testament in the presence of Wyllyame Brauntley, Thomas Fowler, John Thorne and Richard Tinker. The fact that he did not sign his name suggests that he had been seriously weakened by illness, for he was an educated and versatile man. As henchman and agent of the Hoby family (Lords of the Manor of Evesham after the Reformation) he served for many years as one of the six bailiffs in whom the government of the town was vested. At the Goat Inn he probably furnished with accommodation and sustenance whenever they visited Evesham, for they had no permanent quarters in the town.

No vestige of the Goat Inn at present remains; but lying, as it did, on the Merstowe Green within sight of the Abbey gatehouse, it may well have sheltered many an abbot's guests before the monastery itself was destroyed in 1540. Its earlier sign, the Bear, may relate to the badge of the Warwick Beauchamps who held Evesham Castle[29] and lands in Bengeworth after the Norman Conquest. The sign of the Goat is not very common but does not appear to have had any particular significance in this case.

George Hawkins died in 1584, having been relieved of his stewardship by Bartholomew Kighley who had been commissioned by the Queen to occupy the office. The events leading to the royal patent may be read in May's *History of Evesham*, 1845, chapter XIII. Of more immediate interest is the inventory of his possessions dated 11th September 1584, signed and sealed by the appraisers Gyles Horwell, John Thorne, Wyllyam Brauntley, and Thomas Fowler, and preserved with the will in the Worcester Probate Registry. From this document we may conjure a fascinating image of the interior of the Elizabethan inn on Merstowe Green known by the Signe of the Goat.

In the Hall, "a table bord, two formes, a deysborde, a coobborde, two square tables, a seate, two carpets, four quishions and the othere implements in the same" were valued at 20 shillings. The "deysborde" was probably the raised platform or dais commonly situated at one end of the dining room where the innkeeper and his family entertained

---

[29] That is, the castle that once stood in Castle Street, Bengeworth. SBB

the more important guests, rather like the captain's table on board a liner. The carpets and cushions were much less common, reflecting the discrimination and social standing of innkeeper Hawkins and wife.

In the parlour, "a bedsteede, a fetherbed and flockbed, a bolster, a pillowe, a blanket and a coverlett" were valued at 20s.; "seven chests and a tableborde" at 13s. 4d.; "eighteene peare of sheets, six pillow bures, two doson of table napkins and six table cloathes" at £4 18s.; "two silver cuppes, two Masser bowles, one Creuse (drinking cup) with a cover gilt and a doson silver spoones" at £6 14s. 4d.; "the peynted cloathes about the parlour" at 13s. 4d. A mazer bowl was a shallow drinking vessel without handles generally manufactured from birds-eye maple wood. Normally there was a chased silver band round the rim of the cup bearing an inscription; many of them had silver covers and bases. A mazer bowl of this description is exhibited in Buckland Church. It was used in the sixteenth and seventeenth centuries as a bridal bowl. The parlour seems to have been the repository for most of the valuables in the house. The presence of the bed in a downstairs room may indicate that George Hawkins lay there directing his multifarious interests as best he could during his last illness.

"In the mayds chamber, two bedst', two beds with furnyture and two chests" were assessed at 20s. It is interesting to contrast the value of the domestic items in the parlour above with those in this room. "In the newe chamber" were "two bedst, two table bords, two carpets, 16s., one cheyre, four quishions and one peare of andirons 5s., two fetherbeds, two flockbeds, two blankets, two coverletts with courteynes and the peynted cloathes, £4 5s." The andirons or firedogs show that this room had a fireplace; there were probably five in the whole of the inn if the "other implements" in the hall included the andirons. Chairs were still rare at this period and there were only six all told in this residence. The "peynted cloathes" covered the walls, like tapestries.

In the "greate chamber" – "one bedst, a trocklebed, two fetherbeds, a flockbed, a bolster, one blanket, one cov'lett and the curtynes" were estimated to be worth £8 13s. 4d. and "two tablebords, two carpets, four formes, one coobborde, a bason and ewer, one cheyre, four quishions, one peare of aundirons and the peynted cloathes" at £10 6s. 8d.

The "bason and ewer" and the quality of the appointments in this chamber suggest that it may have been reserved for the lodging of the Hobys, their relatives and friends, when visiting or passing through Evesham.

Then follow the inventories of the "inner chamber", the "Plo'r [parlour] chamber" and four other chambers "of the Row." The "Gott Chamber" had furnishings to the value of 30s. and probably overhung the sign of the Goat in the forecourt of the inn. The "Close Plo'r" may have overlooked the Merstowe Close mentioned in the will and contained among other items "hys library" accounted by the bailiff's friends at 30s. In the Buttery, "all the pewter and such like" was entered at £4.

In the "kychin, seven brasse potts, three pannes, a chafferne and a chaffrindishe, one skym'r, three dabnetts, one kettle, two dripping pans, a mortar and pestle" are valued at £3, "six broaches, one peare aundirons, a fire pike, three peare of racks, two gridirons, a fyreshovle, a peare of tongs, the poot hooks and linckes" at 33s. 4d., a "great leade and a furnace [for brewing]" at £3 6s. 8d. In the "bowltinge house" were "four coolinge boards," 20s., "two malt mills and cowp'y [coopery] ware" 18s.

"In the backside [rear of the premises] all the wood, timber, cart beds, plowes and such lyke" was appraised at 40s., "all the corne" at £18, "three kine £4, four horses and theyre harness, £4, and a cisterne and two stone troughs" at 20s.

Finally, "hys apparel 40s." and "his leazes and tacks £4" brought the sum to £97 4s. 6d., an amount which might not unreasonably be represented by five or six thousand pounds sterling at the present time.

Golden Cross

Behind a modest stucco façade at 14, Market Place lies a building which must be unique among the architectural antiquities of Evesham: of cruck construction and in a most satisfactory state of preservation for a dwelling house over four hundred years old, the Golden Cross was probably one of the earliest inns in the town.

Its unusual features include an internal well in the kitchen, now covered with a concrete slab, and – affixed to the ceiling above the stair head – a remarkable carved oak boss. The latter, consisting of four trefoils with incised central veins and stalks entwined, has been skilfully executed in the decorated Gothic style: almost certainly ecclesiastical in origin, it is a striking example of the wood carver's art.

The owner, Mr H.C. Grimes, has allowed me to examine the deeds of this ancient building, and from other varied sources, it is evident that the Golden Cross was a flourishing inn early in the eighteenth century, though it probably existed as such long before then, taking the sign of the Golden Cross because of its proximity to the Abbey.

Bearing the date 6th December 1729 (3 Geo. II) a deed exists between Joseph Rose, of the City of London, mason, and John Bayzand, of Evesham, baker, whereby the latter was granted possession of an inn "called the Golden Crosse lyinge in the Pig Market att Evesham." Bayzand lived at the inn for about fifty years and figured prominently in public affairs. From 1721 to 1724 he was one of the churchwardens of St Lawrence parish and at the Easter vestry of 1726 "it was ordered that Mr Bayzand's bill of seventeen shillings for going to Worcester be allowed him for searching whether St Laurence was a chappell."

He again filled the office of churchwarden from 1734 to 1737 and at a parish meeting held on 15th April 1737, he and Mr William Rowney, his co-warden, were asked to continue another two years "in consideration that we are going to repair our ruinous church and that it will require extraordinary care and attendance, we likewise choose two more churchwardens for this year and also in 1739." Whereupon Mr Nicholas Field and Mr William Biddle were called upon to complete the quota.

8th January 1742, found John Bayzand host to the Evesham Company of Mercers who adjourned their meeting at the Guildhall to the Golden Cross when Thomas Dunn, a mercer, was "admitted and gave a hansum treet." Four years earlier, Mr Dunn had acquired the shop at the corner of High Street and Bewdley Street, now known as Rightons (Evesham) Ltd, and it is interesting to note that the drapery trade has been carried on continuously from these premises for over two and a quarter centuries. Thomas Dunn presumably footed the bill of £6 14s. (which included £1 18s. 4d. for a previous feast) for the party enjoyed by the mercers at the Golden Cross. At the same meeting, Richard Horne, the mayor, was elected Master of the Company "provided that he gives a hansum treet."

Meeting at the Guildhall on 15th January 1744, the assembled Company of Mercers discussed the questionable conduct of Joseph Pearce "who hath for sum time past sold a quantity of goods of the mercers' business within the said borough" without paying his dues. Consequently it was ordered:

> …that Mr Nicholas Field, the present mayor, and Mr William Plesto and Mr Bayzand, the wardens of ye said Company, do forthwith proceed in law against Mr Joseph Pearce in order to restrain him from so doing any more.

Fortunately the rigour of the law was softened. Mr Pearce quickly saw reason. He was magnanimously excused, and the dispute was amicably settled to the complete satisfaction of all concerned with the customary "hansum treet" at the Golden Cross.

In 1758 John Bayzand paid the Corporation a chief rent of eight pence for his inn and on 2nd April 1761, he was admitted a freeman of the borough. By 1788 the inn had changed hands and was described in the deed as "lately known by the name and sign of the Golden Cross but now by the name of the Sawyers." How long it remained licensed after this date is unknown. It seems to have become an ordinary dwelling house by the time John New, woolstapler, bought the property from William Dobbins, a plasterer, in 1811. Four years earlier, tragedy had visited Dobbins and his wife, for their son, John, had been hanged for murder.

Details of the Craycomb Hill murder, as it was known, are given in a broadsheet from that time. Displaying a crude representation of a felon suspended from a gallows and attended by his executioner and several soldiers with halberds, the paper professes to be:

> A Full, True and Particular Account of John Dobbins, Who was executed at Worcester on Thursday 16th March 1797, for the Robbery and Murder of Mr Partington of Wyre Piddle near Evesham in the county of Worcester.

These grim souvenirs were commonly hawked among the gin-swigging crowds that flocked to make a public holiday of executions in those days and often purported to contain the "dying speech and confession" of the person to be "turned off," though it was not so in this case. The preamble continues:

> The above John Dobbins was a strong robust man, about 28 years of age, born in the Borough of Evesham, of honest and creditable parents. He was by trade a

slater and plaisterer, which he followed, but being of a wild disposition he gave himself up to bad company and other nefarious designs, till he was at last overtaken.

He was convicted for having on 3ʳᵈ October last, between the hours of 6 and 9, stopped and robbed Mr Jonathan Partington, of Wyre Piddle, Pig Dealer, and taken from him 7 guineas, and a half in gold, 3s. 6d. in silver, and three country bank notes of 5 guineas each; also for wilful murder of the said Jonathan Partington.

The grisly description of the murderous assault which follows are included under the section on the Horse and Groom inn, where the fatal episode began. It seems that John Dobbins was no newcomer to a life of crime. Many years later, when the property at 14, Market Place had come into the ownership of John White, structural alterations caused part of a ceiling to collapse. This revealed a quantity of new shoes, presumably hidden there by Dobbins after one of his thieving expeditions.

To conclude on a less sombre note, the following note taken from the diary of the Rev. W.B. Bonaker, who lived at Prussia House, Greenhill, is of both historical and horticultural interest:

September, 1801, William Dobbins gave me an apple that grew behind his house in Market Place. It weighted 17¼ ounces and girthed 13½ inches.

Golden Fleece

On a site now occupied by public walks, ornamental gardens, pergolas and shelters, forming the entrance to the lower Abbey Park, stood the Golden Fleece. Many recall the lively campaign to save the picturesque Fleece cottages fronting Bridge Street which ensued when the inn was demolished in September 1929. In the end, both inn and cottages suffered the same fate. Some may remember the iron sheep which hung for many years as a sign in front of the inn, though it disappeared before the house ceased to be licensed in April 1914. the Fleece is a very ancient sign, recalling the time when the woolstaplers were powerful and Jason's golden fleece of Greek legend was an allegory of their trade.

The British Museum holds the earliest documentary references to the Fleece inn and by a curious coincidence the name Jason features prominently. In an "Act to dissolve the marriage of Sir John Dinely, Bart., with Mary Lawford, and to enable him to marry again, and for other purposes therein mentioned," Sir Robert Jason (to use modern parlance) was cited as co-respondent.

Lady Dinely eloped from the matrimonial home, Charlton Manor, on 13ᵗʰ August 1730, and had "unlawful familiarity and adulterous conversation with Sir Robert Jason" at "ye sign of ye Fleece at Bengwith," where – if the lawyer's notes are accepted – they drank till eleven and other conduct of a more scandalous nature followed. The details are in British Museum Additional Manuscripts 36153.

23: Fleece Inn, Bridge Street (c.1925)

Hodgett's Cycle Shop, which can be seen in the background, was the site of the Angel, Bridge Street. The Golden Fleece Inn and the cottages above it were demolished about 1931 to provide access to the Crown Meadow.

24: Site of the Fleece Inn (2008)

The Fleece appeared very early in the minutes of the Watch Committee established in 1836 to supervise the newly constituted Evesham Constabulary. Policeman No. 4 reported having seen two of his colleagues "on 5th May 1836 at a quarter before four o'clock at the Fleece where a man was brewing." Three days later the same two officers were discovered by the inspector "sitting on the steps of Charles Burlingham's house in Bridge Street about half past two on a Sunday morning fast asleep." He took a lamp from the other without waking either. The implications were clear to the Watch Committee.

As a favourite rendezvous for the bargees on the Avon, the Fleece at one time enjoyed anything but a reputable name in the town. There were rumours of questionable activities on the wharves adjoining the inn when all respectable townsfolk should be abed; and tavern tales, which lost nothing with the passage of time, hinted at underground passages below the house for secret access to the river. More than a century later (*Evesham Journal*, 'Notes and Queries', November 1911) 'C.T.' of Evesham boldly asserted:

> Years ago I remember being told that the barges which came up the river to Evesham in the last years of the eighteenth century brought contraband goods among their cargoes, such as tobacco, rum and lace, and that such goods were brought into Evesham at dead of night and hidden in the large cellar underneath the Alley.

Brandy for the parson, baccy for the clerk? Perhaps, if you like your history flavoured with a dash of romance…

25: Fleece Yard (c.1925)

Of the earlier Fleece landlords, Thomas Hodges was so successful that he moved to the Crown, a much more important hostelry, in 1751. Ten years later, Moses Stickley, brother of John Stickley, who was thrice mayor of Evesham, paid a window tax of twenty-four shillings on fourteen lights when he was owner of the Golden Fleece, William Allard was landlord in 1820, followed by William Collins in 1834.

John Collins, son of William, succeeded his father and was proprietor from 1839 to 1859 when he retired to Oxstalls Farm. "In consideration of his integrity through a long and active business career and his generous and warm hearted qualities," his friends and neighbours presented him with his portrait, in February 1864. According to the *Evesham Journal*, those present included Messrs John Nind (chairman), G. Tredwell (vice-chairman), Dunn, Field, Harris, Collins, Humphris, Whitford, Fitton, Liley, Summers, Julien, Jones, Walker and Bedenham. The picture hung for many years in the town hall and later in the Public Hall, where it is at present stored in a basement room.

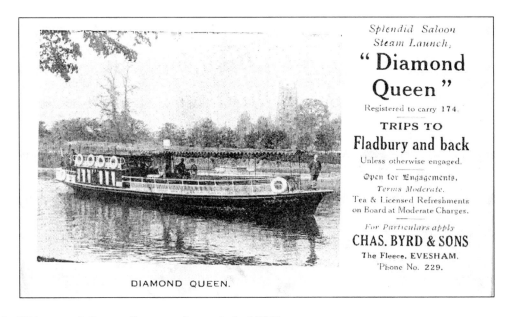

26: "Diamond Queen" steam launch (c.1925)

The last landlord of the Fleece, Charles Byrd (born at Bretforton in February 1845, died 11th August 1925) took over the licence from William Hook in 1871. After farming at Wickhamford, where he served as District Road Surveyor when each parish was responsible for the upkeep of its own roads, he later moved to Clarke's Hill Farm. Settling finally at the Fleece, he entered business as a fruit, cider and timber merchant, caterer and pleasure boat proprietor. In Littlebury's *Directory*, 1873, his advertisement read:

> Fleece Agricultural Inn, Bridge Foot, Evesham. Ales, wines and spirits of the best quality. An ordinary every Monday at half past one o'clock. Every accommodation for pleasure parties. Boats for hire. Good stabling and coach house.

Mr Byrd also manufactured cider for wholesale in a yard quite close to the present bowling green in the Lower Abbey Park, formerly known as the Fleece Meadow. Every autumn the cider making acted as a magnet on the Evesham boys of Victoria's reign. After sufficient "dares" had been voiced and accepted in the school playground, a few "bright sparks" (now respected, sober and discreet members of the community) would enter the yard at dusk, armed with long straws carefully selected from the nearby stables, to practice the art of "cider sucking" from the freshly filled barrels. The penalty for being "copped" was a ducking in a brimming barrel, or a cuffing when the devil – usually in the guise of Sergeant Charlie Yarnold – took the hindmost… and he had to be quick!

Charles Byrd began a long association with the Avon which was later continued by his sons. His first passenger craft was *The Princess Royal*, a small steam boat which eventually met her end in a severe frost in the eighties. Next came the aptly named Golden Fleece, which lasted ten years until superseded by the *Lily* in 1890, but was later used as a dining room while lying high and dry during the great frost of 1895, when a sheep was roasted on the frozen river near the bridge. The Lily did duty in her original form until 1907 when she was rebuilt and renamed the *Lilybyrd*, her accommodation having been enhanced by the provision of a saloon. In 1919 she was joined by the saloon steamer *Diamond Queen*. Fladbury Mill and Offenham Boat[30] were the steamers' destinations in those days.

Golden Hart

Early in 1787 the old Evesham Company of Glovers assembled "at the dwelling house of Thomas Knowles known by the sign of the Golden Hart in Cowl Street" to discuss the behaviour of a certain Robert Whitford who was following "the arts and mysteries of a glover not having a right thereto, to the great injury of the said company and their franchised rights." The company agreed to employ Mr Charles Welch, an Evesham attorney, to bring such action against Whitford as he deemed right and proper; the master, Michael Cartwright, and the wardens, Henry Hewgill and John New, to instruct him accordingly. At the same meeting one of the brethren was fined a shilling "for his abuse and ill-treatment of the master at our last meeting, and also for his non-attendance at this meeting, he being properly warned thereto by the beadle by a written notice delivered under the hand of the said master to answer his ill-conduct."

For various reasons no action was taken on the first resolution until 29th August 1787, when the company was informed that Robert Whitford, now designated as a breeches-maker, was prepared to submit to the Glovers. A dispute arose among them concerning the terms upon which he should be admitted; five brethren voted for a fine of five guineas and fees, while four were prepared to settle for three guineas and fees.

---

[30] The inn now called The Bridge Inn, Offenham. SBB

In the event, Robert Whitford refused to pay any fine and Welch, the lawyer, declined to take further action against him.

The dismayed Glovers met once more at the Golden Hart to appoint a successor to Welch. This was Thomas Blayney, who advised that Whitford should be induced to break the Company's rules, so they appointed a cooper named Michael Lynal to act as their decoy. He duly purchased, on behalf of the Glovers' company, "one pair of dogskin leather gloves for one and sixpence including the stamp," in company with John Hemmings who corroborated Lynal's deposition when the company reassembled in Cowl Street. Whitford had also sold a pair of gloves for 1s. 2d. and a pair of breeches priced four shillings on other occasions, making himself liable to fines of forty shillings each time.

27: Golden Hart, Cowl Street (2003)

Unfortunately, the result of the dispute is not recorded in the Glovers' account book, now lodged in the Birmingham reference library, but one cannot help feeling that probably Messrs Welch, Blayney and Thomas Knowles, the innkeeper, gained most profit from the affair. Knowles was himself master of the Glovers' company in 1784 and as sergeant-in-mace he kept the corporation accounts in 1804.

The next landlord of the inn of whom we have cognisance was Thomas New (about 1835) who was later commemorated in the house of his cousin (The Why Not?) in the same street by this rhyme:

> *William Gladwin is able to brew*
> *As well as his uncle Thomas New.*

The quality of New's brew may be estimated from the remarks of Police Inspector Arton in June 1838: "About 40 men and women have been parading the streets and creating a disturbance. They had been a tea-drinking in the Golden Hart."

Thomas was succeeded by William New (1842), Joseph Gould (1850), Thomas Haines (1852), Thomas Dawes (1857), Charles Brotherton (1873), William Price (1880), Walter Stanley (1897), Herbert Major (1904), and Harry Morton (1907). The present landlord of the Golden Hart is Mr Ernest S. Wilmot who took the licence from Mr Harry Morton on 18th March 1930, when the latter removed to the Falcon in Vine Street. Mr Wilmot, who has been secretary of the Evesham and District Licensed Victuallers' Association since 1937, has seen many changes in the trade during his quarter of a century at the inn. Among them has been the alteration in the sign board which depicted a "true GOLDEN HEART" (as Mr Sharpe described it in his ballad in praise of Evesham inns about 1810) when Mr Wilmot took over. It reverted to the earlier Golden Hart only five or six years ago.

Which is correct? The name Golden Hart appears in a number of eighteenth century records but has no known significance in heraldry or legend. A golden heart is an emblem of the Virgin Mary. In old almanacks her feasts were indicated by this symbol. If we discount the haphazard spelling of our forbears the balance appears to favour the religious sign in an old part of the town dominated from earliest times by a great Benedictine foundation. In any case, both these signs have the distinction of being extremely rare nowadays.

Recalling his early days at the Golden Hart for me recently, Mr Wilmot mentioned the forty-eight spittoons which he inherited from his predecessor. These had to be cleaned out, black-leaded and polished, then refilled with fresh sawdust, every morning, as was the trough in front of the bar – until the day they all went, in one fell swoop, to their doom in Jimmy Randall's scrap yard, much lamented by their former patrons but not by the landlord and his wife.

Then there were the clay pipes delivered in large sawdust-filled boxes to be freely given to any purchaser of twist or shag tobacco. Locally known as 'duts', these short clay pipes were very popular among the children of the neighbourhood for blowing bubbles. The Sunday evening entertainment provided by the gramophone with the big horn and the Saturday night fracas in the travellers' room were other features of those days which have long since passed away.

The inn was completely rebuilt in 1934 and among the excellent accommodation provided was the large clubroom at the rear, where the Evesham and District Darts League was formed by a band of enthusiasts that included Cyril 'Pinky' Green, their secretary, who died in an air crash during the war. Many old customers recall jaunts with the darts club to Winchcombe, Toddington, Ford and other places.

Consulting his old account book, Mr Wilmot was able to tell me that gin was £2 19s. a gallon to the trade in 1930, Martell brandy 14s. a bottle and Black Label whisky 11s. 6d. He could buy a dozen pint cider mugs for 6s. 9d. and a hundredweight of coal for 2s. 2d.; the charlady came daily from 8 am to 3 pm for 15s. a week; and the rates were £24 a year. Today he pays just £100 more for rates alone.

On the retail side, he sold cider at 2d. a pint and bread and cheese at the same price. Mild ale was 4d. a pint, Guinness was 6d. and he "tipped his hat to anyone who ordered a glass of whisky at 8d."

But even then not everyone was entirely satisfied as this anecdote of Mr Wilmot's reveals: A man walked into the four-ale bar and ordered a glass of ale with bread and cheese. On being supplied, he asked if any pickles were available and was offered the choice of onions or walnuts. Indicating the walnuts, he prepared to pay as half a dozen were served to him on a plate. Fivepence was the sum requested, whereupon the man turned on his heel and left the inn, declaring that he would not be 'stung' a penny extra for pickles, which he considered should be 'on the house'.

Green Dragon

The old Evesham Glovers Company met at the Golden Hart in the eighteenth century. But by the early nineteenth century, now calling themselves the Evesham Company of Fellmongers, they had gone round the corner to the Green Dragon in Oat Street. Here they enjoyed a number of 'feasts' just as they had at the Hart.

28: Green Dragon, Oat Street (1952)
In this view down Oat Street towards High Street, the Green Dragon is on the left.

On 5th November 1816, for instance, they consumed a leg of mutton and around of beef costing £1 15s. – the same commodities having cost them exactly 3s. 8d. on 6th November 1787. The vast difference in price was accounted for by the effects of the

Napoleonic wars, which had occurred in the meantime. A detailed account of a feast provided by Mr Souch, the landlord in 1817, shows:

	£	s.	d.
Mutton and beef consumed	1	1	6
Pastry, vegetables, cooking, servants, etc	1	5	0
Beer	2	2	5

The last figure was beaten in 1819 when £2 10s. was expended on ale, and 3s. 6d. on tobacco. In 1820, 30lb. of rump beef cost 14s. 4d., 11lb. of mutton 4s. 7d, and 9¾lb. of 'sparrib' 4s. 10½d. The brethren paid 2s. a head for their feast, which included dinner, tea and supper and, it would appear, beer and baccy *ad lib* to make a day of it.

By 1835 the Green Dragon had become the property of William Stephens who developed an extensive malting business there which was continued by his son John. John Stephens achieved a position of importance in the business and civic life of the town, being a member of the town council, chairman of the gas committee, building society, Sladden and Collier Ltd, and the Vale of Evesham Flour Mills, a governor of the Grammar School, treasurer of the Oddfellows, and a member of the Foresters when he died, aged 66, in November 1893, at the Lodge, Greenhill.

Later landlords were Harry Byrd (1897), G. Stanley (1898), H.J. Jenks (1901), G.S. Vivian (1904), Joseph Porter (1907), Mrs Porter (1920), Frank Ovard (1925), Leonard Swinbourne (1935), and more recently Jim Stanley, now at the Railway Hotel. The sign of the Green Dragon is quite common, being one of the oldest heraldic charges of this kingdom. It is generally reckoned to be a compliment to the Welsh origins of the Tudors.

29: Green Dragon, Oat Street (2003)

Hop Pole Inn

Charles Williams of the Hop Pole inn was listed as a subscriber to May's *History of Evesham* in 1845; Bentley's *Directory* for 1840 described him as a wines and spirits merchant of Bridge Street. By 1850 he had removed his business to 1, Vine Street (King Charles Bar) where it was continued by Charles Williams and his descendants until 1920. At the rear of these premises, opposite the junction of Brick-kiln Street with Bewdley Street, the stone sign of Williams' Brewery still appears on an extensive range of premises now occupied by Messrs A.H. Wright and Son and others[31].

Williams probably took the sign of the Hop Pole to indicate that he was a dealer in hops as well as a brewer, maltster and vendor of wines and spirits. While the hop-yards at Wick are familiar to most people in the Vale today, it is not generally appreciated that hops were grown much more extensively in this area during the last century, though never on the same scale as in the noted hop country to the west of Worcester. Mr Raymond Webb, who has an unsurpassed knowledge of agricultural land in the district, assures me that hops were grown in Fladbury, Harvington, Cleeve Prior, Badsey, Aldington, Wickhamford and in a field known as the hop-ground at the back of Bengeworth Vicarage.

Hop growing was such a very chancy business and, as such, probably appealed to the independent spirits of the Vale agriculturalists until hops were superseded by plums as the 'hit or miss' crop. Dr Nash (*History of Worcestershire*, 1781) had a poor opinion of 'Robin Hop':

> A few acres of hop ground," he wrote, "swallow up the manure of the whole farm; and the crop being very precarious, occasions the landlord often to give long credit for his rents, and gives the tenant at turn for gaming and traffic which frequently proves his ruin.

Those familiar with the vagaries of weather, diseases, pests, supply and demand, and other natural and unnatural phenomena affecting the staple industry in the Vale will detect a familiar note in this extract from *A General View of the Agriculture of the County of Worcester* drawn up for the consideration of the Board of Agriculture by W. Pitt in 1807 and published in 1813.

> The distempers to which hops are subject, are blight and mildew, for the prevention or cure of which no remedy is known; they are supposed entirely dependent on the season, as a crop is very precarious and subject to changes so sudden as to baffle all human care or foresight.

> In the month of July, a sudden blight has often been known to raise the price of stock in hand in a few days, sometimes to double their former value, and the

---

[31] Now called Rowland Court, as Rowland Breweries took over brewing operations there from the Williams family. SBB

dealer who has before been pushing off the articles in expectation of the price lowering has on a sudden locked up his warehouse and refused to supply his customer.

Arthur H. Savory, who introduced hop growing at Aldington Manor in 1875, wrote (in his book *Grain and Chaff from an English Manor*) about journeys for hop poles, with men and teams of horses, to Blockley, Broadway, Winchcombe and Farmcote.

> "When unloaded at home," he explained, "the poles have to be trimmed, cut to proper length, twelve to fourteen feet, 'sharped', 'shaved' at the butt, two or three feet upwards, and finally boiled so far for twenty-four hours, standing upright in creosote, which doubles the lasting period of their existence. They were chiefly ash, larch, maple, wych elm, and sallow, and the rough butts when sawn off before the sharping supplied the firing for the boiling."

> "Some of our journeys took us to the estate of the Duc d'Aumale on the Worcester side of Evesham, where some excellent ash poles were grown. In one lot of some thousands I bought, every pole had a crook in it ('like a dog's hind leg,' my men said), about two or three feet from the ground, which was caused by the Duc having given orders some years previously, on the occasion of a visit from the Prince of Wales [the future Edward VII] to have a large area of young coppice cut off at that height to make a specially convenient piece of walking and pheasant shooting for the Prince."

Early in the eighteenth century the government had realised that a duty on hops would provide an acceptable source of revenue. In 1710 an act was passed to prohibit brewers or innkeepers from adding any other bitter ingredients to ale. The next year, an excise duty of a penny per pound on all home-grown hops was introduced, and all hop grounds had to be registered. In 1720 this duty was made permanent and subsequently increased over the years until 1862.

In the intervening period, betting on the probable total of the duty to be paid on the year's crop became a feature in Worcestershire, until the scene at Worcester Hop Market in August was likened to "the hurley-burley among the stock jobbers in London."

On 5th March 1862, a deputation of hop growers and factors waited upon the Chancellor of the Exchequer, "urging him the justice and policy of providing for the repeal of the excise duty on hops." Later in the same year the government annulled all duties on hops and the hop growers celebrated their success with a dinner "within the walls of the Great Exhibition in London," where John P. Smith of Lower Wick represented Worcestershire.

The next year Mr Smith earned fame for his *Prize Essay on Hop Cultivation* and in 1866 he introduced the system of posts and wires from which modern methods of hop culture had derived.

Horse and Groom

Three inns made up the corner of the Market Place and Vine Street in the latter part of the eighteenth century: the Plough, which survives; the Golden Cross, later called the Sawyers tavern; and the Horse and Groom.

Sometimes known as the Horse and Jockey, the latter was kept by Samuel Tymbs when it was a favourite rendezvous for pig dealers visiting the pig market then regularly held in the Swine Street, now euphonised as Vine Street. The backyard of the Horse and Groom was overlooked by a small window in the south gable of the Sawyers tavern at 14, Market Place.

From this point John Dobbins, the Craycomb Hill murderer, may have spied upon Jonathan Partington, the pig dealer, before hatching the "nefarious design" which proved fatal to them both.

Dated 6th October 1796, now yellowing with age, "the deposition of the dying Jonathan Partington of Wyre Piddle... now lying on his bed, touching a Highway Robbery of the said Jonathan Partington on Monday night last at which time he was violently beat and his skull fractured" tells the grisly story.

Two pages of rather stilted legal prose in the handwriting of George Perrott, J.P., of Craycomb House, record the evidence against Dobbins, concluding with this paragraph:

> That this Examinant well recollects the said John Dobbins being in the Parlour of the House of Samuel Tymbs in Evesham aforesaid on last Monday afternoon whilst the Examinant was trying to sell two pigs. That sometime after this Examinant quitted the parlour and went into the Kitchen of the same house and the said John Dobbins soon after came into the kitchen and near this Examinant and then this Examinant received a Five Guinea Bill, the said John Dobbins being present.

Then follow the pathetic attempts of the unfortunate dealer to write his signature. In one place he found it possible to put "Jon"; elsewhere may be seen a capital "P," after which, the strain evidently having proved too great for him, there are no further attempts. The neat script of the examining magistrate goes on to certify "the Mark made by Jonathan Partington in the presence of and sworn to the above by me George Perrott"; the statement is initialled by three witnesses and a marginal note states "Is not certain when the blows were given."

For a description of the murder to conclude the story of Dobbins, we return to the broadsheet. Untrammelled by any legal considerations, the author has allowed his grisly imaginative powers full play in the broadsheet which presumably sold like hot cakes in Evesham and Worcester on 16th March 1797.

> As Mr Partington was returning home from Evesham market, he was accosted on the road by the said Dobbins, who walked and entered into conversation with him for nearly two miles, when stopping behind on some frivolous

pretence, suddenly came up and struck him on the head with his axe in such a furious manner, that it was with difficulty he could draw it forth from the skull; the poor man begged for mercy, and he told him he was welcome to what he had; but the villain after taking his money repeated the blows, by which his skull was fractured, and he very much mangled; when believing him dead he threw him in a ditch close by.

After lying some time he recovered so as to be able to crawl home, and had even sense enough next day to describe the man. Dobbins was taken up whilst at work and on searching his lodgings his lathing axe was found bloody, which fitted the wound in the head and cut in the hat, his breeches stained with blood, a pistol and silver spoon in his box, and four guineas and a half in his pockets; being taken to Mr Partington he declared himself perfectly satisfied, both from Dobbins's voice and what he could discern of his person.

The unfortunate man languished ten days in the most excruciating torture and then expired; whereon the Coroner's Jury, after the examination of several witnesses, brought in a verdict of Wilful Murder against the said John Dobbins.

Before and on his trial which lasted six hours, he seemed rather hardened; and when the solemn Sentence of the Law was passed upon him, it only brought one solitary tear. He was conveyed to the Place of Execution about the usual time, lying prostrate in the Cart all the way. After a short time spent he was turned off.[32]

The Horse and Groom yielded one other item of historical interest some fifty years later when James Hands was landlord. First noted by George May, *History of Evesham*, 1845, when describing the armorial bearings of Evesham Abbey – *azure, a chain in chevron with a bolt in the dexter and a horse-lock in the sinister, between three mitres labelled, or* – the writer states:

We here present them, copied from a fragment of ancient carving in oak, removed from an old tenement in Vine Street, at present known as the Horse and Groom inn. The relic – enfolded in the still graceful arms of a mutilated though angelic bearer – is now preserved from further injury within the summer house of Mr Anthony New in the same street.

The same relic, which had been coloured and restored, is now fixed in the porch of a house in Greenhill Park Road formerly occupied by Mr Geoffrey New, who placed it there on removal from his father's house in Vine Street. The first photograph ever taken of this interesting link with Evesham Abbey is published now through the courtesy of Mr L.C. Cox, the present owner.

---

[32] Additional details of the Craycombe Murder are given under the sign of the *Golden Cross*. SBB

Horse Shoe

In 1820 a tavern bearing the comparatively rare sign of the Horse Shoe existed in Bengeworth. The landlord was Joseph Watkins. Both inn and sign appear to have had a very brief career for no references concerning either appear after that date.

The common horse shoe has always enjoyed a vogue in the English countryside as a symbol of good luck and protection against witch craft. Certain traditional usages surround it. The shoe, in the first instance, must be found or stolen, those obtained as gifts or purchases being useless. Secondly, it must be nailed up over the threshold with the two ends upright to hold the luck in, because the luck would run out from a ∩.[33]

The famous London brewing firm of Meux use a horse shoe as their trademark, derived, it is said, from the original sign of the inn which was the forerunner of the great modern enterprise.

Jolly Gardeners

> Use of the word *jolly*, on the sign board, formerly so common in our Merry England, is now gradually dying away. Whatever the opinion of our workmen upon the subject of national good humour, they no longer desire to be advertised as *Jolly*; it is vulgar, and they prefer *Arms* like their betters.

Thus wrote Jacob Larwood and John Camden Hotten in their classic work, *The History of Signboards from the Earliest Times to the Present Day.*

The Jolly Gardeners was an established beerhouse at 16, Bewdley Street by 1869, though nothing is known of its history before that date. Contrary, however, to the prediction of the experts, the Evesham inn resisted the wave of Victorian gentility and remained Jolly to the bitter end, which came in 1936, when the licence was not renewed. The old sign, faded, but still legible, remains painted on the wall of the adjoining house, but it seems that both inn and sign must soon disappear in the cause of municipal progress.

I am informed that the Jolly Gardeners was in the possession of the Cooke family, still well known in Evesham, for upwards of a century before passing into the ownership of Mr Harry Byrd about 1915 and to Messrs Hunt, Edmunds and Co. Ltd of Banbury in 1919. The latter were the owners when the inn was unsuccessfully referred to the Compensation Authority at Worcester by the Evesham justices in 1921.

---

[33] In many parts of the United Kingdom the horseshoe, fixed above a doorway, should have the prongs pointing downwards in order to direct the good luck at those passing underneath. The superstition is that horseshoes not only protect the good luck of the household, but also deter witches. SBB

Evidence was given that the Jolly Gardeners did a good trade, with a turnover of £50 to £60 a week and that it was the headquarters of several flourishing clubs, angling and football being particularly mentioned. Three hundred and four customers signed a petition requesting the continuance of the licence, which the committee decided should be renewed. The brewery spent about £1,000 on alterations to make the premises more suitable for the trade, Mr George John Huxley being the licensee.

Mr George James Brotherton was the landlord in March 1934, when the Evesham justices again heard the police object to the renewal of the licence. Superintendent Pass agreed that the house had been well conducted and said his chief objection was on the ground of redundancy. There were twenty-nine licensed houses in the borough, which gave once licence to every three hundred and sixty-five inhabitants.

In support of the objection, Sergeant Davis said he had visited the house frequently in the course of his duties. He had never seen anyone in the tap room and the most he had seen in the smoke room at one time were seven or eight people. Sometimes only the landlord and his wife were present. He agreed with Superintendent Pass that the licence could be done without.

> *Mr A.H. Cross*: Well, I suppose, Sergeant, that a good many of us could easily be done without?

> *P.S. Davis*: Very easily, I should think (Laughter in court)

It was stated that the takings were reduced to £5 to £6 a week – a striking commentary upon the parlous state of agriculture in Evesham during the depression. Despite an eloquent appeal by Mr Cross, the renewal was referred to the Worcestershire Licensing Committee, who decided to close the inn and pay £1,100 compensation to the owners and tenant. The Jolly Gardeners finally closed on 27th July 1936.

Of the earlier landlords, Mr W. Cooke was host in 1873, and his son William in 1894. In the autumn of 1889 the Jolly Gardeners attained a certain incidental notoriety as the place where a band of poachers, who became involved in a fatal fracas with a gamekeeper, planned their nocturnal expedition to the Duc d'Aumale's coverts at Lenchwick.

On 8th June 1904, Mr Louis Sprosen was host when the newly formed air gun club held their first dinner, Mr A. Grove presided, Mr Harry C. Dentith was landlord in 1908, and was succeeded by Mr Herbert Pettit in 1909. In 1917 Mr George John Huxley became the licensee and also took land at Hampton where he achieved fame as the originator of the strawberry variety which still bears his name. He was also a town councillor between 1922 and 1925.

Starting work at eleven, Jack Huxley, despite the loss of a hand, remained an active market gardener throughout his life. He died in December 1949, aged 72. The story goes that one day in the early 1920s he chanced upon a strawberry seedling struggling for existence among the weeds under a gooseberry bush. Struck by its unusual appearance, he decided to nurture it and take runners. After six years of patient perseverance he crossed it with an established variety to produce the well known

Huxley's Unknown, which rapidly took its place with the leading sorts of that time. Later, he evolved and introduced a number of new varieties to the trade, including Huxley's Supreme, Perfection and Bountiful, the latter a cross between Royal Sovereign and Doctor Pillnitze, a German variety. Once he told an *Evesham Journal* reporter:

> Many times a year I am visited by people from all over England who want to know how I cross two varieties. It's as easy as snapping your fingers, but nobody can find out, not even the experts with all their theory. They think I cross the pollen, but they are wrong. Nobody else knows the secret. I have sons but they don't know it. My secret will go with me to the grave.

And so, it seems, it has.

King's Arms

> To be sold by Auction at Garraway's Coffee House, Change Alley, Cornhill, on Monday, April 22nd, 1805, at Twelve O'clock. Lot 12, The King's Arms Public House with a Brew House, Stable, Yards and Outbuildings and a capital Piece of Garden Ground well planted with Fruit trees adjoining the London Turnpike Road containing 3 Acres 8 Poles in possession of Mr Harris, Tenant-in-Will, at the rent of £24 0s. 0d. per annum.

The above details, obtained from a sale bill, are, at present, insufficient to indicate the exact location of the premises. Writing in 1900, Mr A.W. Ward, in a short paper on licensed houses, mentions a former beerhouse "opposite the Talbot on the site of Mr F.K. Gardiner's house" also "a house on Bench Hill where Mr H. Masters lived was an outdoor beer shop." Both of the places mentioned are "adjoining the London Turnpike Road" but the latter, now known as 'Fairways' and in the ownership of Mr B.G. Cox, answers best to the other particulars at the present time. Perhaps a reader can help with additional evidence concerning either location. The King's Arms sign was, of course, the familiar royal escutcheon with the lion and unicorn as supporters.

King of Prussia

About 1760 a private house on the crest of Greenhill, just south of the pool and almost directly opposite the entrance to Gallows Lane, was converted into an inn. The following newspaper report appeared in 1766:

> Baptised in a Horse Pond – One Sunday in the merry month of May, six women and two men belonging to the Anabaptists meeting at Evesham were publicly baptised at the common horse pond, near the Evesham Turnpike, in the presence of about 1,500 spectators.

Undoubtedly, the King of Prussia, as the inn was called, did good business on that occasion. It is likely that in general the pool was used by cattle drovers proceeding to and from the Evesham markets and fairs as a watering place for their beasts. A house of refreshment for men in such a spot supplied an obvious need. Furthermore, Evesham wake and donkey races were held regularly on Gallows Hill until 1819, when the mayor of Evesham issued the following decree:

> The mayor and justices being at all times desirous of promoting the general welfare by preventing, as far as they have power, any unlawful assemblage which may tend to the increase of vice and disobedience of the laws, do order that in future no *Raceing* or other disorderly proceedings be held within this borough; of which innholders and inhabitants are hereby desired to take notice, as all persons offending contrary to this order will be prosecuted with the utmost rigour of the law. Daniel Edge, mayor, May 28, 1819.

This was probably the reason why the King of Prussia was demolished a few years afterwards.

This inn sign was quite a common sight up to the outbreak of the 1914-18 war with Germany and derived from Frederick the Great, the "glorious Protestant hero" of the Seven Years' War. In his essay on the King of Prussia, in the *Edinburgh Review*, April 1824, Macaulay paid him this tribute:

> At Rosbach in Prussia, a great battle was fought between the Prussians commanded by Frederick the Great and the combined army of Frenchmen and Austrians in which the latter were defeated with severe losses, 5th November 1757.

> After this event, Frederick the Great, our ally, became the popular hero in England, and his name was accorded signboard honour in all parts of the country. Ballads were made in which he was called 'Frederick of Prussia' or the 'Hero of Rosbach.' The birthday of our ally was celebrated with as much enthusiasm as that of our own sovereign and at nights the streets of London were in a blaze of illumination.

> Portraits of the hero of Rosbach with a cocked hat and long pigtail were in every house. An attentive observer will at this day in the parlours of old-fashioned inns and in the folios of printsellers, find twenty portraits of Frederick the Great for one of George II. The sign painters were everywhere employed in touching up Admiral Vernon into the King of Prussia.

Rosbach, Napoleon said, "was a masterpiece. Of itself, it is sufficient to entitle Frederick to a place in the first rank among generals." And among inn signs, apparently!

Actually, the glorious Protestant hero held complete sway for two years in the public imagination, until the French were defeated at Minden in August 1759, when two more popular soldiers emerged for public acknowledgement – Prince Ferdinand and the Marquis of Granby, the latter remaining, particularly in the East Midlands, a popular sign to the present day.

Certainly in 18th-century Evesham there was no lack of admiration for his Prussian majesty, even before Rosbach. The parish records of All Saints' show that Evesham tower bells pealed merrily all day on 22nd December 1756, it being "ye King of Porwsa's Accession Day." In contrast it is rather amusing to recount that a serious proposition was placed before Evesham Town Council in 1916, which suggested that Prussia Pool, which derives its name from the forgotten tavern, should be filled in as "being more or less a nuisance." The obvious inference is that it was the name which gave offence more than the pool itself. Fortunately, common sense gave the idea short shrift.

Another 18th-century association with Frederick the Great was forged by William Baylies, doctor of physic, a native of Evesham and son of a local apothecary. His second wife was Elizabeth, daughter of Robert Cookes who built Dresden House, to which Dr Baylis succeeded. When she died in February 1754, the doctor left Evesham and travelled abroad. Eventually he settled in Prussia and became personal physician to Frederick in 1774, remaining in court until the emperor's death in 1786.

'An act for paving, cleansing, lighting, watching, regulating and improving the Borough of Evesham, 5 Geo. IV May 28, 1824' to meet the cost of improvements in the town, decreed that certain common lands in the borough should be sold. One of these plots was described as "that common including pool having the turnpike road east, the land of William Bonaker west and north, and a house called the King of Prussia south."

A year earlier the corporation had leased a tract of land north and west of Prussia Pool to William Bonaker, surgeon and former mayor of Evesham (1787) for a term of 99 years at an annual rent of £1. On the land thus acquired he built a mansion which he called Prussia House. At his death the residence passed to his only son, the Rev. W.B. Bonaker, who was vicar of Cow Honeybourne for many years. The latter became very proud of Prussia House and its appointments and in his 84th year, when he lay dying, he called his general factotum to his bedside and addressed him thus:

> Look here, Tom, when I'm gone don't you let the undertaker's men carry the coffin down the front stairs. They will scrape all the paper off the walls. You borrow a couple of ropes and a plank and let it down out of the window.

His instructions were faithfully observed but he need not have worried: he left no heirs and consequently when the property came on the market in 1865 it was bought by the late Edward Charles Rudge, who promptly took it into his estate and razed the house to the ground, only the stables being spared.

I well remember those stables standing in an advanced state of decay for many years, thus gaining a reputation among my school friends for being haunted, presumably owing to their gaunt aspect and proximity to Gallows Lane. Pool House occupies the site now.

King's Head

The patriotic sign of the King's Head has ever been a favourite with innkeepers all over England and old Evesham was no exception in making this loyal gesture. At least two Evesham inns dispensed hospitality beneath the sign of the King's Head in the course of the centuries.

The first documentary reference to the sign appears in the files of the Public Record Office concerning a lawsuit in 1676 between Henry Halford and Francis Younge. The former, who was a mercer of Evesham, mentions that on 15th October 1641, the property known as the King's Head came into the ownership of Edmund Younge and Elizabeth, his wife.

When Edward Clemens was mine host in 1744 and 1750, the Company of Mercers were regularly patronising the King's Head as also were the Glovers' Company, whose fascinating record books may be consulted at Birmingham Reference Library.

A good many local residents will recall the demolition of the last King's Head in 1938 to make way for the present multiple shop of Timothy Whites and Taylors Ltd, at 60, High Street. Through the courtesy of the directors and management of the latter I have been supplied with relevant extracts from the deeds relating to the former King's Head inn, which have been of great assistance in compiling this history.

The evidence from the deeds makes it clear that the King's Head of Edmund Younge and Edward Clemens was not the property at 60, High Street. The earliest document, a mortgage dated 19th November 1778, describes the inn as the Butchers' Arms, in the ownership of James Welsborne, baker and maltster, the son of Charles Welsborne, innholder, who in turn was the son of John Welsborne, innholder. The same document states that the premises had previously been in the occupation of Thomas Baylis.

I have been unable to trace the location of the original King's Head inn, but the reason why the sign of the Butchers' Arms flourished for two centuries in the south-east corner of High Street is not far to seek.

The inn was purchased by James New at an auction sale on 7th December 1807, when it was described as "lately known as the 'Butchers' Arms' but now known as 'King's Head'." At this period and for many years to come the hustings were erected immediately in front of the King's Head on the cobble stones of the High Street. Without doubt this custom contributed much to the prosperity of the King's Head, especially as elections frequently last for a week or more and strong liquors were considered to be *sine qua non* of polling in those days.

Mr New was still at the King's Head in 1818, to be followed by John Lewis, then by William Grove, at whose death the premises were offered for sale by the auctioneer, H.W. Smith, on 30th November 1846. from the contents of his sale bill much can be learned of the appearance and function of a nineteenth century market inn. The preamble describes it as an:

...old established and convenient freehold market inn, situate near the corn market and in one of the best parts for business within the borough of Evesham. This desirable property has a frontage of 36 feet and extends in depth 232 feet and is within view of the site of the intended station of the Oxford, Worcester and Wolverhampton railway and of the terminus of the contemplated railway from Cheltenham to Evesham.

I cannot refrain from remarking upon the extraordinary powers of eyesight possessed by our Evesham forebears. The Bill continues:

...the house comprises two kitchens, a bar, four parlours, six bedrooms with closets, a good larder; and the cellaring is capable of holding 25 hogsheads; the brewhouse and scullery are very compact. There is also a good walled-in garden. The other outbuildings of which was heretofore a malthouse and may now be easily restored, consists of stables sufficient for between 30 and 40 horses with lofts over, coach houses, piggeries, cisterns, etc.; also roomy warehouses for many years past used by Messrs Ward and other carriers.

Littlebury's *Directory* for 1873 records that carriers by land left the King's Head on one or more days each week for Ashton-under-Hill, Bretforton, Campden, Cookhill, Cleeve Prior, Dunnington, Gotherington, Laverton, the Lenches, the Littletons, Long Marston, Marl Cleeve (Marlcliffe), Stanton, Throckmorton and Welford. Many readers will recall the rows of carriers' carts drawn up on the cobble-stoned forecourts in High Street, and the comings and goings through the carriage entrance of the King's Head on a market day, before the advent of the motor omnibus changed the scene in the 1920s.

Jonathan Thorp became the owner of the King's Head after William Grove but does not seem to have lived there himself. The names of Alfred James Memmory, Frederick Shakespeare Shenton, Thomas Taylor, Henry Hemming and Mary Hemming, appear as tenants before 18th November 1879, when Thomas Partington, a retired butcher, took possession. When he died in 1886, his widow, Laura Partington, conveyed the inn to Wilson Herbert Coles, who remained there as owner and host until December 1898.

On 13th December 1898, "this well known public house" was offered for auction by Mr E.G. Righton. "There was a large attendance. The bidding, which started at £3,000 was not over brisk, but the property being eventually bought at £4,500 by G.L. Eades for Mr J. Lloyd Felton." About eight years earlier the first photograph of an ox-roast in Evesham had been taken in front of the King's Head. It became a popular site for such occasions and readers will remember several other roasts taking place there during the hospital carnival weeks in more recent times.

In 1901, E.C. Meadows was landlord of the King's Head – now generally described as an hotel – and by 1909 William Salmon was the tenant. He was still there in 1920 when the inn came into the property market again, was withdrawn at £6,000 but eventually passed to the Cheltenham Original Brewery Co. Ltd, who put in a number of tenants.

Jack Brotherton's Rules

(displayed at the King's Head by one of its later licensees)

1. When thirsty thou shalt come to my house and drink. Thou shalt honour me and my barmen, so that thou mayest live long in the land and continue to drink at my house for ever.

2. Thou shalt not take anything from me that is unjust, for I need all I have and more too.

3. Thou shalt not expect glasses too large nor filled too full for we must pay our rent.

4. Thou shall not sing or dance only when they spirit movest thee to do thy best.

5. Thou shalt honour me and mine that thou mayest live long and see me often.

6. Thou shalt not destroy or break anything on my premises else thou shalt pay for double the value. Thou shalt not care to pay me in bad money nor even say "Chalk" or "Slate".

7. Thou shalt call at my place daily; if unable to come we shall feel it an insult unless thou sendest a substitute or an apology.

8. Thou shalt not abuse thy fellow Cummers nor cause base insinuations upon their characters by hinting that they can't drink too much.

9. Neither shalt thou take the name of my goods in vain by calling my beer "Slops" for I always keep the best the market affords and am always at home to my friends.

10. Thou shalt not so far forget thy honourable position and high standing in the community as to ask the bar keeper to stand a treat.

Maiden's Head

Throughout the country a welcome revival of interest in pictorial inn signs is now in full swing and Evesham is happily no exception. Many first-class artists are exercising their talents in this traditional sphere of art. It is a sphere that has been graced in the past by such painters as Samuel Wale, R.A. (d.1786), Richard Wilson, R.A. (d.1782), David Cox and Sir John Millais. The recent preview (on this page) of the new sign of the Maiden's Head which is to replace the sign of the Plough was specially interesting in that it revives an old Evesham inn sign which passed into obscurity many years ago.

The sign of the Maiden's Head was first mentioned in Evesham borough records on 3rd May 1667, when the Corporation made a decree that the sheep market should be moved from its traditional site in High Street to be held between the Maiden's Head corner and the church gate. In the event the transfer never took place because the householders in High Street who had objected to a rate imposed by the Council, realised that the latter meant to carry out their threat to move the market and paid up. In consequence the pig market continued its existence between the Maiden's Head corner and the church gate for at least another 200 years.

Since the reign of Elizabeth I, the Maid's or Maiden's Head has usually been associated with the 'Virgin Queen' but previously it was the crest of the Mercers' Company, the Duke of Buckingham and, oddly enough, Katherine Parr, sixth wife and widow of Henry VIII, who died at Sudeley Castle as the wife of Lord Thomas Seymour and was buried in Winchcombe church.

Thomas Williment (1786-1871), an authority on heraldry from the reign of George IV to his death, gives the only description of the Maiden's Head crest of which I am aware. He writes:

> The house of Parr had before this time (the royal marriage) assumed as one of their devices a maiden's head couped below the breast, vested in ermine and gold, the hair of the head and temples encircled with a wreath of red and white roses.

The Mercers' crest takes precedence, being the oldest of the three emblems, and in Evesham it was probably adopted as an inn sign in deference to the Company of Mercers who formed an influential section of the trading community in the borough, at least from the granting of the charter (1605) and perhaps for centuries previously.

Messrs Mitchells and Butlers are certainly to be congratulated upon "ringing the changes" and restoring to Evesham a lost link with a worthy past. No less should Mr Francis Warren be thanked for his impression of:

> *A tender, timid maid who knew not how*
> *To pass a pig sty, or to face a cow*

…though personally I would plead for the wreath of red and white roses if there is still   time.

Masons' Arms

For the addition of this obsolete inn sign to my list I am indebted in the first instance to the mayor of Evesham, Councillor E.A. Andrews, whose interest in this series prompted him to tell me of a small wayside inn which he believed existed in Hampton many years ago. It was the cottage owned by Mr James Grove, and situated a short distance east of his house, 'Berryfield', at present the last house in Pershore Road on the way to Worcester.

My inquiries led me to one of Hampton's oldest residents, Mr Henry Birch, who was able to confirm that the house had once displayed an inn sign. He recollected the faded paintwork of the sign of the Masons' Arms which could still be discerned on the façade of the house in the last century.

Mr Birch was unable to remember the place being used as a licensed premises in his lifetime, but he said he always understood that a cattle pound or enclosure existed where the road bends southward just east of the old alehouse. This is very likely, as drovers' inns existed on all the main routes out of Evesham at the ends of the town. Thus it is probable that for many years the Masons' Arms at Hampton was the first or last port of call for wayfarers en route from Evesham to Pershore or vice versa.

If the inn sign was ever a pictorial one it would depict the various squares, dividers and other instruments associated with the stone mason's trade and Masonic tradition.

Nag's Head

Little is known about the Nag's Head except that it was located in Vine Street, in 1751, when John Gardiner, the landlord, entertained the Company of Mercers there, as he did once again in 1760. The signboard probably displayed a representation of a horse's head, in deference to the folk who attended Evesham's famous horse fairs. In Studley I have seen a public house sign where the expressive portrait of a sour-faced woman serves as an appropriate and amusing alternative.

Navigation

Best known as the Navvy (or Navigation), but later known as the Crown Inn, is first referred to in the notice for a vestry meeting of All Saints' parish dated 8th November 1807:

> ...to hear a proposal from the proprietors of the Navigation for settling the dispute between them and the said Parish, without applying to a Court of Law and thus incurring great Expense.

The dispute may have concerned the obligations of the owner to pay or not to pay a poor rate to the overseers of All Saints', since the inn was situated on the borders of

Evesham and Hampton, the latter parish not them being in the borough. In 1818 the appeal of one John Milton against the poor rate levied upon him lost the parish the considerable sum of £76 13s. 3d. and this may have been the final outcome of the dispute referred to above.

30: Crown Inn, Waterside

The Navigation inn quite naturally took its first name in deference to the prosperous waterway which flowed past its door. In 1840 John Lightborne, the landlord, was also in business as a coal merchant and had his own wharf on the river bank opposite the inn. His successor, Charles Phillips (1873), was a shoemaker as well as a victualler. He was an early Forester and regularly supplied the annual dinner of the Court Vale of Evesham Ancient Order of Foresters held in the Farmers' Hall. I believe he was succeeded about 1894 by the late Mr H. Leach, who held the licence until about four years ago when Mr K.H. Legitt took over.

Recently I came across a letter written to the *Journal* in January 1910, which describes the surroundings of the inn some century ago. It reads as follows:

> I well remember travelling along the road from Pershore to Evesham more than sixty years ago and was specially pleased with the part from Hampton to Evesham. At that time there was no fence between the riverside and the road from opposite the Northwick Arms hotel to near the Bridge over the River Isbourne at Hampton. At that period Mr John Lightborne kept the Navigation inn. There was a ferry boat just opposite the inn to take people across the river; there was also a wharf opposite Cheltenham Road for loading and unloading merchandise from boats and barges. There was also a toll house and two toll gates crossing the two roads. There was another wharf at Battleton's Bridge at the lower end of the Pleasure Gardens.

Tom Baylis wrote an additional article on the Navigation for the *Journal* (6th December 1973)[34]:

Mrs. R.E. Shepherd writes:

> ...as every local person refers to it as 'The Navi' we can't help wondering if at any time in the past it was in fact called The Navigation Inn. We hope, in the near future, to change the name of the pub to The Navigation Inn.

To the best of my knowledge, no sign bearing any name or illustration relating to waterborne transport has hung outside the inn within living memory yet, as Mrs Shepherd rightly indicates, to every local patron it is still the 'Navvy' and not the Crown.

Why, when or how the house took its present name is not clear. My own idea is that following revisions of the licensing laws towards the end of the last century about the time of Victoria's Jubilee or Edward VII's Coronation when patriotism reached a zenith, the house was drastically altered or rebuilt, the word 'navvy' was not socially acceptable and the navigation itself was no longer significant commercially – hence the Crown instead of the original name.

By that time the Avon navigation across the road from the inn was in decline and well on the way to dereliction, in the best financial interest of the shareholder in the Great Western Railway Company, who quite obviously saw little profit in the maintenance of ancient waterways. From September 8, 1666, the Avon navigation of 14 locks and weirs between Shakespeare's birthplace and King John's Bridge had served the riparian settlements well and contributed in no small way to the growth and prosperity of Tewkesbury, Pershore, Evesham and Stratford, but those days were over, unless history could repeat itself in a fresh guise.

Evesham itself had important wharfage and warehousing on either side of the river just below Evesham Bridge. Once known as High Street, Bengeworth, modern Port Street almost certainly took its present name from the from the busy boat basins near the Bridge foot.

Today it is not possible to visualise the Old Angel with its yards, stables and barns standing on a triangular site directly opposite Burlingham's showrooms or the narrow 'gullet' between the New and Old Angel inns, just wide enough for a coach or waggon to navigate a clear passage. The New Angel was not the present pub on the corner of Castle Street but the house now masquerading as Cassidy's, the jewellers, on the corner of Port Street and Waterside.

---

[34] H.R. Elliston (Regional Director, Mitchells & Butlers Limited) replied in a letter to the *Journal* (14th March 1974) noting: "In view of this local tradition and the good historical reasons for the house originally being called 'The Navigation' until the end of the 19th century, we are taking steps to revert to this original name by application to the Licensing Committee. We will also arrange to put up in the house a record of the change of names and the reasons for them and a mention that this came about through your good services." SBB

Inn, port, warehouses and wharfs, all were demolished between 1854 and 1856 following the successful appear by Henry Workman for public subscriptions to build a new Bengeworth Bridge. A plaque on the bridge records the achievement which replaced the old bridge, cleared away several large aits, canalised the river and deposited the debris over the old port of Bengeworth between the 'cut' and the turnpike road now known as Waterside. Soon afterwards the spoil heaps were levelled and landscaped to make a site for the Workman Pleasure Gardens.

It may not be stretching imagination too far in surmising that the navvy gangs that undertook the canalisation of the river between Evesham Weir and the Hampton Turnpike were not always wholly welcomed by the innkeepers in the town, especially at houses like the Old Red Lion which, by that time, had pretensions as the Northwick Arms Hotel. The Navigation Inn was well out of town and probably did very nicely, thank you, out of the hungry, thirsty navigational men who gave Evesham such a fine river vista between the Bengeworth and Battleton bridges.

Certainly, when the railways came to Evesham, the landlord of 'Paddy's Duck' at the other end of Bengeworth made hay while the sun shone. The wharfage, lost under the soil of the Pleasure Gardens, moved down river to Battleton's Bridge and below. Thus, for a time at least, the landlords of the Navigation Inn took further advantage from the river trade.

31: Crown Inn, Waterside (2003)
The Crown Inn, Waterside, formerly known as the Navigation.

Nelson

Variously described as the Admiral or Lord Nelson, a 19th-century tavern sign paid tribute to the memory of Sir Horatio Nelson. His victories at sea in the wars against Napoleon earned enduring fame; so did his stirring signal to the Fleet at Trafalgar, "England expects that every man this day shall do his duty."

Nelson was victorious in the Battle of Aboukir Bay (1798) and the Battle of Copenhagen (1801), losing an arm and an eye in these encounters. His personal bravery and striking success rapidly made him a popular hero and his death in his flagship, the *Victory*, at Trafalgar in 1805, shocked the nation, overshadowing the national rejoicing engendered by his most famous victory. "It does not become me to make comparisons," Lord St Vincent had written previously, "there is but one Nelson."

For years after Trafalgar, prints and oleographs depicting the hero's death were to be found in the parlours of inns up and down the country, and a few still exist today, a century and a half after the event. Of these, a black and white print of 'The Death of Nelson,' from the painting by Sir Benjamin West, R.A., may be seen at the Fleece Inn, Bretforton, and I have seen several coloured reproductions of the same work hung in private houses in Evesham.

An interesting local story concerning 'The Death of Nelson' was recently confirmed for me by Alderman Alfred Johns, of Bengeworth. He affirms that when he was a boy in the nineties, he well remembers how Mr Basil Cull, a baker living at 68, Port Street (now occupied by J. Webb, butcher), cleared his shop window of goods on each anniversary of Trafalgar (21st October) in order to display an illustration of the death of Nelson to advantage. Alderman Johns attributed this odd practice to political motives, for which I sought a reason.

From at least 1820 until the licence lapsed in 1885, the Nelson tavern seems to have been the Bengeworth rendezvous of the Tory Party in the borough. The inn regularly "opened with Ale and Pipes for Sir Charles's friends" at election times during the twenty years that Sir Charles Cockerell, of Sezincote, represented Evesham at Westminster in the Tory interests.

As one of the inns where non-resident voters were lodged at the candidate's (unofficial) expense during the poll, it presumably accommodated those fortunate voters who, to use the words of George May, "feast upon the best, appear when wanted at the poll, remain to witness the result and receive in person a liberal remuneration for their expenses and loss of time." Thus it would appear that by this usage the name of Nelson became inextricably associated with political objectives, and, in the course of time, a sort of touchstone for the Tory faction in Bengeworth. How else could Mr Cull's curious observance of the British hero's death be explained?

Lying as it did alongside the yards of the fellmongers where the ancient gloving and parchment industries of Bengeworth flourished, the Nelson – as might be expected – served for many years as the acknowledged headquarters of the old Evesham

Company of Fellmongers, formerly Glovers. The inn itself remained continuously in the occupation of a family of fellmongers called Cook, who appear as landlords from 1820 to 1870.

Quarterly and annual meetings of the Company were held at "the dwelling house of John Cook called or known by the sign of the Lord Nelson" for at least seven of the years between 1812 and 1821. In the former year the record book showed that the Company sent 36 dozen sheep's pelts and 44 dozen lambs' pelts to be dressed in oil at Mr Smart's mill for the autumn quarter.

It is, however, the annual feast of the Company of Glovers or Fellmongers, held at the Nelson on Gunpowder Plot Day, which reveals their prosperity as Napoleon began his disastrous retreat from Moscow. The inflated sum of £7 5s. 10d. for the banquet of 1812 prompted me to search for the detailed account concerning the event, which appeared as follows:

	£	s.	d.
A leg of mutton		9	0
23lb. of beef		15	4
A roasting pig		9	6
Vegetables, bread, puddings and pies, etc	1	5	6
Servants		5	0
Ale	4	1	6
total	7	5	10

As the sum total is correctly returned as £7 5s. 10d., there can be no reasonable doubt about the staggering amount expended on ale. Fellmongering in 1812 must have been a dry job as well as a profitable one. The bill for the annual feast held at the same inn in November 1826, renders an interesting comparison with the above:

	£	s.	d.
17 dinners, 2s. each	1	14	0
Servants		2	6
Biddle		2	0
14 teas, 6d. each		7	0
13 suppers, 9d. each		9	9
Ale and tobacco	1	1	3
total	3	16	6

At £3 16s. 6d. it will be noticed that the expenses of the feast had been very much reduced, as indeed they continued to diminish until in 1832 the Company of Glovers, ceasing to meet, became extinct.

The gloving and parchment trades continued for some considerable period and readers may be interested in the following few details which I have been able to glean concerning the parchment works in Bengeworth:

The premises, situated roughly on the site of Burford Road, were in the hands of a Mr Payne before 1850. About that year, Mr J.J. Tipper took over the business to be succeeded eventually by his son, Mr J.H. Tipper, who was conspicuous in the Evesham of his time for proceeding to and from his place of business in a top hat.

For a good many years local and other solicitors were supplied with skins for deeds from this source while occasionally orders for the War Office were executed at the Bengeworth manufactory. A craftsman named Charles Tombs was the last journeyman to be employed in the works, where his father and grandfather had preceded him. The manufacture of parchment in Bengeworth ceased in 1894.

New Anchor

Closed in 1910 under the terms of the Licensing (Consolidation) Act of that year was the New Anchor, situated at 1, Brick-kiln Street. Opened about 1865 by James Callow, who later became landlord of the Old Angel at the foot of Port Street, lived to be 90 and retired to Fairfield Cottages at Hampton, the inn took its sign from the house next door, now the Old Anchor. Until then, the Anchor Inn at 3, Bewdley Street had been the sole possessor of the ancient sign. But the advent of a new iron anchor, complete with rope attached and painted bright blue, caused the original inn to change its sign to that of the Old Anchor, and it has been so ever since.

When Mr Callow left the New Anchor is passed into the hands of John Brotherton who, in 1873, was also in business as a fruit and potato salesman and commission agent. His advertisement appears in Littlebury's *Directory of Worcestershire* for that year and displays his trade mark – an anchor on a shield. Twenty years later, Mr G.J. Brotherton was landlord of the New Anchor; he was succeeded by Mr Louis Sprosen, who left in 1908, becoming host at the Jolly Gardeners in adjoining Bewdley Street.

New Angel

The New Angel inn was opened at 79 (now 11), Port Street, about 1897 when E. Fennel was the proprietor. W. Ellis was landlord the following year and George Williams in 1901. From 1906, when Richard C. Vant was the host, the inn was variously known as the New Angel or Angel Vaults. James Andrews took over in 1910 and was eventually succeeded by his son, F.S. Andrews, who kept the inn until 1941, when Mr H.C. Maries became the licensee.

Northwick Arms

> Northwick Arms is a sign where travellers will find:
> Good dinners, kind landlord and plenty of wine;
> Where the gentry oft meet and in full bumpers;
> Church, King and the Constitution we boast.

Thus sang Mr Sharpe in the days of the Old Evesham Theatre early in the nineteenth century and everything I have discovered about the inn since shows that tradition dies hard in Evesham. To salute the elevation of the owner, Sir John Rushout, to the peerage about 1800, the Old Red Lion in Waterside became the Northwick Arms and Posting House. Baron Northwick took his title from his seat at Northwick Park, near Blockley, which had been occupied by the family since the middle of the seventeenth century.

32: Northwick Arms, Waterside (c.1920)

The Rushouts had forged a long connection with Evesham as Members of Parliament for the borough for the long periods in the seventeenth and eighteenth centuries. One of them, who in his later years was 'Father of the House', shared the expense of adding the present council chamber to Evesham town hall with his co-member, Edward Rudge. The present post-sign outside the hotel displays an adaptation of the Northwick Arms, which were:

Sable, two lions guardant within a bordure engrailed, *or*. Crest: a lion passant guardant, *or*. Supporters: two angels proper, wings displayed and inverted, habited *argent*, semee of mullets and fleur de lis alternately, *or*; about the waist a girdle *azure*, the end flowing and fringed: the interior arm bent at the elbow and the hand pointing upwards, the exterior holding a parl branch *vert*. Motto: *Par ternis suppar* ('a pair nearly equal to three').

On 30th August 1803, John, Lord Northwick, gave a feast at the inn to his successor in the mayoralty of Evesham, George Day, another Bengeworth landowner. The details of this banquet are worthy of notice and are listed as follows:

	£	s.	d.
To cakes and wines before dinner		17	0
Twenty-three dinners	5	15	0
Port wine and Lisbon	6	8	0
Punch	1	7	6
Rum, brandy and gin	1	5	6
Ale and porter		17	0
Cyder		7	0
Fruit	1	3	6
Tobacco		2	6
Tea and coffee		10	0
Servants' dinners		9	0
Punch and rum, etc.		12	6
Ale and porter		7	6
Customary gratuity to servants	1	1	0
total	21	3	6

From this account we learn that the twenty-three Evesham worthies concerned managed to dispose of £10 5s. worth of strongish stuff with their dinners. Their capacity for strong waters may be estimated from this wine list of 1804:

	£	s.	d.
Superior old Port (a dozen)		38	0
Lisbon (a dozen)		38	0
Old Jamaica rum (a gallon)		15	0
Cognac brandy (a gallon)		20	0
Gin (a gallon)		10	0

As Mr Sharpe observed, the dinners provided at the Northwick were well worthy of notice and it is interesting to find the tradition of dining and wining there still preserved in the Tuesday lunch meetings of the Evesham Rotary Club (though hardly in the 1803 style) over a century and a half later.

In 1864 the Northwick was considerably enlarged and its accommodation increased. The alterations were carried out by William Gardner, a Bengeworth builder, on behalf of the landlord, Mr David Saunders, giving the "spacious and commanding front of handsome elevation and imposing appearance" described by a contemporary journalist who also noted "the very excellent dining room." The latter was put to immediate use by the Vale of Evesham Agricultural Society under their chairman, Sir John Pakington, Bt, M.P., following the agricultural show held on Wednesday, 21st September, when the society held its annual exhibition of stock and roots in conjunction with the Horticultural Society, the latter exhibiting fruit, flowers and vegetables.

The show was held in the orchard adjoining the Northwick Arms while the Workman Gardens were devoted to the flower show and promenade. "The dinner, wines and dessert were all that the most fastidious could desire, comprising all the delicacies of the season, being superabundant in quantity, excellent in quality, well cooked and quickly served," according to the *Evesham Journal* of 24th September 1864.

Recently I came across a printed invitation to a function at the Northwick Arms which is typical of its period and consequently is reproduced here in full.

> Evesham. 7th August, 1865. Dear Sir – To celebrate Mr Holland's return to Parliament for this Borough for the fifth time, his Committee and Supporters intend to entertain him at a Dinner, to be given at the Northwick Arms Hotel, on Friday, the 18th instant, and to which you are respectfully invited. The mayor has kindly consented to preside. Dinner on the table at five o'clock. Tickets, 4s. each, to be had at the Hotel. I remain, dear sir, Yours faithfully, Herbert New.

The Toast List:

By the Chair	1	The Queen
Ditto	2	The Prince and Princess of Wales and the Rest of the Royal Family
By Mr H. New	3	Edward Holland, Esq., Our Liberal Member (Mr Holland to reply)
By the Chair	4	The Army, Navy and Volunteers (Mr T. Holland)
By Mr Holland	5	The mayor (The mayor)
By Mr Wright	6	The Corporation, with the health of the Town Clerk. (Mr Cheek)
By the Chair	7	The Watchwords of the Party: Civil and Religious Liberty all the World over.
By Mr Prance	8	Her Majesty's Ministers
By Mr Wadams	9	Prosperity to the Town and Trade of Evesham (Mr H.W. Smith)
By Mr Warmington	10	The Vice Chairman (Mr H. New)
By Mr H. New	11	The Good Old Friends of the Good Old Cause (Mr B. Workman)
By Mr Cole	12	The Press (Mr W. Smith)

The opposition, in the person of the Evesham Lodge of our National Conservative League, with Colonel Long, M.P., presiding, held their annual meeting at the Northwick Hotel on 11th December 1901, when "Mr and Mrs J.H. Matthews placed an excellent dinner on the tables" as you might anticipate.

In June 1902, Mr Matthews, who had been in occupation of the inn for some years as a yearly tenant, bought the property for £3,250 when Lady Northwick disposed of the Rushout estate in Bengeworth. She died in 1912, thus ending the long connection of the Rushout family with the town.

Mr Alfred Phillips, of Leamington, acquired the hotel for £2,500 in 1905 after a large parcel of land had been sold to Dr Leslie for £700. Dr Leslie built in Coopers Lane the house now known as 'Fairwater', reputedly to the design of the late Sir Edwin Lutyens, P.R.I.B.A. Mr Phillips made great improvements at the Northwick and laid down the present bowling green which affords so much pleasure to its patrons, but he died suddenly, early in 1906. In September of the same year, Sladden and Collier Ltd bought the Northwick Arms for £2,450 and later their whole interest passed to the present owners, Cheltenham and Hereford Breweries Ltd.

33: Northwick Arms, Waterside (1937)

Landlords I have not yet noted included: C. Hundley (1796), George Taylor (1818), John Mayfield (1830), Thomas Gates (1835), William Bushell (1840), Elizabeth Stanley (1850), John Brown Saunders (1854), J. Mayor (1880), John West (1908), Mrs Lloyd (1912), Mrs Grace Tanner (1917), B.N.T. Owers (1925), F.J. Machin (1930), and the late R.L. Nicholson (1935) who will be recalled with great affection by many of his old friends in Evesham and district.

Old Anchor

Evesham being, to all intents and purposes, a hundred miles or so as the crow flies from any blue water, the adoption of the anchor as an inn sign here strikes an incongruous note until the use of it as an emblem is understood. It is, surprisingly, ecclesiastical in origin. From the earliest days of Christian belief, the anchor has been regarded as a symbol of true faith. St Paul described hope as "the anchor of the soul, both sure and steadfast" and St Ambrose said "it was this which keeps Christians from being carried away by the storm of life." Frequently found among the Christian symbols still to be observed under Rome, the anchor later (about AD100) became the sign of St Clement, the patron saint of tanners. He is believed to have suffered martyrdom by having an anchor tied about his neck before being cast into his ocean grave.

34: Old Anchor, Brick-kiln Street (c.1900)

It required little consideration to link the martyr's name with that of Clement Wych, the Abbot Lichfield whose bell tower remains, after over four-hundred years, the unchallenged architectural masterpiece of this district. Adopting the nautical emblem of his saintly namesake as his own, Clement Lichfield caused it to be carved on his escutcheon over the eastern archway of the bell tower.

The Dinely manuscripts of about 1684 as published by the Camden Society in 1868 under the title *History from Marble*, contain a free-hand sketch of the bell tower as it then appeared. The eye is at once attracted to the flag flying above the Tower, plainly emblazoned with an anchor. It seems reasonable, therefore, to assume that the gilded anchor which hung over the door of No. 3, Bewdley Street, for over a century, was the successor, perhaps, to a similar sign displayed in the days when tenants of monastic lands sought favour with their landlord by simple gestures of respect.

The history of the Golden Anchor Inn is void before it appears in the first local directory of 1820. While retaining the actual sign of the Golden Anchor until about twenty years ago, the inn changed its name to the Old Anchor about 1865. At about this time, the house next door, No. 1, Brick-kiln Street, opened as a beerhouse with the sign of the New Anchor; it had a sign similar to the old one except that it was painted bright blue. It may be that in the political hot-bed of the Bewdley at this period the rival landlords thus advertised their allegiance to the Blue or Yellow factions.

According to the old police book, on 15th March 1836, Kinchin reported that he heard "Murder" cried several times and went into the Anchor public house. John G.'s wife was crying in the passage and the cups were being broken in the house. "I desired G. to go home," he wrote, "but he then caught hold of me, tore the stock from me neck and broke me lamp." Fined 2s. 6d., lamp 5s., costs 2s. On New Year's day, 1857, Sergeant Mann: "…found four men at the Anchor Inn, kept by John Simpson, Bewdley Street, smoking and drinking at 1 am. The landlord said they were all lodgers." In May, 1841, the previous landlord, Enoch Smith, had brought charges against a Hampton man for being drunk and wilfully damaging the inn door and insulting his daughter, Miss Mary Ann Smith. Fined 5s. and one month's hard labour.

35: Site of the Old Anchor, Brick-kiln Street (2008)

Enoch Smith kept the Anchor from 1820 to 1854, Charles Rogers (1864), John Watkins (1873), George Watkins (1894), William Grove (1897), Arthur Smith (1906), David Churchley (1907). Subsequent landlords have been H. Smith, Miss Fisher, Frank Short, Frank Dingley, Jack Nightingale, and the present licensee, Mr George

Halford. During Mr Dingley's time at the Anchor, the Evesham Rovers Football Club was formed there and had several successful seasons in local leagues. In the early part of the century the Anchor was noted for its smoking concerts and tripe suppers. The 'main dish' at the latter functions was supplied, prepared and cooked by the late Horace Wheatley, who kept the butcher's shop on the opposite corner to the Anchor, now owned by Mrs Tandy.

Oddfellows' Arms

The retirement of Mrs Annie Spiers from the licensed trade earlier this month severed a long family connection with the Oddfellows' Arms in Briar-close. Taking its name from the Loyal Avon Lodge of Oddfellows (No. 6352) Manchester Unity, established there on 28th January 1880, the public house had been kept by successive members of the Spiers family from 1860, when it had originally opened as a beer and cider house. The late Mr Joseph Spiers bought the house in 1925, and after spending over £2,000 on rebuilding and enlarging the premises, was granted a licence to retail wines and spirits in addition to beers, cider and porter, in 1929.

Recently [1956] the inn was purchased by Messrs Atkinson's Brewery, who have been in occupation since 11th October, when the Oddfellows' Arms ceased to be a free house and joined the ranks of the 'tied' public houses.

36: Oddfellows' Arms, Briar Close (2003)

Old Red Horse

Surely the Old Red Horse is the most photogenic pub in Evesham. Even the most casual observer cannot fail to notice its popularity, together with the stocks and Almonry opposite, as the 'bit of Old Evesham' most favoured by photographers in search of the picturesque. Unquestionably the black and white exterior of the Vine Street inn is a salient feature of the southern approach to the town centre. But it hasn't always been so.

Like its contemporary neighbours the Royal Oak and Almonry, now fortunately restored, it had been endowed at some period with heavy layers of featureless stucco which entirely disguised the true nature of the earlier workmanship.

37: Old Red Horse, Vine Street (c.1900)

In 1932, the new owners, Hunt, Edmunds and Co. Ltd, acting on the advice of the Vale of Evesham Antiquarian Society, re-exposed the ancient timberwork and jettied construction to view and have since maintained the original fabric of the Red Horse in a manner which reflects the utmost credit on them, deserving of the gratitude of all true admirers of Old Evesham.

The sign of the Old Red Horse is very rare: it actually derives from the old English roan or red horse long since extinct as a breed and now almost equally so as an inn sign. In Evesham it serves as the last link with an important aspect of the town's development as a market centre since its incorporation in 1605. The Old Red Horse is the sole survivor of a cluster of inns in the vicinity which set out to attract the custom of the 'horsy' fraternity attending the famous horse fairs held four times a year in the shadow of the town hall for at least three centuries.

Between the Red Horse and the corner of Genesis Lane[35] lay the Farriers' Arms, now the King Charles Bar, and the Nag's Head. Across the road Mr Pearce's shop displayed the sign of the Horse and Groom while the White Horse Inn once occupied the site of the Post Office in the Market Place. Horse trading was probably well established as a feature of the commercial life of Evesham when the Red Horse was built in the 15th or 16th century and continued until the internal combustion engine created a new era in road transport.

Plenty of Evesham folk will remember the droves of Welsh ponies and other sturdy breeds of horses offered for sale by dealers for use with the light Evesham dray, a useful vehicle which will soon be as rare as red horses. But it is not so well known that the prototype of the dray was made for a man called Joseph Cook, who had land in the Abbey Gardens, by Thomas Stokes in his wheelwright's shop a few doors from the Old Red Horse itself.

> Red Horse is a sign I know naught what to say!
> For a red horse I ne'er saw, by night or day;
> But for my part I wish it, I cannot say less,
> May her endeavours to please be crowned with success.

The lady proprietor of the Red Horse who was wished well by Mr Sharpe in his *Song of Signs* was Mary Roper, who kept the inn in 1820. She was followed by S. Sheppard (1835), Henry Parr (1842), Thomas Hunting (1850), John Groves (1863), William George (1873), William Brotherton (1894), A. Brotherton (1913) and W. Grove (1920). More recent landlords have been W. Hill (1930), F. Woods (1935), and A.H. Gilbert (1945), who was succeeded by the present tenant Mr Raymond Frankum in 1953.

38: Old Red Horse, Vine Street (c.1900 and 2008)

---

[35] Presumably called Genesis Lane because it was at the beginning of the Bewdley. SBB

Pheasant

This little 18th-century inn was situated in Bridge Street opposite the present Duke of York public house. It does not appear in the earliest directory of Evesham (dated 1820) and presumably had disappeared before then.

Plough

In July 1955, when Mitchells and Butlers Ltd, the Birmingham brewers, replaced the sign of their sole Evesham inn with a Maiden's Head in lieu of a Plough, a link with the past was restored. The Mayden's Head Corner at the junction of Vine Street with the Market Place was a familiar landmark in old Evesham, as entries in the corporation books dating back to 1667 indicate. In that year, the pig market was designated as:

> ...the street leading from the New Hall to Merstowe Green on both sides from the dore of Mr Thomas Harewell to the corner house in the possession of William Roberts on one side, and from the Mayden's Head Corner to the Church gate on the other side.

In 1684, the corporation received 1s. 2d. chief rent from William Gardner for his house, the Mayden's Head, and paid him 8s. 10d. "for mending five buckets and a journey to Worcester" – reimbursement due to him in his office as sergeant-at-mace.

39: Plough Inn, Vine Street (c.1910)

Early in the following year he undertook a longer journey on behalf of the corporation in order to deliver an address of loyalty on behalf of the inhabitants of Evesham to James II. For this service he charged the mayor £2 8s. – a very modest item in the civic expense accounts for 1685, which included £13 19s. 4d. for the proclamation of the new king, £6 18s. for Coronation celebrations and, later in the year, £7 "att ye Thanksgiving for ye taking of Monmouth and the defeat of ye Rebells" – every penny of which was spent on alcoholic refreshments.

Gardner's name continued to appear in borough records until 1699 when, for some reason undisclosed, he was discharged from his position, disenfranchised and debarred from the liberties and freedoms of the borough.

The earliest deed relating to the inn now in the owner's possession is dated 10th April 1790, and refers to the Plough and Harrow in the occupation of Richard Cook. In 1833 the owners were Charles and Maria Partington, the former being described as a butcher. The earliest local directory (Lewis's) shows J. Cull as the landlord in 1820 and Pigot's *Directory of Worcestershire* gives Charles Frederick Stratton as the landlord in 1835. An interesting story linking the Plough and Harrow with the Dover's Hill sports at Campden was recounted in 1908 by Stratton's son, George M. Stratton.

Charles Stratton became foreman of his grandfather's silk mills at Badsey, where he married Miss Ann Knight and took a beerhouse. Two years later he removed to the Plough and Harrow, opposite which stood the old Evesham gaol at the south end of the town hall. He befriended a stranger who had been locked up in the gaol for some trivial offence, providing the man with food and drink during his imprisonment and financing the legal aid which eventually effected his release.

Mrs Stratton used to attend the Dover's Hill games every year, taking with her a large tent, a good supply of ale, cider, wines, spirits and viands to sell during the week of gaming. She made a considerable profit which, in the form of golden sovereigns, was "banked" through the bunghole of a barrel of ale or cider, for safety's sake. She also kept a brace of pistols, loaded and primed for use, under the counter. The lawless behaviour of the various criminal classes who battened on the countryfolk attending the sports made these precautions essential.

One year, every stall and booth on the ground, except Mrs Stratton's, was razed to the ground and pillaged. Scores of people found refuge in Mrs Stratton's tent; yet she, her maid and men were never molested or robbed in all the years she attended the games; nor was any pedlar, or benighted person who sought shelter in her tent, ever harmed in any way. The reason for her immunity from attack was the good deed by Charles Stratton in Evesham to the unfortunate stranger who turned out to be a sort of captain in one of the gangs that raided the folk attending the Dover's Hill games. One day he had entered Mrs Stratton's tent for refreshment and had recognised his benefactor's wife. Thereafter, the Stratton's tent was safe, even during the wildest riots on Dover's Hill.

Mrs Stratton also pioneered a new branch of the victualling business by supplying refreshments at country farm sales. Subsequently this became a popular and remunerative line with many innkeepers and a particular boon to those attending sales of several days' duration in the more isolated areas of the countryside. In 1836, the Strattons removed to the New Inn at Cropthorne, where the good-natured and jovial Charles continued, well liked, for another forty years or more.

The new occupant of the Plough, as it was hereafter described, was Thomas Walker, who soon got an unwelcome guest in the person of one described in the old police book as "an old offender," charged in 1837 with "being drunk and creating a disturbance in the Plough and resisting an officer." As this gentleman was being escorted across the road to the police station his custodians were attacked by his mother who also had to be taken into custody for "attempting to rescue her son." Blood, as we well know, is reputedly thicker than water; and we suspect that the ale was thicker in those days, too. The next landlord, George Weightman, had his troubles of a similar sort.

40: Plough Inn, Vine Street (c.1910)

In a *Journal* of January 1865, this notice appeared:

> Pigeon shooting – The subscriber respectfully announces a grand match for £15 bet between two gentlemen of Evesham, and a second match for £6 between a gentleman of Evesham and a gentleman of Cropthorne, to take place on Tuesday next, the 23rd instant, in Mr Hunt's field at the bottom of Bewdley Street. A fat pig will also be shot for, entrance 5s. each, to be followed by a sweepstakes, open to all comers. Shooting to commence at 10:30 o'clock. A dinner will take place at the above inn at 4:30 o'clock when the company of any gentleman will be esteemed a favour – W. Kings, proprietor.

Later landlords of the Plough were – James Major (1873), John Phipps (1894), Mrs Phipps (1901), Louis Newbury (1902), and Mrs Annie Newbury who, on 31st March 1930, assigned the lease to Mitchells and Butlers. The brewers acquired the freehold of the premises from Mrs Fanny Grove on 21st December 1935 and rebuilt the house in its present form during 1936-37, the architect being the late Mr H.E. Dicks, of Evesham.

Mr Hector C. Morris, now of the Cross Keys, was landlord of the Plough for about twenty-five years until Mr Edward Bladon took over in 1951, to be succeeded this year by the present landlord, Mr Harry Andrew.

Prince of Wales

A small Bridge Street inn proudly displayed the familiar princely badge of three feathers together with the motto 'Ich Dien' (I serve) for the better part of the last century. Although the name of the Prince of Wales is absent from trade directories of the period it appears in other public records such as those of the police.

On 29th December 1847, for example, a Bengeworth man was committed to the sessions after being accused by Hannah Keen, the Prince of Wales, Bridge Street, of stealing a bottle jack[36]. The latter seems to have been either a bottle-shaped spit for roasting meat before an open fire or a gadget for lifting purposes.

Bentley's *Directory of Worcestershire* for 1840 lists the names of both Hannah Glover (page 29) and Joseph Keen (page 31) as being hosts at the Duke of York in Bridge Street, which is unlikely. Slater's *Directory* for 1850 (page 26) shows Charles Badger as landlord of the Duke of York and Hannah Keen as proprietor of an eating

---

[36] The bottle jack was so described because of its supposed resemblance to the ancient type of wine bottle with a long neck and bulbous container. The jack was a mechanical device for roasting meat before an open-hearth fire. A clockwork device inside the 'bottle' caused a wheel beneath it to click back and forth at a steady tempo, thus the joints suspended from hooks on the wheel were regularly exposed to the source of the heat on all sides. Sometimes a semi-circular metal screen having dripping pans in the base, known as a 'hastener', was placed in the hearth, thus enclosing the jack and fire in a rough-and-ready kind of oven. TJSB

house in Bridge Street. It is reasonable to assume that Hannah was the widow of Joseph Keen who probably should have been credited with the Prince of Wales and not the Duke of York by Mr Bentley ten years previously.

From the incorporation of the borough, three hundred and fifty years ago, Evesham has been closely associated with the various titles of the Prince of Wales through the Borough Arms. Before that, the three ostrich feathers of Wales were carved into the row of quatrefoil decorations which appear over the north door of All Saints' porch, probably in honour of Prince Arthur, eldest son of Henry VIII, before his death in 1502. But there is no evidence to show that the royal crest was adopted as an Evesham inn sign before the 19th century.

Evidence of Evesham's regard for the royal heirs to the throne in the last century is not lacking. On 25th January 1842, for instance, the bells pealed merrily from Abbot Lichfield's bell tower as the infant Prince of Wales, later Edward VII, was baptised at Windsor. Twenty-five years later, His Royal Highness visited the Duc d'Aumale at Wood Norton and was presented on arrival at Evesham station, with an address of welcome on behalf of the loyal burgesses by the mayor, Mr W.T. Allard. A few days later, the Prince drove through the town in an open carriage, when the schoolchildren were assembled in High Street to watch him pass.

Possibly the sign of the Prince of Wales was adopted by an existing inn as a patriotic gesture during the Napoleonic Wars when the Prince of Wales and the Duke of Clarence drove through the town on 5th September 1806, after attending a review of the East Worcestershire Regiment of Volunteers which had been recruited in Evesham and Pershore.

Somewhere about the same time, the spendthrift Prince Regent paid his first visit to Sezincote, the Cotswold seat of Sir Charles Cockerell, a retired director of the East India Company who became Tory M.P. for Evesham in 1818. The exotic eastern styling fascinated the Regent, who later spent years of time and a mint of money on his Pavilion at Brighton.

The Regent had a mania for fantastic expenditure: £160,000 for furniture at Carlton House; a silversmith's bill for £130,000; £50,000 spent on furniture at Brighton in excess of the half-million already allowed in his Civil List. It is hardly surprising therefore that when the Whig Party revealed these facts in Parliament, the populace – impoverished to the point of starvation by the struggle with France – should resent the thoughtless extravagance of the pleasure-sated Prince.

In 1817, while returning by coach to Carlton House after the State opening of Parliament, the Regent was pelted with cobble stones and garbage from the streets by a hostile mob. No real harm ensued but a small round hole, appearing in one of the windows of the vehicle, was attributed to an air gun shot, no sound having been heard. The Prince promptly ordered prayers of thanksgiving to be read in all places of worship for his "safe deliverance from the barbarous assault of a lawless multitude."

The loyal address to his Royal Highness which was at once dispatched from Evesham for presentation by the High Steward, the Earl of Coventry, and the two Members for the borough, William Manning and Humphrey Howarth, is a typical effusion of its day:

> May it please your Royal Highness. We, His Majesty's dutiful and loyal Subjects, the mayor, Aldermen and Burgesses of the Borough of Evesham, in Common Council assembled, humbly beg leave to approach your Royal Highness with assurances of our unfeigned Loyalty, Attachment and Respect.
>
> We beg to express our Abhorrence and detestation of the daring and atrocious Attack of a misguided and lawless Multitude on the Sacred Person of your Royal Highness in the discharge of one of the most solemn functions of the highest office of the Empire.
>
> To offer our most sincere Congratulations to your Royal Highness on your happy Escape from injury and to render thanks to that Merciful Providence by which the infamous Attempts of Domestic Traitors have been so entirely frustrated.
>
> We cannot too strongly deprecate the evil designs of those base and factious Characters who, taking advantage of unavoidable public distress, under specious pretences go about culminating their Superiors, spreading dangerous delusions and endeavouring to enflame the minds of the ignorant and unwary against the Constitutional Authorities of every description, who represent resistance to Governments as a Duty, and even dare to stigmatise Charity as a Crime; who being themselves destitute of virtuous feelings would have us forget that England (with all her faults) has long been and we trust will ever continue to be, the Nurse of Patriotism and Virtue, the Land of Liberty, the Abode of Happiness, the refuge of the Honorable Exile, the Mother of Heroes, and the Avenger of the Rights and Liberties of the World.
>
> We beg to assure your Royal Highness that we have a firm reliance under Providence, on the Wisdom, firmness and enlightened policy of the British Parliament, the constitutional representative of a free people, that it is our unalterable determination to support and defend to the utmost of our power the Glorious and uncorrupted Constitution, as transmitted to us by our Ancestors, and we confidently trust that under the Paternal, Mild and Benevolent Administration of Your Royal Highness, the time is not far distant when difficulties we now experience (inevitably resulting from the great Change in Circumstances in the Common Wealth of Europe) will by a patient Co-operation be overcome; the Agriculture, Commerce and Manufactures of the Country will recover their wonted activity, and England, proving as pre-eminent in Peace as she has been triumphant in War, bidding defiance to dastardly calumniators of enviable establishments, will proudly remain the first of Nations in an admiring World.

Quart Pot

Taking an attribute of his own trade for a sign, William Wheeler kept the Quart Pot, a Bengeworth alehouse, in 1820. This 'tiddleywink' is generally supposed to have occupied the site of Ivy House in Elm Road, near the junction with Badsey Lane. A hundred years ago the corner thus formed was known as Bishop's Corner after Henry Bishop, a gardener who lived there during the first quarter of the 19th century.

Kelly's *Directory of Worcestershire*, 1863, confirms that the alehouse, possibly re-built, was then known by the sign of the New Inn, a name which had been adopted at least six years earlier.

The earlier case-books of Evesham police force show that on 22nd February 1857, six pounds of candles were stolen out of the tap room of the New Inn, the property of John Nightingale, of Offenham. The thief was not found, though several houses were searched.

Mrs Susan Wheeler was proprietor of the inn when the licence lapsed in 1877. It is said in Bengeworth that this was engineered by the owner of the brickyards opposite, now the premises of the Bredon Package Company, who considered that the proximity of the alehouse to his newly-established kilns was not conducive to the sobriety of his workmen. Whether he achieved his object by regaling his employees with snuff as an alternative to ale is undisclosed, but he appears to have passed into Evesham history with the acknowledged soubriquet of 'Snuffy'.

An Evesham worthy born at the Quart Pot, or New Inn, was Frederick Wheeler, son of William and Susan, who became very well-known as town crier of the borough. Resplendent in his official habit of top hat with gold band, white cravat and gloves, blue coat with brass buttons and red waistcoat similarly adorned, blue plush breeches with red bows at the knee, white stockings and black-laced shoes: with voice and bearing to match his fine appearance, Frederick Wheeler was acknowledged to be a credit to his native Bengeworth as he toured the streets crying the public notices of sales and entertainments, property lost and found; and, in winter, telling where relief might be obtained by those suffering hardship or distress.

In private life, Frederick Wheeler owned several livery stables from which he hired out horses and traps, the main establishment being situated just west of New Street in the Leys. Not many yards away at 17, Burford Road, lives Mrs S. Cresswell, sole survivor of Mr Wheeler's ten children. Recalling her father's handsome appearance and services to the town with justifiable pride, she told me:

> "They used to say he put padding in his stockings to improve the appearance of his calves, but he never needed to improve on nature."

Then she added, as an afterthought: "But he was very strict with us kids!"

Railway Hotel

Amidst a tumult of noise and exploding cannon, ringing church bells and the vociferous enthusiasm of the populace gathered at the point of departure, a twenty-one coach railway train left Stourbridge Junction at 9 am on Saturday, 1st May 1852. Triumphal arches of flowers and evergreens, flanked by cheering crowds of spectators, greeted the train at every town, village and hamlet upon its route. Shortly before noon, the engine halted before a newly completed bridge decked with flags and a streamer bearing the legend, "Success to the Ox., Wor. and Wol. Railway." Nearby, another banner exhorted all concerned to: "Eat, drink and be merry." As indeed they did at an *al fresco* public luncheon held that afternoon in High Street, Evesham, to celebrate the arrival of the first railway train in the town.

By amalgamation with other companies, the line became known as the West Midland Railway (1860) and later as the Great Western Railway in July 1864. In the meantime, another company had built a railway from Evesham to Alcester which later became a branch of the London, Midland and Scottish system, linking Evesham with Birmingham and Ashchurch Junction.

41: Railway Hotel, High Street (1935)

The Midland station first opened on 17th September 1866, and in January 1868, the following appeared in the *Evesham Journal*:

> The want of accommodation for the refreshment of railway travellers connected with or within a reasonable distance of our railway stations at Evesham has long been felt and upon the opening throughout of the Evesham and Redditch line now very near its completion, this want will naturally be very considerably

increased. We learn that the year 1868 is in all probability destined to see this requirement fully and efficiently supplied. A strip of land lying between the Great Western and Midland lines immediately facing the entrance to the railway stations has, we are informed, been purchased by Mr John Meddings, a builder of this town, with a view to erecting upon it an hotel, comprising on the ground floor coffee room and bar, refreshment rooms right and left of the main entrance, with a smokeroom and kitchen behind.

The Railway Hotel was eventually built and licensed, but not before some dispute and difficulties had ensued. Mr Meddings built the hotel abutting on to the public footpath and some members of the Council advocated that he should be proceeded against in law for "bringing the building line up to the footpath and thus causing an encroachment." After several months of indecision, the Council agreed to take no action against the builder in view of the legal expenses involved.

42: Railway Hotel, High Street (2003)

In September 1868, at the Evesham Borough Licensing Sessions, Mr Herbert New applied on behalf of the owner for a licence to sell excisable liquors on the premises lately built by the railway station, to be known by the sign of the Railway Hotel. Mr New regretted that the house was then merely a beerhouse and expressed the hope that the Bench would grant the licence applied for so that it could be at once made into a respectable hotel. But the magistrates refused the application. Mr Meddings had to wait some time before they relented and, presumably, forgave his encroachment offence.

It was described as the Railway Hotel by 18th August 1880, the date of an account from the proprietor, Mr D. Saunders (late of the Northwick Arms) to Mr Lehmann, M.P. The charges may be interesting:

	£	s.	d.
Breakfasts	4	19	0
Luncheons	5	16	0
Dinners	14	10	10
Suppers	2	10	2
Bed, apartments, fire and lights	18	15	0
Brandy, rum, gin, whiskey, hollands	1	7	2
Wine, negus	9	7	0
Biscuits and fruit	1	2	6
Ale, porter, cider	1	13	9
Tobacco and cigars	-	-	-
Lemonade, soda water	2	9	6
Servants' eating and ale	6	2	10
Washing	-	11	8
Parcels	-	-	-
Writing paper stamps	-	7	6
Chambermaid, waiter, ostler, boots	4	5	0
Total	**78**	**15**	**3**

Mr Lehmann, the Liberal candidate, had a majority of two over his Conservative opponent, Mr F. Dixon-Hartland, in the Evesham election of 1880. He presented an Evesham petition to Parliament urging the closing of public houses on Sundays. On a recount, he was unseated... David Saunders was succeeded as proprietor by his daughter, Miss H. Saunders, who kept the hotel for some years with the aid of her sisters. The patronage of Wood Norton was bestowed on them in the nineties, as this *Journal* extract of 13th April 1890, shows:

> T.S.H. the Comte and Comtesse de Paris revived the old tradition of Wood Norton by hunting a pack of harriers throughout the winter. In return for kindness received from landowners and farmers in the neighbourhood they decided to give a complimentary dinner to those over whose land the hounds had hunted. This took place on Tuesday evening at the Railway Hotel when "a truly royal spread" was placed upon the tables. It would have done credit to a larger hotel than that of which the Misses Saunders are proprietors. The health of the Duke d'Aumale and that toast of the Comte and Comtesse de Paris was submitted and received with great heartiness, other toasts and songs followed and the party broke up at midnight.

By 1901, John Smith was landlord of the Railway Hotel. John Levi Wood in 1912, J.H. Roberts in 1920, G.S. Hiles in 1930, H.L. Tigwell in 1935. The late Mr Tigwell went on to the Sandys Arms, Wickhamford, after the war, then Mr F.G. Hickman kept the Railway for some years before returning to Oxford. He was succeeded by Mr John E. Doust, who left last year and was followed by Mr J. Stanley, who removed from the Green Dragon.

Red Lion

Evesham had two Red Lions: one *rampant* in Waterside, now the Northwick Arms; the other *couchant* at 6, Market Place, now the business premises and home of Mr J.D. Woolley, the picture framer. Many will recall the white-painted balustrade of the latter inn which set off its projecting bays, and the signboard surmounted by the iron lion in red that gave the house its name.

Red Lion in the Market Place

In the transactions of the former Evesham Company of Mercers for 1728 appears the first record of the inn. From the town hall the company "a journed to the Red Lyon to complete ye residew of theare business." Later, the secretary was able to report that "wee then a greed to show Mr James Hemming, baker, Thomas Kemp and Mr Henry Mutton a trade that they have no right to." Presumably the customary "handsome treat" had been provided by the gentlemen nominated in acknowledgement of the privilege of calling themselves mercers.

43: Red Lion, Market Place (1903) and Red Lion Yard

From the same source it is learned that Mrs Tovey was hostess to the company in 1760 and that Widow Burlingham filled the role in 1766. A window tax return for the parish of All Saints dated 1761 showed that Mrs Burlingham paid 11s. duty on eight lights, compared with £2 11s. on 32 lights by Thomas Hodges at the Crown. On 19th October 1863, the Red Lion was offered for sale by the trustees of the late Miss Barnes:

...with the brew house, stabling yards and out-offices, as now occupied by Mrs Gee, who is carrying on there a most thriving business, the house from its situation being admirably adapted for and having a capital market custom.

In the same year, an omnibus was advertised to run on Mondays and Fridays from the Red Lion to Tewkesbury; it was probably the successor to Stanley the carrier, who left on the same days of the week in 1840. By 1873 the number of carriers departing from the inn had increased considerably; there were regular services to Buckland, Cropthorne, Dumbleton, Gretton, Laverton, Saintbury, and Willersey.

Owning the Red Lion in 1865 was Thomas Walker, who saw the establishment there of a court of the Ancient Order of Foresters, the founders of which were Job Smith, Walter Goodall and George Dixon.

The hospitable reputation of the Red Lion was again emphasised when "in accordance with their custom, the staff of the *Evesham Journal* supped together" there on New Year's Eve, 1878. A report says "a number of complimentary toasts were proposed and some excellent songs were sung. The catering of Mr and Mrs Underwood gave real satisfaction." A convivial and no doubt nostalgic annual event for Mr William Smith, co-founder of the *Journal* in 1860, whose father, Joseph Smith, kept the Red Lion between 1835 and 1850, in succession to John Smith, mine host in 1820.

Later landlords included George Byrd (1894), H.J. Phipps (1897) and T. Stanley (1898). It closed as a licensed house in 1910.

The last landlord but one was Mr William Salmon, who is well known for his long – almost 50 years – association with the office of borough Sergeant-at-Mace, an office in which he remains active. He was landlord of the Red Lion from 1900 until 1908, when he took another well known market inn, the King's Head. Recalling his years at the Red Lion to me recently, Mr Salmon spoke of the thriving trade carried on there when the country carriages used the inn as a point of arrival and departure for their passengers. He especially remembered how busy he used to be when Evesham mop fair took place since it was then held in the Market Place and not on Merstow Green as at present.

The last landlord of the inn was Mr Frederick William Stafford.

Another very well known and respected Evesham tradesman vouches for the tale of why the Red Lion was sadly missed by a particular section of the community when it was closed in 1910. The Rev. Dr Walker's sermons were, it seems, both erudite and lengthy and in consequence the custom grew up among the choirmen at All Saints' to leave quietly by the vestry door as the vicar began to preach. They would slip round the corner for "a quick 'un" at the Lion while the sand in the pulpit hourglass ran its measured course. It is further said that the learned doctor was wont to congratulate the choir from time to time upon the improvement in the quality of their singing after the sermon.

Red Lion in Waterside

If you could put the clock back to a September day in 1655, it is most probable that you would find the inn parlours of Evesham agog for the latest news of the "Quaking folk in Bengard." Fearlessly attacking all forms of accepted religion amidst the growing hostility of established order everywhere, the Quakers, more properly the Society of Friends, roused strong feelings throughout the country and nowhere more than in Evesham, as we shall see. Led by Humphrey Smith, a former minister of religion, the sect gained a following in Bengeworth which attracted the unfavourable notice of the Puritan clergy and their supporters, who were implacably opposed to non-conformity. In the centre of the storm which ensued stood Edward Pittway, ex-officer in Cromwell's new model army, mayor of Evesham in 1648, and landlord of the Red Lion in Waterside, now known as the Northwick Hotel.

44: Old Red Lion Inn, Waterside

The Bengeworth troubles began on Sunday morning, 19th August 1655, with a meeting of Friends at the house of a sympathiser. Being forewarned, George Hopkins, the Presbyterian Vicar of All Saints, led his "whole congregation, both those called justices and magistrates, and rude people several hundred, to the steeple house in Bengard," according to our Quaker chronicler, where he proceeded to "vent forth sorcery" in the form of a sermon in which he likened "that which is called Quaking unto witchcraft" and rose. He incited the magistrates and justices to take civil action against the disciples of George Fox and urged them to put the oath of Abjuration into effect forthwith.

That same evening Humphrey Smith and Thomas Cartwright were arrested and taken to the house of Samuel Gardner, a magistrate, where they were subjected to what in modern parlance would be termed 'the third degree'. This went on for several days as the enemies of the men roused mob violence among the populace to the pitch where stones and dirt were being hurled at the prisoners, and Robert Martin, a magistrate, ordered other Quaker prisoners to be hauled out naked for the amusement of the crowd:

> But one, Captain Pittway, being there, and seeing the rage of the people and the outragiousness of Robert Martin, for ought he knew to murder the prisoners if they had not gone forth at that time of night, said, 'The prisoners shall not go forth this night. If thou hast anything to do with them, thou mayest do it in the morning', thereby averting what might easily have been a fatal catastrophe.

Thus we have the unusual circumstances of an innkeeper supporting those who were most opposed to the assets of his trade and decried the properties of strong liquors at every opportunity. But Pittway was committed to the cause and became one of the signatories of a complaint, descriptive of the treatment of the Friends, printed and despatched to the Lord Protector, "that by it he might know what corrupt men were in authority in the town." Meanwhile, the first wave of ire died down, though the leading Quakers were kept in an underground prison guarded by eight armed men so that none should have conversation with them.

On 25th September, George Kemp, the mayor, sent for the prisoners and other Friends to ask if they admitted authorship of the representation sent to Cromwell. They all replied in the affirmative and that they were prepared to prove its truth in a court of law as they expected justice from the Protector and "knew they would get none in Evesham," whereupon they were committed to the Sessions.

The Borough Sessions took place on 2nd October before Sir Robert Atkyns, the Recorder. When Edward Pittway was arraigned, he said: "I understand that you have been a magistrate and one of the chiefest of the Bench, and I do much admire that you show no more reverence to the court than to come here with your hat on and now a ringleader of this sect. I will take a course with you." "I see little justice done," rejoined Pittway, whereupon the Recorder exploded "Take off his hat! That's one piece of justice."

Admitting that he called Martin a drunkard because he "did pluck the people out of their beds, and bred such a disturbance in the night," Pittway was recalled next day to hear another indictment against him for signing the complaint – said to be malicious – against the magistrates. "All malice and spight, I deny," he declared, "but for the printed paper I own it true and am ready to prove it." But the Recorder did not allow the innkeeper to call his witnesses and fined him £20, the heaviest penalty, forthwith. Three days later Edward Pittway was removed from his place among the capital burgesses by an entry in the Corporation book signed by the new mayor, Edmund Young, and eleven other burgesses, including Robert Martin and his two sons, who later went away to London and founded Martin's Bank.

For once, however, the success of the magistrates and their minions was short lived, for their conduct came to the notice of Cromwell, who instructed Major-General Berry at Worcester to inform the mayor and magistrates of Evesham "that it is his Highness's Promise and especial pleasure, that the said Fines (imposed at the Sessions) shall be remitted and taken off."

But this only spurred Edmund Young to prove himself more spiteful towards the Quakers than his predecessor, vowing to break their meetings, "or else his bones should lie in dirt," whatever that meant. So on the morning of 14th October he arrested two Friends as they walked to a private meeting at the Red Lion, and another large group who endeavoured to assemble in the street later in the day. Among those taken into custody once again was Humphrey Smith, who left this grim record of *The Sufferings, Tryals and Purgings of the Saints of Evesham* in a pamphlet form:

> The prison, or hole, where we are kept is not 12 foot square, and one gaol hole belonging to it not four inches wide, wherein we take our food and straw to lie upon. And we are forced to burn a candle every day by reason the prison is so dark, and so close, and so many in one little room, and so little air, with the stink of our own dung, all of which might have occasioned the death of some of us o'er this time.... Sometimes when the days were hot, the breath of some prisoners were almost stopped and they lay for several days like men asleep, and when the days were at the coldest we have not room nor place to make a fire, or to walk to keep our bodies warm.

In this, their extremity, the Friends were uplifted in their resolve by a visit from George Fox, their mentor, who sent for:

> Edward Pittway, a Friend, that lived near Eovesholme, and asked him the truth of the thing, and he said it was so. Then I went that night with him to Eovesholme, and in the evening we had a large precious meeting, whereine people were refreshed with the Word of Life, and with the Power of the Lord.

Next morning he rode to the various places of imprisonment in Evesham to encourage his followers and was just leaving the gaol when he:

> ...espied the Magistrates coming up the town to have seized me in prison. But the Lord frustrated their intents, that the innocent escaped their snare, and the Lord's blessed power came over them all. But exceedingly rude and envious were the priests and professors about this time in those parts.

During that winter there were further meetings at the Red Lion and further persecutions. Edward Pittway gave the sect a piece of garden ground at the back of his inn, as a burial ground; Stephen Pittway, his brother, "suffered imprisonment about sixteen weeks for speaking to a priest in a steeple-house." But gradually opposition waned. Samuel Gardner went off his head and drowned himself in 1660, Robert Martin is said to have died after a fall from his horse, till eventually in 1676 the Quaker community removed from the shelter so long afforded by Edward Pittway at the sign of the Red Lion to the meeting room they built in Cowl Street, where the meetings of the Society continue to this day.

Rose and Crown

The Rose and Crown is one of the several badges of the House of Tudor now perpetuated on inn signs all over England. The earliest local reference to it appears in the transactions of the Evesham Company of Mercers for 1762 when Hannah Warran entertained the guild at her inn of that name. George Harber was mine host in 1803 and the old Masonic Lodge of Mercy and Truth held several meetings of instruction there during 1818 and 1819.

By 1820 George Laurence was conducting the inn as a posting house, being licensed to let horses for public hire. In 1840 a coach left the Rose and Crown for Worcester every Wednesday and Saturday morning at 8 am. The fare was 2s. 6d. single and 4s. return, the route was through Pershore and the journey was slower and less costly than the service provided by the coaches which posted at the Northwick Arms. The inn continued for many years as a popular rendezvous for carriers. Littlebury's *Directory* for 1873 gives details of close on twenty services a week starting from the inn and serving a dozen villages within ten miles radius of Evesham. At this time Edward Lawrence was landlord in succession to J. Sears (1840), William Williams (1842), George Brotherton (1850), and William Cox (1870).

On 7th February 1843, the United Patriots' National Benefit Society instituted an Evesham branch at the Rose and Crown and from time to time thereafter reports of their annual dinner appeared in the local Press. This Society was particularly strong at Bidford-on-Avon where they held an annual 'Club' Day (on Whit-Monday) attended by other friendly societies from Evesham until comparatively recent times.

Admirers of the Victorian author, George Gissing, will be interested to learn that he once spent a night at the Rose and Crown inn which he recounts in *The Private Papers of Henry Ryecroft*, published in 1903 and probably his best known work.

> I once passed a night in a little market town [he wrote] where I had arrived tired and went to bed early. I slept forthwith, but was awakened by I knew not what; in the darkness there sounded a sort of music, and, as my brain cleared, I was aware of the soft chiming of church bells. Why, what hours could it be? I struck a light and looked at my watch. Midnight. Then a glow came over me. 'We have heard the chimes at midnight, Master Shallow!' Never till then had *I* heard them. And the town in which I slept was Evesham, but a few miles from Stratford-on-Avon.

From the 1890s to the mid thirties of the present century, W.J.R. Partridge owned the Rose and Crown, then George Bell took over on behalf of Messrs Flowers, the Stratford brewers, who rebuilt the house in a modern styling. Mr J.A. Burton the present landlord succeeded Mr Bell in 1949. During this period the Rose and Crown has frequently been the venue for important property sales for which purposes it is well accommodated.

Each Tuesday evening one of the main rooms is given over to the Earl of Coventry Lodge of the Royal Antediluvian Order of Buffaloes wherein to practice the rites and mysteries in pursuance of their worthy precept: 'Justice, Truth and Philanthropy.' The

Earl of Coventry Lodge was established at the Northwick Arms in 1925, removing to its present home in 1936. The senior Buff Lodge in the borough was inaugurated at the Golden Heart in 1921 but has met at the Railway Hotel since 1941. It is named in honour of Simon de Montfort.

Round House

Few visitors to Evesham can fail to be impressed by the well-preserved fifteenth century building that dominates the Market Place. Copies of the late E.A.B. Barnard's *History of the Round House* (1915) are now extremely rare. Mr Barnard based his account on papers which are now at the County Records Office in Worcester, where they were lodged by the National Providential Bank Ltd, present owners of the building, in 1951. This account is drawn from both sources.

45: Round House, Market Place (1900 and 1937)

The first owner of the property who can be traced was Richard Baylye, draper, of Evesham, who made his will on 15th March 1579, and died before 13th June 1580, the day on which his estate was appraised. The valuation of £24 11s. 6d. establishes the Round House Tavern as quite a modest hostelry compared, for instance, with the Goat Inn on Merstow Green, the contents of which, only four years later, were valued at £97 4s. 6d. But the description and inventory remains of great interest, since it refers to one room in the house as "the taverne," that is, the wine shop.

Mr W.A. Cox, of the Abbey Gate, possesses a wine merchant's cork seal, dated about 1650, which he found during alterations to the Round House in August 1916. He has expressed his intention of presenting it, together with other local antiquities, to Evesham Museum when this is established in the Almonry. The 1580 inventory has been transcribed and includes:

The Hall – one cupborde, one longe tableborde with his frame and two formes, 13s. 9d., flower potts of pewter and 13 quyshyns 8s. All the waynes cott in the hall 20s.

Chamber over the Shoppe – one joyned bedsted, one fetherbed, one flock bed, two bolsters, one old coverlett and one curtayne 26s. 8d. Three coverletts, five pillowes, twentie payre of sheets, four chests and one coffer £7. Three dosyn of napkyns, six table clothes and twelve towells 36s.

Chamber over the Hall – two joyned bedsteds, one truckle bedsted, one fetherbed, one flockbed, one mattresse, one old coverlett, and three buckaram curteynes. Twelve old bords, one short ladder with other small implements.

An Other Chamber over the Hall – one boulting whytche, two kneading skeles, one kneeding trough, one long bord, one beating hurdle with other implements there.

Parlor – four square tables with theire frames and two formes and one candle plate.

Kytchin – six brasse potts, three brasse pannes, two yron drypping pannes 36s. Two payre of pott-hooks, one payre of ondeyrons and one payre of cobberts 2s. 6d. Four broches, two chafyne dishes, one strainer and one fyre shovel 3s. Nine candlesticks, one paire of tongs and one frying pan 9s. One garnyshe of pewter 26s. Two counter dishes and one laver 2s. 4d. Three pewter chamber potts 18d. One Brewinge ffurnes and one little boyling furnes 13s. 4d. One fyre forke, three wooden platterns and one brandyron 12d. Six pewter scones, one pewter bottell and one pynte pott 16d. One chaffron, one grydyron, two posnetts with other small implements there 4s.

Buttery – halfe a garnyshe of pewter vessels 14s. One brazen spyce morter with other smale implements there 20d.

Taverne – four morte (malt) skales, two brewing ffats and six other vessells 5s. Four old payles, one gallon, one malte myll with other small implements there 5s.

The Shoppe – six old chests and three cheares with other implements there 20s. One sherte of mayle old 11s. 6d. His apparrell £5 – Sum total £24 11s. 6d.

On 13th June 1646, Richard Baylyes, of Evesham, innholder, sold to Daniel Kemble, of Tewkesbury, mercer, for £275, "a messuage and appurtenances used as a tavern near the Markettplace, a stable and garden in the Black Lane near Bewdly stile, a barn in the Horse Lane"[37] with other property in Long Street[38] alias Bewdley Stile Lane (now Bewdley Street) and elsewhere.

---

[37] Now Swan Lane. SBB

[38] Identification of 'longstrete' as Bewdley Street is suggested again by T.J.S. Baylis in *Evesham in Old Postcards* (comment to postcard no. 74). B.G. Cox, in *The Book of Evesham* p.49, thought 'longstrete' was High Street/Vine Street unbroken by the Town Hall (which was built c.1550). SBB

On 4th August 1654, the property was purchased by Daniel Lysons, woollen draper of Gloucester, for £300 to be paid in instalments. When he defaulted, Kemble having died, the property reverted to Daniel Kemble junior and his wife. They disposed of their interests, in 1663, for £25, to Jarrett Roberts, a London wine cooper.

On 2nd October 1677, Roberts and Milberrow, his wife, sold "the tavern, shops and appurtenances near the Market Place, Evesham," for £200 to George Hopkins, of Evesham, mercer, who was a son of George Hopkins, M.A., vicar of Evesham from 1642 to 1662. Ejected from the living at the Restoration the vicar retired to Dumbleton, where he died in 1666.

George Hopkins junior was born in Evesham in 1650 and became mayor in 1678. An indenture made in June 1678 describes "the messuage heretofore known as the Round House" as the jointure of Jane Martin upon her marriage to George Hopkins. This is the first recorded instance I know of when the premises are referred to as the Round House.

At Christmas 1685 during the mayoralty of Theophilus Leigh, a chief rent of 1s. 8d. for the Round House was paid to the Corporation of Evesham by George Hopkins, being only exceeded by Thomas Harris at the Trumpet (2s.) and Thomas Bouts at the Ledden Post (1s. 9d.) in amount. The Round House remained in the Hopkins family until 2nd June 1774, when, for £190, it was sold to John Benton, of Fladbury, gent, by William Hopkins, of Cheapside, London. And it was then described as "formerly used as a tavern."

Royal Oak

The Midlands are liberally sprinkled with inns bearing the sign of the Royal Oak commemorating the arboreal refuge of 'Charles, King of the Scots', following his flight from the Battle of Worcester on 3rd September 1651. He was forced to hide in an oak tree near Boscobel in Staffordshire while his enemies combed the district around. After a series of thrilling adventures and escapes, he eventually reached Brighton, whence, forty days after Cromwell's 'Crowning Mercy' of Worcester he succeeded in escaping to France.

In Evesham, the Vine Street inn probably took its name during the massive burst of public jubilation coincident with the Restoration of the erstwhile fugitive as King Charles II on 29th May 1660 – his birthday – a date observed annually in Evesham as a public holiday for over two hundred years thereafter.

Mr Sharpe's ballad in praise of Evesham pubs seems to advertise the "speciality of the house" early in the nineteenth century:

> Royal Oak is renowned, for it sheltered a king
> When snug in the oak you may laugh, drink and sing
> And once in a week if you call and not glutton
> They'll ask you to sup off a good leg of mutton.

46: Royal Oak, Vine Street (2003)

The "General Sessions of Peace, Oyer and Terminer presided over by the mayor, Thomas Beale Cooper, deputy recorder, John Hunter, Esq., and others assigned to keep the King's Peace" sat at the Royal Oak in the Pig Market "to hear and determine divers felonies, trespasses and other misdemeanours and offences" on 7th November 1809.

Actually, despite the high sounding official language, the gentlemen were only required to settle one case, that of a young woman who had been 'betrayed'. No doubt the matter was dealt with expeditiously for this type of complaint was all too familiar to the Bench in those days. Sgt Pardoe struck a contrasting note when he entered in his record book for 11th October 1866: "Received information that an old-fashioned silver watch was stolen from the person of J.H. at the Royal Oak inn while in a state of intoxication about 11:30 last night."

A Masonic Lodge[39] was held at the Oak when William Penny was landlord in 1818. Other landlords have been W. George (1840), Thomas Melen (1850), Mrs Elizabeth

---

[39] The Masonic Mercy and Truth Lodge (No.703) was founded in 1818. The Lodge was scheduled to meet at the Cross Keys, but did not use the accommodation there until 1824. The first two years were

Melen (1873), W. Nash (1894), C. Brotherton (1898), C.H. Bell (1902), George Brearley (1908), George Bell (1920), and William Grove (1930), who was succeeded by his son George, familiarly known as 'Chas' to the regulars. During his time the Oak was the headquarters of many sporting organisations including the old Evesham Town F.C., 'The Robins', flying, shooting, darts clubs, etc. Mrs Kate Grove carried on the inn for a decade after her husband's decease but gave up the licence to Mr Streatfield last year.

In the first half of 1935 the interesting old house was carefully restored by Flowers and Sons Ltd Only necessary repairs were effected on the original fabric of the steeply pitched gables when the stucco façade had been removed but the bargeboards had to be renewed. Inside, several walls were swept away to reveal the fine timbers in the ceilings. The architect left a block of stone over the doorway for the date of the house, but as this could not be accurately determined (probably fifteenth century) it was decided to cut the name of the house instead. This task was begun by Mr Fred Cox, the noted Evesham sculptor, who was unable to complete because of an infirmity of the hands. The unfinished inscription will surely provide many generations who pass through with food for thought.

47: Block of stone over the door of the Royal Oak (2008)

On 24th June 1939, *The Times* published an illustration of a new sign painted by Mr Hubert Williams which depicted a Crown set in an oak tree with the bell tower of Evesham Abbey in the background – certainly the first Evesham sign to be thus distinguished. Unfortunately it has now been replaced by a very inferior substitute.

---

spent at the Rose and Crown and the next four at the Crown. Interest in Masonry was thin in Evesham. There were no meetings in 1829, only one in 1830, and the Lodge closed on November 9th 1831, and was erased from the Grand Register in 1833 (details from Ray Sheppard, *History of the Masonic Province of Worcestershire* (Worcestershire Masonic Study Circle, 1989)). SBB

Shoe and Boot

"On the box" – synonymous with "on the panel" or "on the sick list" – this old expression had its origin in the rules of the friendly societies established by the patrons of certain Evesham inns. One of the earliest forerunners of the modern "sick and divvy" was the Evesham Union Society which began on 19th July 1785, at the Shoe and Boot Inn, Bengeworth.

Their thirty seven articles were printed by H. Smith, of Evesham. With the intention "to promote Friendship and true Christian Love, and upon all just Occasions to assist and support each other," the members of the Union Society agreed to assemble once in every four weeks at the Shoe and Boot on Tuesday night at seven o'clock, and to stay together till nine o'clock from "Lady Day 'till S. Michael; and from St Michael to Lady Day from Six 'till Eight." Mine host, John Walker, undertook to provide a private room, suitably heated, from Michaelmas to Lady Day for the use of the Society during Club hours.

He was forbidden to admit strangers to the room on pain of a shilling fine unless the said strangers had first obtained leave from the stewards of the society and "a beer ticket that he has paid fourpence." Each member present was required to pay eightpence "to the Box" and spend fourpence in addition – evidently on beer and tobacco, while every absent member must send a shilling to be put in the Box.

Rule two decrees "that there shall be a Box kept with three locks and three keys for the use of the Society, each steward to keep one key and the person who gives security for the said Box to [keep] the other. And no member shall receive benefit from the Box till two years are expired from his first entrance."

Any member falling sick, lame or blind must send word to the club house, the landlords immediately to inform the stewards who visit the distressed member forthwith to arrange a payment of seven shillings a week. Should the member have the misfortune to become incurable he was entitled to receive 4s. a week "tho' the illness continue till death" and at his funeral every member of the Union must appear with gloves and hat band "otherwise as decent as they can." Failure to attend a deceased comrade's funeral caused a fine of one shilling, exclusive of the shilling that each member was required to pay into the Box to defray the funeral expenses, upon pain of being expelled from the Society. The sum of £2 was given towards the undertaker's charges while the widow or next-of-kin was granted £6 from the Box.

In the case of a member dying, and money being urgently needed for funeral expenses, the stewards were to go to the landlord of the house and borrow the necessary cash from him. John Walker was to be reimbursed from the Box on the next club night "when there is company in the room which shall be five men at least beside the stewards."

Rule 35 envisages an old age pension of 2s. a week for any member over seventy "notwithstanding he may be able to labour"; and as long as £20 remains in the Box he "shall be suffered to follow his Business until totally disabled by some infirmity when he shall receive the benefit of the Box during life." During his superannuation the member was required "to attend the church or some other place of worship as often as there shall be divine service, if he is able, or forfeit sixpence for each neglect."

The administration of the Box was in the hands of two stewards and a clerk. The former, elected in rotation every quarter, were responsible for the accounts of the society, visiting infirm members twice each week, disbursing sick pay and safeguarding the keys of the Box.

The clerk, chosen by majority vote and remaining in office until another be chosen likewise, was required to attend all club nights and to make all fines. His perquisites of office were "that he shall not pay for Beer at any time" and receive sixpence from the Box for calling extraordinary meetings when so desired by the stewards. He was supplied with a hammer to call for silence when the stewards ordered it; when three knocks had been struck a fine of 3d. for the Box was levied on all chatterboxes. The rules were designed to ensure that no unseemly conduct whatsoever marred the club nights at the Shoe and Boot, and to this end rule 20 decreed that:

> ...no Atheist nor known Deist, Waterman or Porter shall be admitted a member of the Society, and if any shall unknowingly be admitted he shall be excluded as soon as discovered.

This may have been a safeguard against the company of bargees who plied the Avon navigation and had a reputation for being a particularly rough lot. The clerk was to impose a fine of 6d. upon any member who "curses, swears, or calls nicknames in the club room" and the penalty was increased to 5s. for any member so indecorous as to quarrel or offer to fight at the club house – with expulsion as the penalty for a second offence. Rule 26 said:

> that if any member get any hurt thro' drunkenness, fighting, wrestling, backsword, cudgel playing... he shall in no wise receive any benefit from the Box for such accident.

Gambling was frowned upon by the Society: if any member "proposes to game and doth play in the club room he shall pay sixpence or be excluded." Similarly, "if any sick member who lies upon the Box shall be caught at gaming, he shall lose his week's pay." Any member who enters the club room "disguised in liquor" must forfeit 2d. but if they be stewards or clerk the fine is increased to 6d.

Finally, good manners must be observed at all times in the club room, so that if any member rises off his seat and another takes it without permission the latter forfeits 2d.; and if any member drinks out of his turn he, too, shall pay a similar amount to the Box. On this note we leave the Union Society safe in their club room and

> *Thus all from dread of Penury secured,*
> *From wounds and Sickness, as it were, insured,*
> *In social Ties of Friendship, all combined,*
> *To be to one another good and kind*

as it says in the poem preceding the articles on the broadsheet.

The sign of the Shoe and Boot is unusual. The late Alderman Henry Masters, J.P., suggested in 1916 that the inn stood at the conjunction of Gardener's Square with Church Street and but a few yards from the churchyard wall. Three cottages, Nos. 41, 40 and 39, Church Street, now occupy this site; and one, No. 39, bears the date 1712.

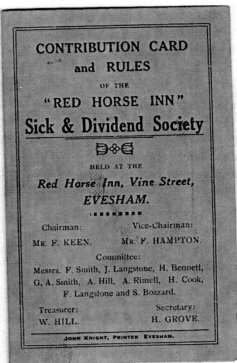

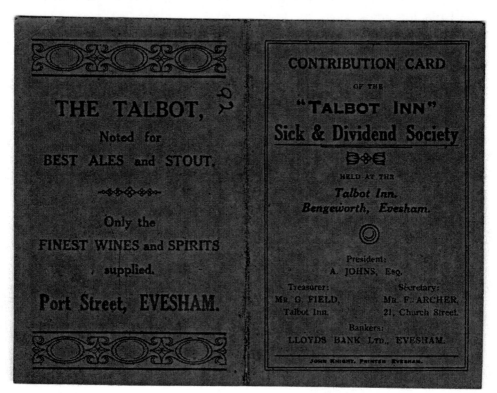

48: Sick & Dividend Society cards (Talbot, Bear, Red Horse)

Shoulder of Mutton

Shoulder of Mutton – the name of this popular old English inn sign appears only once in Evesham annals and this in the record book of the Evesham Company of Mercers, 1612-1833, now preserved in Birmingham Reference Library. The Glovers or Fellmongers as they later became known, were a notoriously thirsty lot. The consumption of ale seems to have taken a regular and important position on the agenda of their meetings. Thus, in 1720, two sums of 11s. and one of 10s. 6d. were spent on that indispensable commodity at quarterly meetings held at the Shoulder of Mutton inn.

At the end of 1721, the sum of £1 9s. 7d. was spent, presumably on the feast, when a new Master of the Company was elected, with an addition of 18s. for ale and a shilling for the gaoler – the latter probably for turning a blind eye to the course of events at the Shoulder of Mutton.

These particular jollifications caused the Glovers to face the new year with a debit balance of £4. Consequently, it is not surprising to discover that about this time there were several instances of masters being elected who refused to meet their predecessors' liabilities, and for whom the Company had no further use. A number of brethren also "denied their privileges" and were "dismissed and put out of the Company" by their gravel-throated colleagues.

Star and Garter

The Star and Garter, still widely favoured as an inn sign, is the insignia of the Most Noble Order of the Garter instituted in the reign of Edward III (1327-1377). Originally, the garter appeared on signboards without the star; thus, Shakespeare, in the *Merry Wives of Windsor*, speaks correctly of the Garter inn at Windsor, where "as an emperor in his expense," Falstaff lived in enviable style. The star was added to the insignia by Charles I and, in the course of time, innkeepers adopted the innovation.

Recently I examined a deed of 1823 which referred to certain premises in Vine Street, Evesham, as "formerly a victualling house and known by the sign of the Star and Garter." From evidence in hand I judge the inn to have been situated on or about the site of 15, Vine Street, at the rear of which there still stands a most interesting three-storey barn in the half-timbered style of construction.

Star Hotel

The earliest document relating to the Star Hotel, Evesham, is an indenture dated 10th February 1586, made between Sir Edward Hoby, of the Isle of Sheppey in Kent, George Tottey and Thomas Dalmare, and Edward Freame, of Evesham, yeoman, by which "the Swanne Inne, Evesham, in High Street between the messuage in the occupation of Thomas Piers on the south side and the Horslane on the north side" was sold to the latter for £55. Sir Edward Hoby was the nephew and heir of Sir Philip Hoby, purchaser of the Abbey lands at the Dissolution. Sir Edward married Margaret Hunsdon, one of the Carey family whose coat of arms bore a swan for their crest. A magnificent swan may still be seen on the tomb of Margaret Hoby in Bisham Church, Berkshire. Surely the High Street inn was first named in her honour.

49: The Swan Inn, High Street (1914)

Of Edward Freame, the other party to the bargain, there is much to be told and little to his credit. He first comes to notice as an innholder in 1578 when called upon to give evidence in a case of homicide against a man called Arnold Tickeridge, who was accused of killing Abraham Dobbyns, a servant of Thomas Bigge, of Lenchwick Manor, in a running fight in High Street, by stabbing him. Freame described how Dobbyns was carried into his inn and lay there until he died. After a prolonged trial Tickeridge was finally acquitted. In 1600 Freame was presented at Worcester for allowing unlawful games in his house, but these were mere straws in the wind compared with what was to follow soon after Evesham attained corporate status in

April 1605. Regrettably the original colourful language of this story, centred on the Swanne Inne, is such that discretion has been required in its presentation. Those who seek the unvarnished version may find it in the Bill of Complaint to the Court of Star Chamber lodged by George Hawkins on 7 Feb. 3 James I (1605/6) (P.R.O. C.P. James I H 178/20).

The complainant, George Hawkins, attorney of Clifford's Inn and Evesham, was the son of George Hawkins who kept the Goat Inn on Merstowe Green and was for many years Steward of the Leet for the Hoby family. George, the son, had also been appointed to the same office on 18th June 1604, according to the Borough Charter and had practised his profession in the Evesham Court over a period, enabling him to build up a reputation of which he was justly proud.

The complaint beings with a statement about a William Hickeman, a Coventry mercer "of lewd, drunken life and bad behaviour" according to Hawkins, whose business in Evesham Market consisted mainly of "evil and cosoning practices." Hickeman seems to have encountered the attorney previously for he had been bound over to be of good behaviour and to keep the King's Peace at Evesham several times with others of his ilk. These were known to George Hawkins, who nominated thirteen more men, including Edward Freame, and Elizabeth Hickeman, a widow. Hawkins said that all of them conspired to defame and overthrow his good character and bring him into disrepute in public life.

50: Star Hotel, High Street (1930)

It appears that in December 1604, several papers, bearing caricatures (described as "images") of the Steward, were posted up in the Swan Inn. Beneath the drawings were what are best described as cheeky verses signed by Launcelotte Rattsey, another of the accused. One of the less noxious extracts scans thus:

> This is the b------------
> With his father the dastard,
> George Hawkyns hight he is,
> In all this sheere
> There is not a squire
> More like a knave, I trow.

Hawkins declared that the libels were still displayed in the Swan Inn on the day of the complaint.

Anne Freame, a widow, leased the Swanne Inne, as it was then designated, to Richard Cresheld, who represented Evesham at Westminster almost without a break from 1624 to 1659, and Philip Harris, mayor of the borough in 1606, 1614 and 1626. Later Mrs Freame's descendants sold the house to Thomas Cresheld but in 1659 the property passed to Samuel Gardner, jun., gent., of Evesham.

In 1666, the Evesham Borough Council resolved "that the sheep market of this burrow be reputed and taken to and shall be in High Street between the Swan inn and the house now in the tenure of Mr John Ballard." Mr Ballard's house has gone but the Swan still stands with sturdy roof timbers, still embellished with red pigments and white scrolls to prove its antiquity. The cattle and sheep markets continued on the very doorstep of the inn, now the Star, for another two and a quarter centuries and the hurdles for penning the animals were stored in its capacious outhouses abutting on the Swan Lane. Traditionally, also, the hustings were erected on the same site, on the cobbles in front of the Star, when Evesham went to the polls.

After Samuel Gardner, jun., the inn was leased to William Gold, of Atch Lench, whose son Nathaniel kept the inn for many years and paid the corporation a chief rent of 8d. "for the Swan" in 1684. By an indenture 19th January 1692, Nathaniel Gold leased the inn to Joseph Field, of Arrow, vintner, who was about to marry Mary Elizabeth, his daughter. On 29th January 1711, Nathaniel leased the inn to Martin Deacon, a maltster, who released it next month to George Gardner, gent., of Evesham, and John Hopkins, yeoman, of Fladbury.

About this time, the inn was divided into two tenements, one kept as the Swan Inn by John Dudley and the other occupied by Nathaniel Gold. In 1724 the tenants were Henry Johnson, who had succeeded Stephen Brown as the innkeeper and Ann Deacon in place of Nathaniel Gold. The northern boundary of the property had now ceased to be Horse Lane and had become the now familiar Swan Lane.

When George Gardner, who had been High Sheriff of Worcestershire in 1708, died in 1729, he bequeathed £150 for the relief of the poor of the three parishes and another £100 for the teaching of poor children of Evesham to read English. His executors agreed to settle this by making a yearly rent charge of £10 for ever out of their revenue from the Swan Inn.

The Bengeworth parish account book for 1755 shows that, following an agreement to inaugurate a new joint system of poor relief, a vestry meeting of the churchwardens of St Peter's, All Saints' and St Lawrence held at the Guildhall[40] decided to purchase the Swan House from William Roberts for £130 "that it may be employed as a workhouse for the use of the poor."[41] It is not clear whether the Swan was ever put to the purpose suggested but on 29th September 1765, it was let to Charles Beaufoy, a grazier, by the wardens.

An indenture dated 1st September 1800, between the churchwardens and Ann Smith, widow, revealed that the premises had once more become a single messuage but had ceased to be an inn. A schedule attached to this deed showed the house to comprise: a common kitchen with a purgatory (pit grate), pantry, dining room, passage, room over laundry, yellow room, green room, nursery, tent room, servants' room, wine cellar and best kitchen; that many rooms had Dutch tiles in the grates, one room had a 'Chinese' Chippendale overmantel while in the garden was "an attractive Chinese Bowery and Chinese work."

51: The Olde Swanne Inne, High Street (2003)

---

[40] That is, the town hall. SBB

[41] The workhouse was finally built in Waterside, Little Hampton on the site now occupied by the community hospital. SBB

Harriot Smith, daughter of Ann and Thomas Smith, occupied the house until her death in 1830 when she left £500 to the rector and churchwardens of All Saints' and St Lawrence's for the relief of the poor (still distributed in money at Christmas). Miss E.M. Rudd then rented the house.

On 26th April 1832, the premises were put up for letting by public auction which resulted in William Bushell, a wine and spirits merchant, of Bridge Street, contracting for £51 per annum, he to spend £150 within two years on necessary repairs to the property. Mr Bushell immediately re-opened the house as licensed premises under the name of the Star Brewery and the sign of the star with sixteen rays, the crest of the Innholders' Company.

In 1842, an ardent Radical, Richard Hemming Hughes, leased the Star Brewery from the managers of the Church Estates for £30 per annum. Hughes, who was mayor in 1848, gloried in the political fire and brimstone that sparked around his house at election times, especially during the election of 1852.

Evesham then returned two members and the 'official candidates' were the Conservative, Sir Henry Willoughby, Bt, and the Liberal, Mr Charles Lennox Grenville Berkeley. Hughes, aided by the Baptist minister, Mr Barnett, and others, induced a leading barrister, Serjeant Wilkins, to be a Radical candidate.

The introduction of a 'Dark Horse' created a sensation in the town – as no doubt it was intended to do by the host at the Star. Serjeant Wilkins was a fine, fiery orator. He harangued the crowd from the upstairs windows of the Star, making fun of the local big-wigs, Oswald Cheek and William Byrch. He urged the working men (who flocked to hear him) to stand up for their rights and privileges, likening them to herrings in the sea – able to choke the whale if they acted together.

But despite the furore, Serjeant Wilkins was always the outsider, and so it proved at the poll, which gave Willoughby 189, Berkeley 170, and Wilkins 87. But his visit to Evesham gave plenty to talk about for many a day to come.

Hughes and his wife Mary were the first couple to be married in the Baptist Chapel, Cowl Street, after an act permitting legal marriages in non-conformist places of worship came into effect in 1839. They had a son who was known in the town as 'Daredevil Dick'. Dick one day dared so far as to accompany Alderman Joseph Masters to a temperance meeting. The results were that he became an ardent teetotaller, emigrated to New Zealand, became a well-known citizen of Auckland and remained prominently associated with the temperance cause all his life.

Hughes was succeeded at the Star by Samuel Butler about 1863; H. Taylor was landlord in 1906, H.W. Morgan (1920), A.W. Jaynes (1925), F. Jones (1935), Mr F.J.A. Dyke (1950), and Mr E.F. Morgan (who died in January 1957). Messrs Sladden and Collier bought the freehold from the Church Estate for £2,400 in 1914 and their interest later passed to Cheltenham and Hereford Breweries Ltd.

Swan Hotel

This inn began life as a little thatched beerhouse on the site of the present Swan Hotel at 78, Port Street. It was common practice for smaller houses to take the signs of old-established inns when they closed down as the Swan in High Street closed at the end of the eighteenth century. The Bengeworth inn probably adopted the sign of the Swan – an emblem of innocence – early in the nineteenth century, for it is first mentioned in the books of the old Evesham company of glovers or fellmongers who held their annual feast "at the house of Elizabeth Byrd, called or known by the sign of the Swan Inn, Bengeworth" on 5th November 1807, and met there regularly thereafter.

But the days of the glovers' company were numbered as the industrial revolution speeded the decay of ancient trading methods by this time more honoured in the breach than the observance. Thus on 7th November 1829, eleven of the dwindling company met at the Swan to elect a new master. These courageous eleven dined together, then had tea together followed by brandy all round – the tea and brandy being supplied by Mr J. Byrd at an inclusive cost of "a bob a nob".

The last feast of the guild took place on 5th November 1831, when the resources of the company were almost exhausted. It was evidently looked upon as being the swan-song of the brethren as an organised body and the final opportunity for the customary conviviality so they then and there proceeded to spend the 'kitty' to the last penny. Only seven die-hards were present at the obsequies, and the very last entry in the accounts of the company of glovers is one of £1 5s. 10d. for "ale, tobacco, liquors, etc." spent at the Swan that night.

52: Swan Hotel, Port Street (1930)

People have asked me how the Swan came to get its nickname of Paddy's Duck. I have never come across any firm evidence on the point but my own idea is that it stems from the days when the Irish navvies brought the railroad from Oxford to Evesham. It seems possible that they pitched a camp on the Bengeworth side of the Avon (at Donneybrook?) while the river was bridged and few of those hardy gentlemen would bother to explore the countryside beyond the nearest pub. In August 1851, the contractors at work on the Oxford, Worcester and Wolverhampton Railway "in progress through the borough" asked the Watch Committee to swear in one of their watchers named Charles Barnet as a special constable "as numerous men were employed thereon," which may be significant. It is a fact that landlord John Bedenham at the Swan was involved in several disturbances in his house about this time but the delinquents were usually described as "travellers" in the records.

John Bedenham, who was a victualler and hop merchant, was very well known in Bengeworth for his political activities. He was a very strong protagonist of the Blue party and acted as their local agent in several elections. In 1830, 1833 and 1838 he was called to Westminster to give evidence in election petitions, which make very interesting reading when you have time. Frederick Bedenham kept the Swan in 1863 when the Berkeley Hunt coach called there every Monday at 5 pm. By this time a good posting business had been built up and a farrier's shop was established on the premises which continued in business until comparatively recent times. Mr F.A. Holder, a builder, was landlord of the Swan from 1872 to 1903 when Alfred Hicken took over. He was followed by Mr W. (Doctor) Bell in 1910 and Mr A. Bell is the present licensee.

53: Swan Inn, Port Street (2003)

Talbot

In 1956 the Talbot Inn at 36, Port Street, Evesham, was given a new pictorial sign to replace the interesting eighteenth century lettered board now preserved in the Almonry Museum through the generosity of Hunt, Edmunds and Co. Ltd, of Banbury. The Talbot takes its name from the old English hunting dog which is believed to be the ancestor of all present breeds of bloodhounds and hunting dogs. The talbot hound on the new sign is represented in a naturalistic style though there is little doubt that the original sign of the Talbot was of heraldic derivation both in Evesham and elsewhere.

54: Talbot Inn, Port Street (1930)

On the sign boards the Talbot appears in a number of heraldic forms usually statant (standing) and sometimes 'passant arg. langued gu.' (a walking hound, plain white with a red tongue), very occasionally it appears as a Spotted Dog, and rarely in its proper form as a 'talbot rampant arg.' (white hunting dog standing on its hind legs). The badge itself was adopted long ago by the ancient and noble family of Talbot (earls of Shrewsbury) whose recorded history began about a century after the Norman Conquest. No-one knows whether the family took its name from the dog or *vice versa*.

The Bengeworth Talbot seems to have had a long history, as a house known by the sign of the Bell before adopting its present name, and may well be the oldest inn on the east bank of the Avon at Evesham. Standing in the shadow of the twelfth century church of the Blessed Trinity[42], which was said to have been built from stones from Bengeworth Castle, the old Bell Inn was almost certainly one of the main centres of social intercourse in its day.

The name itself recalls the customs of ancient times when Christmas, Easter, New Year's Day, Restoration Day (29th May) and the Fifth of November were celebrated by tradition with the music of bells so that the parish records are liberally sprinkled with entries of payments made to the ringers on these and many other festive occasions.

The original house was probably quite small, consisting of four or five rooms, and built of brick, stone and heavy timber beams with a high stone wall at the back. Outside this wall the village pump faced Church Street, later another pump was erected on the Port Street side of the inn. This ancient inn is probably unique, not only in Evesham but in the country, for it has its own running water supply rising from a spring in the cellar and flowing in a piped channel through Port Street and Castle Street to the river, surely a great boon to the brewmasters of the past and not without value at the present day.

The Bell was the only inn ever mentioned in the parish register of Bengeworth: "Items 29th daie of November John houlle bell in was buried 1573." It would be about a quarter of the way through the seventeenth century that the Bell became the Talbot. Bearing the coat of arms 'Or, a talbot sable' (a black talbot on a gold shield), Sir William Courteen or Courteene acquired the manor of Bengeworth about 1625. He had been knighted in 1622 and was one of the most prominent merchants of his time, being connected with the Merchant Strangers Company in overseas enterprises.

In 1628 he incurred very heavy losses by the failure of his attempt to colonise the Barbados Islands in the West Indies which had been granted to him for his services to the Crown. His settlers were expelled by the Earl of Carlisle in 1629 and he was further embarrassed by the fact that large sums of money lent to James I and Charles I had never been repaid. By 1636, when he died, he had been forced to dispose of his Bengeworth estates and much other land elsewhere, but what he had lost in material possessions he seems to have regained in the esteem of his contemporaries, which probably accounts for the Bell becoming the Talbot. Of him and his son Peter, who died in 1625, Habingdon, the famous Worcestershire historian, writes:

---

[42] According to Shawcross and Barnard, *Bengeworth* (1927), p.12, the church was originally dedicated to the Blessed Trinity, but after the Dissolution this dedication seems to have been forgotten and the church was dedicated to Almighty God and in honour of St. Peter. D.C. Cox in an article in the *Transactions of the Worcestershire Archaeological Society* (3rd series, vol. 12 (1990) p.124) points out that since the Blessed Trinity, built by Earl Leofric and his famous wife Godiva, was for the honour of the Abbey, it presumably stood near the abbey church, perhaps being structurally attached. That is, the Church of the Blessed Trinity is a different church to the old church of Bengeworth. SBB

He leafte to Mr William Courteyne who now succeedeth him, yea, to us all, suche an example of bountie and pietie in beinge more like parentes than landlordes to theyre tenantes as all must needes prayse, and I wish all able gentlemen would imitate.

In 1713 the Talbot was mentioned in a law suit between people called Halford and Cooke and in 1758 Sir John Rushout paid a chief rent of three shillings "for the Talbot" to the Corporation. Charles Baylis was landlord in 1854 followed by Thomas Cull (1857), Mr Schofield (1861), George Pitman (1873), Charles Pitman (1895), Mrs Pitman (1873), Thomas Taylor (1908), Thomas Osborne (1910), G.H. Field (1915/25), A.A. Milward (1930), Percy Shakles (1935), J. Matthews and Mrs Matthews (1940 to 1955), and the present licensee Mr R.A. Teague in 1956.

Three Tuns

The Three Tuns – the sign bearing the Three Tuns was derived from the Vintners' or Brewers' Arms. In 1720, when the King's officers came to inspect the stamps of the Evesham Company of Glovers, the sum of 4s. 6d. was spent on their entertainment at the Three Tuns Inn. In the same year, the Company also spent a shilling "at ye Tuns receiving ye Flag." On 12th November 1741, the Mercers' Company "adjourned to the house of Mrs Field by the sign of the Three Tuns."

By courtesy of Mr H.C. Spiers, of West Ridge, Greenhill, I have lately examined the deeds of Nos. 26 and 27, High Street, which clearly indicate that these two houses together constituted the Three Tuns Inn. An indenture tripartite made on 2nd May 1765, between George Middleton, of Birmingham, William Baylies, doctor of physick, formerly of Evesham now of Middlesex, and John Heath, clothier, of Tamworth, describes the premises.

Approached by an elegant early Georgian staircase, of considerable merit, an upstairs room in No. 26 contains a fine piece of ornamental oak panelling in the Elizabethan style. Mr Spiers thinks it originally came from the cabin or state room of some wooden man o'war or merchant ship broken up at Bristol, reaching Evesham by way of the Severn and Avon navigations. The lower portions of the panelling on either side of the Queen Anne fireplace are later copies of the original, or extensions, but the whole forms a most interesting feature of the well-known premises adjoining Dresden House.

Three Crowns

The Three Crowns – Bagford, the 17th-century antiquary, says this sign was used by the mercers trading with Cologne, the arms of that city being the crowns of the magi, or three wise men. The Empress Helena, British mother of Constantine the Great, is said to have discovered their bodies in the Holy Land in AD326 during her search for the cross on which Christ died. She removed the bones to Constantinople, where they remained in the church of St Sophia until the Crusades began, when they were transferred to Milan Cathedral.

When Milan fell in 1164 the relics were given by the emperor Frederick to Reynaldus, archbishop of Cologne, whose successor, Philip von Heinsburg, placed them in a magnificent reliquary. The shrine is now one of the most remarkable in the world. The relics consist of three skulls, enveloped in velvet and heavily jewelled embroidery so that only the upper portion of each skull is visible.

Favouring the sign introduced into this country by their forbears, the Evesham Company of Mercers met regularly at the Three Crowns, in Bridge Street, where Benjamin Symonds was their host.

After the 18th century, the sign came into general use and in one Buckinghamshire village at the present day the inn has "15s" on its signboard – a humorous play on the ancient sign of the Three Crowns.

Trumpet

The Trumpet Inn at 13, Merstowe Green, Evesham, first appears in a corporation minute for 1685, when Thomas Harris paid a chief rent of 2s., the highest on a list of eight inns.

55: Trumpet Inn and Trumpet Yard, Merstow Green (c.1900)
Trumpet Yard was demolished in 1972.

The sign of the house is popularly associated with the military but it's just possible that this sign originally depicted an 'Angel and Trumpet', that is, the Angel Gabriel, for the inn stands near the former gateway to Evesham Abbey, in a place where one would expect to find one of the early religious signs. Many angels disappeared from signboards after the Dissolution and during the Commonwealth.

On 1st April 1799, a young Evesham attorney noted in his diary that the attended the Trumpet Club dinner. This was a friendly society which did good work among the gardeners until the competition from more powerful bodies like the Foresters, established at the Red Lion in 1865, eventually killed it about 1880. In its later stages the members were called to meetings by the club beadle, a man named Langstone who lived in Merstowe Court. He used to go round the houses calling "Club night tomorrow and a woman's funeral." Perhaps one of the old customers at the Trumpet can tell us what that meant. In Whit week, the traditional gardeners' holiday, the members of the club marched round the town in procession and dined at the Trumpet.

No account of the Trumpet Inn would be complete without mention of 'Bodger' Hughes who followed Samuel Clements (1813), William Drinkwater (1818), Thomas Allard (1835/50), Joseph Robbins (1863), William Cooke (1866), and John Iorns (1873) as landlord there.

Born in 1842, George Hughes attended the British School, joined the Worcestershire Militia at 16, and was later employed by a fruit and vegetable salesman in Birmingham Market before returning to his native town, where he worked for the Great Western Railway company, chiefly on repairs to the two wooden bridges over the Avon. Next he took ground at Hampton adjoining his father's and the two earned a fine reputation as asparagus growers. George used to go to Birmingham three times a week with the produce on a dray, for their 'grass' was much sought after in the season.

George Hughes was a keen politician, ever ready with his wit, tongue, and fists if need be. In 1868 his zest for action led him into trouble when, together with six other young Radical zealots, he chased the Rector of Rous Lench, a leading local Tory, away from the scene of the poll and forced him to take refuge in the Railway Hotel. A charge of riotous assembly and assault followed at the assizes but tempers had cooled by then and the affair was settled with apologies tendered and a donation of £50 to Worcester Infirmary.

Years later, Mr Hughes took a keen interest in the question of tenant-right and gave staunch support and help to Colonel Long, M.P. (to whom he had been politically opposed) when the Member sought to get the Evesham Custom on the statute book.

'Bodger' took the Trumpet soon after his marriage in 1880 and remained there until his death, aged 74, in 1916. In 1889 he was elected to the Town Council, became mayor in 1901 and in 1902, attended King Edward VII's Coronation and was made alderman in 1904. He worked tirelessly for the board of guardians and instigated the cottage homes project to get children away from the workhouse atmosphere. When he died, he was eulogised on all sides but one epitaph is worth quoting "George Hughes loved this Evesham and to the utmost of his power he sought to serve it."

Mr H. Petitt was the next landlord of the Trumpet until the early thirties when S. Smith took over. The latter was succeeded by Mr N.J. Brown in 1951.

56: Trumpet Inn, Merstow Green (1952)

57: Trumpet Inn, Merstow Green (2008)

Unicorn

A fabulous beast, with horse's body and single straight horn, graced the signboard of a thriving coaching inn formerly existing at 27, Port Street. Allusions to the unicorn appear quite frequently in the Old Testament, thus causing it to be adopted as a religious emblem by early printers as well as innkeepers.

The horn, as a reputed antidote to all poisons, was incorporated into the apothecaries' arms and often appeared on chemists' signboards as a token of their skill. The great value set upon the unicorn's horn in the Middle Ages caused the goldsmiths also to adopt the creature as their emblem.

58: Port Street (1927)
Although there was no inn, the sign of the Unicorn can just be made out.

It was believed that a unicorn could be captured by leaving a beautiful young maiden alone near its haunt. When the animal saw the decoy he would approach and lie down at the virgin's side, rest his head in her lap and fall asleep; and in this state he might be ensnared by the hunters lying in wait for him.

Whatever it was that passed for a unicorn's horn (probably a narwhal's horn) was of sufficient value to appear at the head of an inventory of royal jewels taken in the first year of Elizabeth Tudor (1559) as the most precious item in her treasury. About the same time, when gold was worth £2 3s. 6d. per ounce, the unicorn's horn was being sold by apothecaries at £24 per ounce.

The sign of the Unicorn is noted first in Evesham Corporation minutes for 1st October 1658, when:

The same date and yeare it is consented and agreed that the house or Inne comonly called the Unicorne in Bengworth be and shall be henceforth taken and esteemed as a comon fund and that William Woodward the landlord of the house in respect of the allowance thereof doe pay XXd. to the use of the poore of the pishe of Bengeworth to be disposed of as we shall think fitt and this order to be approved and confirmed by the justices of peace att the next Sessions to be holden for this Borrough.

The name of the house appears twice in private records kept during the next century. In his diary from 10th February 1793, the Rev. Thomas Beale (vicar of Bengeworth 1771-1793) noted "a most extraordinary flood within about 14 inches as high as that of November, 1770, and more injurious. It was in ye parlours of ye Unicorn and in Mr Stickley's oven."

Of the flood in November 1770, George May writes:

The highest flood within living memory occurred here. The water reached almost to the key-stone of the main arch of the Bridge and extended up Port Street to the public pump on the south side[43] so that the inhabitants were compelled to pass out of their houses, through the upper windows and were thence conveyed by boats along the street.

Writing in his memorandum book for 1799, Mr Lavender, a local attorney, observed as follows:

November 5: 12 hours of very heavy rain.

Nov. 6: Flood rose in one night to the Unicorn in Bengeworth. Mr Lunn drowned.

The Unicorn inn was often the scene of business transactions during the eighteenth century as, for instance, when landlord Peter Penny was mayor of Evesham in 1724 several sums of 5s. or thereabouts were "spent at the unicorne when the Dole was gin" (given) by the Bengeworth overseers distributing parish relief to the poor. In September 1799, during the wars with France, an important meeting of the parish overseers from Hampton, Bretforton and Bengeworth was convened at the Unicorn to consider the matter of supplying militia men to represent those parishes. Ultimately the parish subscribed £42 7s. 10½d. between them "for raising of two men for the Army and Navy."

Throughout this period, the Unicorn was in the ownership of the Rushout family of Northwick Park near Blockley, as was the major portion of land and property in the parish of St Peter's. Twice a year, the rents of the estate were received at the Unicorn and the inn always served as the political headquarters of the owners at election times.

---

[43] That is, opposite the Regal Cinema. In answers to query 671 on public pumps (*Evesham Journal* 'Notes and Queries' column 327 (7/12/1912) and column 333 (18/1/1913)) there is mention of a public pump in Port Street, near the side window of No.28. SBB

Sir John Rushout, who became member for the borough in 1722, was alluded to in correspondence by Sir Robert Walpole as "father of the House of Commons" in 1766 and lived to be 91. He was succeeded at Westminster by his son and namesake, who later became Lord Northwick. Between them they represented Evesham in the Tory interests continuously for 74 years, a remarkable family record.

In the meantime, William Penny had succeeded his father Peter as host at the unicorn and in 1766 he too became mayor of Evesham when Charles Welsborne, landlord of the Butchers' Arms in High Street, died suddenly soon after taking office for that year. This William Penny was an important and progressive burgess in his day, who made noteworthy contributions in the fields of agriculture and transport. He it was who conceived the idea of setting up a Turnpike Trust to "raise the causeway" between Evesham Bridge and Hampton Turnpike, the roads we now know as Waterside and Avonside.

Previously all vehicular traffic from Worcester passed through Evesham via the old Worcester road turnpike (near Blayney's Lane), Greenhill, High Street, Bridge Street, Port Street and Benge Hill turnpike (near the "Motor House") on the way to London. The 'lower road' or 'bottom road' to Worcester via Hampton was an immediate success, to the satisfaction of the Turnpike trustees who met regularly afterwards to receive their profits at the Unicorn inn. The astute Mr Penny was further rewarded for his enterprise as his coaching and posting business prospered while that of the George in High Street diminished and faded as the fast London coaches and chaises took the new route and ceased to cross Evesham Bridge.

In May, 1760, two meetings of the Bengeworth Field Stewards took place at the old inn. The first set of minutes was signed by John Haines, George Pratt, William Wright (mark). The second meeting was convened to elect George Wheatley and Thomas Banner as stewards for the ensuing year by those present, namely William Penny, William Cox, John Price, Joshua Harris, George Pratt, Samuel Aldington, Charles Acton (parchment maker) and William Wright.

Arthur Young, the 18th-century agriculturalist and social economist, had a great admiration for William Penny and held him in high esteem "as an advanced farmer of his time." William Penny not only kept the inn but also had an extensive farm in Bengeworth Leys to the north of Port Street. About 1769, he was visited by Arthur Young, whose *Farmer's Calendar*, published in 1771, was acknowledged for many years as the best handbook on agriculture in Britain. *The Tour Through the North of England*, from which these extracts are taken, was published in 1770 and after a favourable reception at home and abroad, had been translated into most European languages by 1792. The letters on which the work was based were written after the author had personally inspected the farms concerned.

Young says the experiments and remarks of "Mr William Penny, who keeps the inn at Bendsworth, are much worthy of notice. He is very sensible and intelligent." Of barley, the brewers' crop, he remarks:

> The culture of barley here is excellent. They plough the land in March (but this should be done in October); in May dung it, 20 loads to the acre, 28 bushels per

load. In June, plough it in. The land then lies till September, when it is ploughed again and arched up, and so lays for the winter. In March, it is ploughed down, one half or two bushels per acre of seed being turned in, and the other half or two bushels more being harrowed in at top. This management yields seven quarters per acre on an average. It certainly is most excellent husbandry; and the circumstances of spreading dung on the fallow and mixing it well with the soil by succeeding ploughings preferable, I apprehend, to laying it on in the winter before sowing, which also depends on the coming of sharp frosts.

There is much more agricultural information and advice culled from the landlord of the Unicorn which is of absorbing interest. Those were the days when a farm worker might reckon to earn £18 per annum and a dairymaid £4. A man's board, washing and lodging for a year was reckoned at £12; wheaten bread was 1½d. a loaf, meat was 3d. per pound, milk ½d. a pint, and coals 15s. a ton laid in.

A vivid picture of the furnishings and fare of a prosperous coaching inn of the late eighteenth century may be conjured from the inventory taken at the Unicorn on 8th June 1773, by Joseph Pratt, auctioneer and surveyor, soon after the death of William Penny.

Beginning in the kitchen, he lists among the usual utensils a smoke jack (a machine for turning a roasting spit by means of wheels set in motion by currents of air ascending the chimney), a grate, two sways (flat iron rods, usually working on a pivot from which pots and kettles were hung), spit-irons, four spits, a purgatory (a hole under the fireplace covered by a grating through which ashes could fall), a large trivet and links, a dog-wheel with pulleys and chains complete (a turn-spit worked by a dog treading the attached wheel), three box-irons and heaters and two stands, a cuckold (a portable stove for heating bedrooms), a chafing dish, flesh forks, stake-tongs, many candlesticks and a pair of snuffers, much pewter ware – including six dozen plates, a gross of soup plates and 67 dishes – and 18 dozen assorted china plates; much glassware, cutlery, with various chairs, dressers, shelves, tables, angle drinking tables, a mug case and three bird cages, all valued at £54 14s.

In the bar, adjoining the kitchen could be seen a fireplace, red and white china plates, punch bowls, cups and saucers, decanters (some of them black), punch glasses, wine glasses, gill glasses and tumblers; canisters and pickling jars, a square oak table and a tea table, a large chest of drawers, chairs and ink pots. Unlike the bars of today, it contained no refreshment, but this was stored in the adjoining pantry, together with three (probably silver) tankards valued at £21 and a great many more decanters, china punch bowls and ladles, lemon squeezers and strainers, etc.

Otherwise, the important contents included five bottles of "best French brandy" valued at 16s. the lot, 12 dozen bottles of Port £9, four dozen bottles of sherry £3 12s., three dozen bottles of Mountain (a variety of Malaga wine made from grapes gathered on the mountain sides) £2 4s., 15 gallons of common brandy in a cask £3 15s., 12 gallons of Tent (a Spanish wine of deep red, vino tinto, and of low alcoholic content) £7, four gallons of gin £1, and two quarts of bitters 16s.

Next, the small beer cellar contained no beer but a puncheon (72 gallons) of rum, £38; a cask (20 gallons)[44] of rum £9 5s.; a pipe (115 gallons) of Port, £38; three casks of cider, £4 10s.; ten dozen bottles of bad wine, £5; and 60 dozen empty wine bottles valued at £4 10s.

The brew house contained two large copper furnaces for brewing, a large deal wash tub, a lead cistern and pump, a large cooler, a collection of half-hogsheads, mash tubs, pails, gauns (gallon measures) and stirrers, together with two-and-a-half tons of coal, all estimated at £28 13s. 6d.

The wash house appears to have been used for cheese-making as well as laundry work; containing two copper furnaces, four bucking cauls (washing baskets) and eight wash tubs, with a cheese press, ten cheese vats, two cheese suters and hoops, a cheese caul and ladder, cream jugs and pickling jars. The cheese room proper, situated over the dairy, contained six-and-a-half hundredweights of cheese at 30s. per cwt, two cheese racks and a cheese caul, together with 4½ dozen of porter and some "bad old beer."

The Unicorn was a posting house licensed for the hiring of post horses and chaises under an act of 1746 and did a good business particularly at election times. In the stables, the "chaise horses and arnish" were reckoned as follows: one pair of brown geldings £30, one pair of bays £30, one brown and one grey gelding £25, one pair of black geldings (evidently for funerals) £18, and four post chaises £83. In the outhouses were 40 bushels of damaged barley at 2s. 6d. a bushel, hay worth £8, oats and beans, lanterns, sheppecks, corn bits and shovels. In a nearby barn was "an old coach" valued at £2 10s.

Within the inn, the smoke room had a Staffordshire grate and fender, fire shovel and poker all valued at 6s. 6d., a fire screen and stand 5s., six cherry-tree chairs and two smoking tables £3 2s. and three oak dining tables 16s. Other rooms on the ground floor were named the Blue Parlour, the Old Parlour and the Clock Room, the latter taking its name from an eight-day clock and case valued at £4 4s. Upstairs were the Sunflower Room, the Yellow Room, the Green Room, the Blue Room, and well furnished Tent Room with its four-poster bed, and the Maids' Room. The Men's Room seems to have been a dormitory for coachmen and postillions, while the Soldiers' House provided sleeping accommodation comprising five bedsteads, each of which was supplied with a flock bed, a bolster and a rug.

The "sine of the Unicorn, grapes, board and post" complete were valued at £5 5s., and the whole estate reached a total of £3,526 4s. 3d. [45]

---

[44] Generally speaking a cask is any container of 'barrel' construction, but a standard spirit-cask size of 20 gallons was in use at this time. SBB

[45] On 4th May 1972 the *Evesham Journal* reported that the 20th branch of Super Stores of Shrewsbury (later Kwik Save in Port Street) was being built "on the site of the Old Unicorn Inn." SBB

Vauxhall

The Vauxhall Inn opposite the Almonry was another inn which began life as a 'tiddleywink' or common alehouse. It remained as such until 1928 when the new Abbey bridge and viaduct transformed its quiet backwater at the end of the Vine Street into the section of modern trunk road we know today. Soon afterwards the house became company-owned, and was rebuilt to serve the convenience of the type of trade it enjoys now.

59: Vauxhall Inn, Vine Street (c.1900)

The first reference to the Vauxhall appears in 1859, the year in which the famous Vauxhall Gardens in London were finally closed after being a public resort since 1661. Three years previously a Birmingham resort of pleasure, famous for its fêtes, galas, musical entertainments and firework displays like its London namesake, had been demolished by the Victorian Building Society to make way for the present Vauxhall road district of the city. Either of these events might have suggested the unusual sign of the inn.

Joseph Lawrence was the landlord in 1859, and Richard Careless in 1863. In 1873 George Cole, the proprietor, was described as a fruit and potato salesman, nurseryman and commission agent. In 1888 he catered for the inaugural meeting and dinner of the Loyal Avon Lodge of Oddfellows at the town hall. George F. Cole was landlord from 1894 to 1898, and was succeeded by C.E. Hill, J.G. Porter (1913), A.J. Porter (1920), James Spicer Bailey (1925), H. Rodbourne (1935), Mrs G. Brotherton (1941), Mrs G. Vines (1943), T.N. Cowell (1950), and Mr R.E. Spiers the present licensee in 1952.

60: Vauxhall Inn, Vine Street (1935)

Vine

The Vine[46] was at 54, Port Street, now the Worcester Co-operative Society grocery shop; it existed for many years without a name but eventually became the Vine about 1906; formerly it was a liquor vaults owned by the Glassbrook family. Thomas Talbot was landlord in 1858; and Thomas Glassbrook, also described as a saddler, kept the house in 1898. Harry Byrd owned it in 1906 and, having acquired adjoining properties, established a model brewery by 1910. part of it is still recognisable in premises now used by John Huggan and Co. Ltd. The Vine was kept by R.B. Ballard in 1915, and C.H. Twist in 1916.

In 1919, Mr Byrd disposed of the Vine Brewery and his other licensed houses to Hunt, Edmunds and Co. Ltd, of Banbury, who sent Mr Arthur Hayes to safeguard their interests in Evesham. Mr Haynes, of Benge Hill, remains; but the brewery is no more, having been closed when the Banbury brewers centralised their production over thirty years ago. An interesting reminder of his old inn still remains in the name 'Vine Cottage.'

---

[46] The name 'Vine' was selected presumably, in part, because the inn sat in Vine Street. The old name for this street was 'Pigmarket', though by the 1830s it was occasionally called 'Swine Street'. From the 1840s onwards the name became 'Vine Street', in part perhaps because that has 'more refined' associations and also because Evesham Abbey owned vineyards (Clarke's Hill used to be known as Vineyard Hill). SBB

Volunteer

It seems likely that the Volunteer inn was given its name during or soon after that tremendous outbreak or warlike enthusiasm which swept the country in 1804 when Britain faced invasion by Napoleon. The makeshift Peace of Amiens in 1802 had marked the conclusion of the first phase of the prolonged struggle with revolutionary France begun in 1793; most of the Militia had been disbanded and thousands of English tourists had swarmed into France. Having secured his position on the Continent, however, Napoleon demanded a British evacuation of Malta; when this was refused the Militia was recalled for duty and, on 18th May 1803, war was declared.

Napoleon retaliated by impounding British shipping in Continental ports and imprisoning the hapless tourists. England was without an ally and "the little corporal" prepared his invasion force, gathering a vast fleet of flat-bottomed invasion barges near Boulogne to carry his 'Army of England' In May, he crowned himself emperor. Meanwhile, in England, William Pitt, the Prime Minister, built Martello towers, set up beacons, dug the military canal and encouraged the volunteer movement, which soon supplied the Army with 350,000 willing if untrained and ill-equipped soldiers.

61: The Volunteer Inn, Bridge Street (c.1950 and c.1900)
The location of the Volunteer Inn (tucked behind the Round House at the top of Bridge Street) makes it difficult to find clear pictures. The views above are from along the Alley and from Market Place.

Evesham, in common with other boroughs throughout the kingdom, raised its own corps of volunteers soon after the Worcestershire Militia, on 18th May 1803, had made a forced march to Gosport in consequence of an invasion alarm. On 22nd September a subscription list "to clothe volunteers" raised £20. By December, the ladies responsible had bought up every stitch of flannel they could obtain in order to provide uniforms for the volunteers.

Another committee was formed in Evesham, with the object of growing walnut trees in order to supply wood for gun stocks. It was said that a line of these trees was planted from the middle of High Street to the top of Greenhill on New Year's Day, 1804, the Evesham and Pershore Corps were incorporated by the name of 'the East Worcestershire Regiment of Volunteers' under the command of Major-General Amherst.

62: Site of the Volunteer Inn (2008)
The Volunteer was re-built about 1972 in a style similar to the old building.

Over 300 – more than required under the General Defence Bill – enrolled at Evesham and were mustered into six companies with the usual complement of officers. In March:

> ...the Evesham and Pershore Volunteers were inspected... in a field at Craycombe belonging to George Perrott, Esq., by Colonel Houston; they went through the different evolutions in a manner which gave the highest satisfaction to the Colonel and reflected great credit on both officers and privates.

On 10th April, a pair of colours which had been worked by the ladies of the town and had been consecrated in All Saints' Church were presented to the Regiment by Mrs Perrott. In June, after marching in Campden and Broadway, they:

> …exercised an act of power which reflects great credit upon them, by calling a court martial upon a man who, after having fully been convicted of drunkenness and un-soldier-like behaviour, was sentenced to be drummed out of the corps with every mark of ignominy and disgrace. The prisoner was accordingly marched in front of the line with a halter round his neck and dismissed from the corps, the drummers and fifers of the battalion beating and playing the 'Rogues' March'. So perfectly satisfied were the men with the sentence of the court martial that the prisoner, as he walked along in front of the line, was saluted with the execrations and hisses of the whole battalion.

In September, the battalion paraded with the South Worcestershire Volunteers on Hanley Common where the privates were presented by Mrs Lygon with a purse of 100 guineas "to drink the King's health." Months rolled by, but Napoleon's army did nothing; realising that his fleet must be the key to victory he ordered all the French and Spanish men-of-war to congregate in the English Channel. The encounter waited until 21st October 1805 when Nelson forced the issue at Trafalgar and destroyed the threat of invasion.

On 27th September 1808, the East Worcestershire Regiment volunteered into the Militia and was henceforward known as the "East Worcester Local Militia"; at the same time, a drawing of names took place to meet the requirements of the Additional Forces Act by which each parish had to find a certain number of militia-men or pay an indemnity. Men were called to the colours by means of a 'drawing' or ballot. On 4th November 1803, following a meeting of the Lord and Deputy Lieutenants at the Guildhall, Worcester, a notice was issued by the authorities stating the strength of the Volunteer Force of the country; and in consequence of this the following printed notice appeared in Evesham:

> Insurance for providing substitutes for old and supplementary Militia and Army of Reserve.

> The numerous applications made to R. Gill by persons of this and adjoining counties to open a plan of insurance for providing them substitutes for the old and supplementary Militia, and also for the Army of Reserve, have induced him to make them and the public the following proposals, viz:

> That by paying him the sum of two guineas and a half, he will engage to provide them proper substitutes, without any additional trouble or expense, should they be drawn for either of the above regiments on or before the first day of June 1804. He therefore recommends early applications either at his house, or on Mondays at the White Harte inn, Evesham

> *NB* – Several substitutes wanted, to whom good bounties will be given.

> Dated the 17th day of November, 1803.

Evesham Corporation had agreed, in 1789, that the Borough Prison situated to the north-east of the town hall was "…in so ruinous a state as not to be repairable" and ordered that the "gaol house be taken down and the materials thereof sold for the most money that can be got for the same."

The proceeds of the sale were to be applied to a fund for erecting a clock and market bell at the north end of the town hall. It is probable that the Volunteer inn was erected on the side of the old gaol. The outside of the building still retains the typical appearance of an early Georgian structure despite extensive interior alterations in recent years. An unusual feature is the pseudo-classical decorative mouldings which surround the door and window frames on the east elevation (facing Bridge Street). At first glance, these appear to be part of the woodwork of the frames, but closer attention reveals them to be plaster additions to the architraves.

John Cole appears to have been the first landlord of the Volunteer and in his time a narrow public passage separated the inn from the premises immediately behind it, now the office of Messrs Cross, Son and Hodgetts, solicitors. The passage ran parallel with the Alley[47] and part of it still exists at the back of Mr H.T. Hughes's meat shop. It is clearly marked on the plan of Evesham made by Edward J. Rudge for his *History of Evesham*, published in 1820. John Cole was still landlord in 1840 but by 1850 Sarah Maria Baylis had become the hostess. From 1854, Thomas Millington was the licensee, to be succeeded by his wife for a short time after his death. Mr Phophet took over in 1864 and F.W. Goodall was landlord in 1873 when the inn was generally known as the Old Volunteer. In the intervening years it had become a popular inn with the farmers visiting Evesham market in the days when corn was pitched for sale in the open space beneath the arches of the town hall; in consequence, this convenient inn enjoyed some reputation as a corn exchange.

Subsequent landlords were W.H. Adams, who handed over to Charles Brotherton in 1894[48]; and Thomas Taylor who left the Talbot in 1909 for the Volunteer Bar as it was then described. The last licensee was Frederick William Sallis, who became the tenant in 1928 and vacated the inn on 30th October 1934, when it closed as redundant. The justices had decided that although the Volunteer was a well-conducted house and in good repair, the premises were structurally unsatisfactory with regard to toilet facilities. Compensation set at £1,650 was paid, of which the tenant received £500 and the owners, Rowlands' Brewery, the remainder. Later, the Worcestershire County Council purchased the property to facilitate road widening plans which have not yet matured. Consequently, the old inn had been refurbished to serve as the Old Volunteer Quick Service Cafeteria. During the Second World War, it had served, most appropriately, as the local headquarters of a world-famous voluntary organisation, Toc H, which, like the old inn, took its name in times of strife.

---

[47] The Alley was re-named Allée de Dreux to commemorate the twinning of Evesham with Dreux in June 1977. SBB

[48] Charles Brotherton of the Volunteer Inn is my great-grandfather (on my father's side). SBB

White Hart

White Hart in Bridge Street

> "Goodbye, father – my love at home." A last shake of the hand. Up goes Tom, the guard catches his hat box, holding on with one hand while with the other he claps the horn to his mouth. Toot, toot, toot! the ostlers let go their heads, the four bays plunge at the collar, and away goes the Tally-Ho! into the darkness, forty-five seconds from the time they pulled up; Ostler, Boots and the Squire stand looking after them… "Sharp work!" says the Squire, and goes in again to his bed, the coach being well out of sight and hearing.

How well these graphic lines from *Tom Brown's Schooldays* epitomise the everyday scene in the yards of hundreds of mid nineteenth century commercial inns, of which the White Hart in Bridge Street, Evesham, was an outstanding local example. Auction sales, local government sessions, insurance agency, political gatherings, banquets, protest meetings, congratulatory meetings, were all housed and cared for beneath the hospitable roof of the inn; but coaching was the life-blood of this White Hart and when it ceased the old inn died.

Situated at 19, Bridge Street, now the business premises of Messrs Morris Brothers, fishmongers, the White Hart today evinces but little of its former importance. Gone are the stables, pump, summer house, granary, coach houses, workshops, sheds, piggeries and other outbuildings listed in a deed of 1866 when, having recently ceased to be an inn, it was sold as a basket maker's and cooper's shop. But the curious who venture through the old carriage entrance fronting Bridge Street are rewarded with tokens of former glories in the shape of a well-defined half-timbered gallery, with the former inn yard and gardens under the shadow of the bell tower beyond.[49]

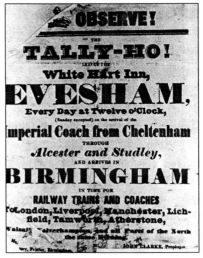 

63: Handbill for coaches from the White Hart and bill heading

---

[49] Now the site of Peacocks, the site having been redeveloped in the 1970s. SBB

Bentley's *Directory of Worcestershire*, 1840, indicated that passengers could join the *Imperial* coach from Cheltenham at the White Hart for Coventry via Stratford, Warwick and Leamington at 12 noon each weekday on payment of 8s. single fare or 16s. return; for Birmingham, as a handbill in the possession of Mrs A. Cox, of the Manor House, Offenham, shows, the *Tally-Ho!* left at the same time each weekday, fare 6s. single or 12s. return. For passengers travelling in the reverse direction, the *Imperial* called at the White Hart each afternoon except Sunday at 4:15.

By 1850, when the railway had approached to within eight miles of Evesham at Bidford and Defford, a coach still left the White Hart for Birmingham every afternoon at 1. On Mondays, Wednesdays and Fridays, the *Star* left at 1 pm for Leamington, and the *Queen* at 2 pm for Cheltenham. Every Tuesday, Thursday and Saturday afternoon at 2, the *Queen* left for Leamington and the *Star* for Worcester. But the station master's bell, which rang at Evesham for the first time just over a century ago, was the passing knell for one more English tradition thereabouts.

A billhead issued from the White Hart Commercial Inn, Evesham, by William Smith in 1827, lists beds, breakfast, dinner, tea and coffee, supper, wine, negus, brandy, rum, gin, ale, tobacco, cyder, porter, hay and corn as the fare available for man and beast. At the top an engraving by Suffield the local artists depicts a white stag lodged, collared and chained. The origin of this White Hart with the collar of gold about its neck with a hanging chain dates from the earliest written history.

Pliny wrote that it was Alexander the Great who first caught a white stag and placed a golden circlet about its throat. Subsequently, the mediaeval historians throughout Europe adopted the legend, altering the details at will to suit their particular fancies, with multifarious, if patriotic, results. In England, the White Hart first appeared as a favourite badge of Richard II (1377-1399). Caxton's continuation of the *Polychronicon* described a tournament at which:

> …all the kynges house were of one sute; theyr cotys, theyr armys, theyr shelds, and theyr trappours, were bowdrid all with white hertys, with crownes of gold abowt theyr neck and cheynes of gold hanging thereon, which hertys was the kinges leverye that he gaf to lordes, ladyes, knyghtes and squyers, to know his household people from others.

By 1450, the king's badge had been adopted as an inn sign; and the most elaborate inn sign of all time was erected in 1655 outside the White Hart, at Scole, in Norfolk; it cost £1,057 and spanned the highway like a triumphal arch for coaches to pass under it.[50]

An entry in the baptismal register of All Saints', Evesham, confirms that the White Hart existed in Bridge Street in 1654: "Phillip the sonne of Mr Philip Smith, a saltpetre maker, was born at the White Hart in Evesham who mother was Jane Smith."

---

[50] It was common in mediaeval times for shop and inn signs to span the highway. SBB

It has been suggested (Barnard, *Notes and Queries*, III. 62) that the inn was called the Bear at one period of its history but I have not been able to establish this point one way or the other. That it was known solely by the sign of the Harte late in the sixteenth century seems certain.

Evesham Borough Minutes for 1684 show that John Roberts paid 1s. 3d. chief rent to the Common Council for the White Hart; and that in 1758 William Cox paid 2s. chief rent for a half-year. In the records of the Mercers' Company this host of the White Hart appeared as William Cox junior when he supplied them with refreshment in 1751. His father had been host to the Company at the same house in 1735. Mr Cox junior paid a window tax on 16 lights amounting to £1 7s. in 1761. By 1728, William Powell was landlord of the White Hart and he was succeeded by Mr White who died on 20th December 1799.

In the early 1800s vituperative political pamphlets were freely bandied about the town whenever an election was due in Evesham. The following example, from 1818, is typical:

> Just arrived and to be seen at the Blue White Hart in the Bridge Street, Evesham, for a few days only an extraordinary animal, supposed to appear only once in seven years, and described by its director, an eminent Grub Picker, to be the principal of the species called A Puppet of a Pocket Borough. This animal was lately caught in the Rous Lench woods. It was by mere chance that the managers procured him, they being in search of some other beast to fill up their menagerie.

> Ten Guineas Reward – Lost in a Mob styling themselves the friends of Mr Rouse-Boughton, between the Post Office and White Hart inn, in the Bridge Street, Evesham – Exchequer Bills to the amount of £3,000, which was intended for the liquidation of the electioneering expenses of Mr Rouse-Boughton, etc., etc. Information to be given at either of the inns in the interest of Mr Boughton.

Posting inns like the White Hart, where representatives of the Whig Party regularly established their headquarters, did a roaring trade in the fetching and carrying of the election agents, their principals and the outside voters during the three days of polling, while the housing, dining and wining of them all brought more welcome grist to the mill of the landlord, at this time one James Doyle. He had been appointed one of the Sergeants-at-Mace for the borough in 1798, but it was probably his reputable table and cellar which caused the Corporation on 26th March 1807, to meet "at the house of James Doyle, known by the name or sign of the White Hart inn."

The inn's reputation for excellent catering had, it seems, by no means diminished in November 1838, when, following a banquet given there in honour of the retiring mayor, Thomas Nelson Foster, the *Worcester Herald* concluded its report in this effusive style:

> The banquet was sumptuous in the extreme, consisting of every delicacy in season including a superb haunch and was served in the neatest possible manner

by the worthy host Councillor William Smith whose wines were of the first quality and gave unbounded satisfaction. The dessert included some remarkably fine grapes from the hot house of Mr Alderman Rudge; the same gentleman also presented an abundant supply of champagne for the occasion.

But the expression 'worthy host' was no misnomer when applied to the landlord of the White Hart for, when, in the previous year, funds for the restoration of St Lawrence's Church were insufficient to cover expenses and a bazaar was held in the town hall, the organisers were able to advertise "a public breakfast which will be most liberally supplied by Mr Smith of the White Hart, and the whole receipts paid over to the Funds for the restoration of the Church." The success of the event may be measured by the fact that the church was opened on the following 16th November.

It was, however, on a previous and even more memorable occasion that William Smith had proved himself to be a caterer "par excellence," giving satisfaction to an even larger body of diners than even he was wont. I refer to the famous Reform Bill Banquet held in Vine Street on Friday, 15th June 1832, when 702 men sat down "while a far greater number, as spectators from the town and neighbourhood, stood around."

The Evesham Reform Association had come into being on 17th October 1831, immediately after the rejection of the First Reform Bill by the House of Lords. The object of the members, who paid monthly subscriptions and assembled weekly at the White Hart, was to keep Evesham "alive" on the burning question of parliamentary reform. Their ultimate satisfaction may be gathered from the following notice published throughout the town in August 1832, and headed "Evesham Reform Association":

> At a general meeting of this Association holden on Tuesday, Mr John Thorp in the chair, it was resolved unanimously that the following intimation be printed and circulated forthwith. The members of this Association anticipate that at their next meeting on Tuesday, August 7, they shall be able to congratulate each other upon that happy and glorious Event, the completion of the great National Measure of Parliamentary Reform, by the Scotch and Irish Bills having then received the Royal Assent and by their having thus become the Law of the Land; and as by the first article of their union, their existence as a political body will cease on the accomplishment of that extraordinary object which justified its creation, they now publicly announce the same, and they also intimate that it is their intention to DINE AT THE WHITE HART, EVESHAM, on Wednesday 8th of August next, with such other Friends of Parliamentary Reform as will favour them with their Company on so grand and memorable an occasion. Dinner on the Table at three o'clock. Tickets 7s. 6d. each, wine included, may be had at the Bar of the White Hart until Monday evening, the 6th August next, but not later.

In confident anticipation of their success, the Reformers had already resolved in June 1832, to collect subscriptions towards a public celebration. These yielded £88 7s. towards the total cost of the festivities, namely £118 12s. spent as follows:

Defraying the expenses of the band, fitting up and fencing Vine Street, constables, ringers, helpers employed to wait on the company and preserve the peace, repairs and breakages, and for taking down and returning the benches, borrowed, and for 700 plates, 700 half pint cups, and 574 pipes purchased.

Seven hundred and two men residents in Evesham partook of roast and boiled beef with bread and vegetables sufficient, and two thousand two hundred and one quarts of good ale, accompanied with pipes and tobacco, each man finding his own knife and fork.

Next day, 1,672 women and children were entertained to tea at the tables previously set out for the men. The aged and infirm who were unable to attend were supplied at their homes, while the indigent poor were regaled with "excellent broth." At this festival, 886lb. of beef was roasted and boiled at the White Hart and Farriers' Arms. Also consumed were:

> 1,000 penny loaves of bread
> 500 sixpenny ditto
> 5 lb. of mustard
> 8 lb. of tobacco
> 14 quarts of vinegar
> 81 lb. of sugar
> 64 lb. of butter
> 21 quarts of milk
> 13 lb. of tea

White Hart in Cowl Street

Readers may be surprised to learn that in addition to the old-established inn of this name in Bridge Street, there was, in 1820, a beerhouse by the same name in Cowl Street, kept by one James Guion, formerly landlord of an Angel inn in Bengeworth. This has led to an error by P.H. Ditchfield (author of *The Parish Clerk*) in his volume of rambles, *Byways in Berkshire and the Cotswolds*; he confuses it with the other White Hart and tells the story of the 'Fool and the Ice'.

The following is from Edmund New's book *Evesham*: [51]

> An amusing story connected with the White Hart Inn has been revived by Mr Halliwell-Phillipps, who by means of it has endeavoured to explain the line in *Troilus and Cressida*, "The fool slides o'er the ice that you should break." The anecdote is related by Robert Armin, who claims to have been an eye-witness of the incident; and this would seem probable, as the local touches are correct

---

[51] This was not included in the original series of articles, but is taken from *Evesham* by Edmund New (London: J.M. Dent, 1904), pp.60-62. SBB

and Armin was for some time a member of the company alluded to. It is to be found in a work entitled *Foole Upon Foole, or Sixte Sortes of Sottes*, published in 1605, and re-edited and issued, with the author's name attached, in 1608, as *A Nest of Ninnies*. The fool referred to in the line quoted above is suspected to be not merely the imaginary representative of a type but the popular local Fool of Shakespeare's time, a fellow of brilliant parts, but eccentric, and, we must suppose, lacking in balance and common sense.

We are told that one winter Lord Chandos's players visited Evesham, and Jack Miller, our Fool, became greatly attached to the company and in particular to Grumball the clown; indeed, so greatly was he enamoured that he "swore he would goe all the world over with Grumball."

The townspeople being loth to lose so popular a character, Jack was locked in a room at the back of the White Hart Inn from which he could see the players journeying on their way to Pershore, their next stage, by the road on the farthest side of the river. With difficulty he contrived to escape by the window, and ran down to the water's edge.

The stream, says our author, "was frozen over thinely," but Miller "makes no more adoe, but venters over the haven, which is by the long bridge, as I gesse some forty yards over; yet he made nothing of it, but my hart aked when my eares heard the ise unto me," continues Armin, "I was amazed, and tooke up a brick-bat[52], which lay there by, and threw it, which no sooner fell upon the ise but it burst. Was not strange that a foole of thirty yeeres was borne of that ise which would not endure the fall of a brick-bat?"!

White Horse

The White Horse is mentioned in only two records at present available in Evesham: a copy deed dated 20th October 1685 (Barnard Collection, O.D. IX), and the Corporation Minute Book of 1687. In the deed, Richard Darling, cooper, in consideration of his marriage, etc., conveys to John Turberville, haberdasher:

> …all that messuage or tenement with the appurtenances situate lying and being in Evesham aforesaid near the Market Place there, having the possession or occupation of Hester Thorne, widow, called or known by the name of the White Horse, on the west side thereof, and the way leading to the church yard gate on the east side thereof…

---

[52] A brick-bat is a piece of brick, especially when used as a missile. The term later came to mean an insult or wounding remark. SBB

This appears to establish the position of the White Horse on the site of the present Post Office[53]. Another deed, dated 14th June of the same year, now displayed in the Gateway Café, records the sale of those premises for £30 to Richard Darling by Sarah Milner, widow and relict of Thomas Milner, tanner. In both deeds there is the same calligraphy; they came from the office of Richard Cave, who was Chamberlain or Town Clerk at the time.

In the mayor's Accounts for 1687 there is a receipt for 5s. from Philip Stone "for his shop at the White Horse"; which gives the impression that the premises had then ceased to be an inn. The sign is generally accepted as being agricultural in connotation; some Saxon kings appear to have used it as an emblem but it was not reckoned to be a royal badge until reintroduced as such by the House of Hanover in the eighteenth century. It is still worn as an emblem on Doggett's coat and badge, or the royal watermen.

William

The William was an insignificant inn, the sole reference to which is in a most imposing document – the minutes of evidence of the Evesham election petition heard at the House of Commons in March 1838, with Sir Robert Peel in the chair, when Robert Salmon and others petitioned against the return of Peter Borthwick, one of the Tory candidates for the borough. In seeking to discredit the evidence of Mr A, a local rate-collector, Mr Cockburn, counsel for the petitioners, attempted to show that he was in the habit of attending meetings of the Blue party at the William public house. He admitted that he knew the William, and that the Blue party had met there.

> "Did you ever attend a meeting of the Blue party there?"
> "I have gone in when there have been parties, but not particularly the Blue party more than others."

I believe the William was situated on Mill Bank and was for many years kept by a man called Thomas Collins.

Why Not?

I began these tales of bygone inns with the story of the American Tavern in Cowl Street; therefore it seems appropriate that this part of the series be concluded with a note on another "tiddleywink" in the same street. The signboard of the house bore this inscription: "Why Not? William Gladwin sells beer and porter the same as his neighbours." Inside there was this notice:

---

[53] Now the site of the recently closed-down 'Home Style' in the Market Place. SBB.

William Gladwin is able to brew
As well as his uncle Thomas New

Since at this time (about 1840) Thomas New was landlord of the old-established Golden Hart inn, we may assume that the nephew's tiddleywink was fairly close to it.

I have reason to believe that the Gladwin family later moved from Cowl Street to the house at the east end of Swan Lane, known as 'The Cottage' for many years. They appear to have continued in business as brewers and retailers of beer and I understand that the house was mainly used by the barge-men who called at the gas works and the public wharf which exists at Collins's bacon factory. The remnants of a painted sign bearing the words 'Licensed to sell' can still be faintly discerned on the brickwork of 45, Swan Lane. I had not previously been able to locate with accuracy a couple of 'Tiddleywinks,' namely the Why Not? and the William. Thanks to the interest of Mr H. Bedenham, of Mill Street, I am now able to site them at 1, Cowl Street, and 8, Mill Street, respectively.

I have heard it said that the Why Not? was one of a row of three alehouses. No. 3, Cowl Street was an alehouse called the Dun Cow, so perhaps 2, Cowl Street, was the Blue Bell or the White Hart, both of which were in Cowl Street. Another tiddleywink existed in Cowl Street next to Mr Edward Parry's shop; its site is now occupied by Coulters Garage. I have been told that this beerhouse was called the Pure Drop, but later the premises were converted to a coffee tavern. I should welcome any further information on this.

In 1840, Evesham had twelve of these little beershops in addition to the other thirty-two fully licensed houses. It has not been easy to obtain information about these smaller alehouses and I include a few comments upon them this week in the hope that some of my older readers may be in possession of knowledge which has so far eluded my researches.

Samuel Alcock had a beershop in Oat Street for which I have neither location nor name. Thomas Bowles kept a similar house at 1, Bewdley Street, now Mrs Tandy's butcher's shop, but no name appears in written records. George Matthews and Charles Rogers had alehouses in High Street, one on or near the site of Tuckwood's Bazaar, the other in the immediate vicinity of Cotswold House.

Round the corner in Cross Keys Lane, as it was called in 1840, Sam Williams had his alehouse. Mr H.L. Goodall informs me that a considerable quantity of clay-pipe fragments was revealed during alterations to the garage some years ago and this leads me to believe that Williams's beershop stood very near to Messrs Goodall's present stores in Swan Lane, but here again no sign has survived.

By tradition, a cider house stood in the yard between Almswood and Yates's seed shop. The premises, now used mainly as a seed warehouse, still bear evidence of having had a good stabling for horses as well as a roomy cellar, now filled in. I have been reliably informed that during alterations to these premises effected some years ago, a quantity of old-fashioned wine bottles of the bulbous pattern with long necks was discovered by a workman – who promptly smashed them up as being useless... to the chagrin of your present historian, not to mention that of the owner when he heard the story from me!

Fortunately, however, another interesting antiquarian feature has survived the course of the years and, by the courtesy of Mr W.D. Yates of Cropthorne Court, I am enabled to publish it here. It is the gravestone, laid flat upon the floor of the warehouse, of a former Evesham publican. The inscription, which still remains clearly visible except for the verse at the end, scans as follows:

> Here Lieth... the Body of William... Barber, Victuler, who Departed... this life, July ye 9th, 1735... Aged 35 years... And also two of his sons. He was respected by his neighbours, Valued by his friends, Beloved by his wife, who ereced this to his memory.

In 1873, Mrs Mary Ann Groves kept a beerhouse under the sign of the Brewers' Arms at 25, High Street, now the dress shop of 'Rebecca.' This is noteworthy as a revival of the Vintners' sign of the Three Tuns which had existed over a century before at 26, High Street, next door – included in my series of obsolete signs last September.

At Dresden House nearby, a school for Young Ladies was opened in 1860 by Mrs Frances Farell and Mrs Moore. The school existed until 1919 under its later and better known name of Watts and Cooper's. In the early days of the school, each young lady pupil was allowed a glass of beer at dinner and half a glass at supper; each servant was allowed a pint a day and the cook three pints a day; the man of all work received two quarts a day. The consumption of beer in term time was eighteen gallons a week. (Please remember this was a school for Young Ladies in 1860.)

"Beer," said Mr Gladstone when Chancellor of the Exchequer in 1860, "is the great national drink of the population, and evidently requires much the largest number of houses licensed for its sale. There are in England 70,000 to 80,000 drinking houses which are in no sense eating houses at all. Is it not obvious that the old system of separating eating and drinking is the most unwise one that we can pursue if we want to promote sober habits?"

This ideal upon which the G.O.M. [Grand Old Man] based his 1860 Act – "of reuniting the business of eating with that of drinking, which by fatal error it had been separated" – has been a feature of all later legislation concerning innkeepers, right up to the Licensing Act of 1953, but it was the Wine and Beerhouse Act of 1869 which set the pattern for the development of pubs as we know them today.

The "fatal error" stigmatised by Gladstone was an act of 1830 generally known as the Duke of Wellington's Beer House Act, "to permit the general sale of beer by retail in England," which caused the advent of little alehouses. The increase in the number of houses selling beer in Evesham was comparatively modest, being in the proportion of one beerhouse to every three established victuallers. But in other parts of the country they multiplied at a fantastic rate. In Liverpool, for instance, over 24,000 beershops opened in the last three months of 1830. The intention had been to wean men from the hard liquors they drank in the public houses to the milder and comparatively harmless beer, but the unforeseen result was a frightening increase in drunkenness, vice and crime.

"The sovereign people," wrote Sydney Smith, "is in a beastly state." Gladstone's act of 1860 did not solve the problem and the "beastly state" of the nation was not effectively altered until 1869 when the control of beerhouse licences came under the jurisdiction of magistrates assembled at their annual licensing sessions…

The policy of licence restriction, inaugurated in 1869 and steadily expanded ever since, accelerated the growth of the 'tied house' system which prevails today. Space precludes me from dealing with the topic in the detail which it deserves; suffice it to say that between 1905 and 1954 the number of on-licensed houses in England and Wales fell from 99,478 to 73,220, while the population increased by eleven millions in the same period. Only two of the 27 on-licensed houses in Evesham are designated as "free houses" today and both rely on one or other of the major brewing concerns for their supplies.

Last Thursday, the chairman of a famous Midland brewery company, after reviewing a year of progress, concluded his report with these words: "Catering at all levels is an expanding side of our business and all our licensees are encouraged to cater." So it seems that William Ewart Gladstone is going to have the last word after all.

Woolpack

The Woolpack Inn at 6, Port Street, wears a name which has probably been familiar in Evesham since the sixteenth century when the name of the town appeared in continental records as "Evesham in the Cotswolds," thus linking it with the famous staple industry of the period. First references to the Bengeworth inn are to be found in the Parish Relief Account Book as follows:

> March 27, 1724. Gave a poore man to Bare his charges at the Wollpack 1s. 0d.

> Apriall 2, 1725. Payd in charges of Removing the man that Died at the Wollpack and for cleaning their Beding and gave the wimmin for waighting on him in His Ilnes com to the sum of £1 4s. 0d.

When the Turnpike road from Evesham Bridge to the Hampton Turnpike (corner of Cheltenham Road) was constructed about 1760 the Woolpack took on considerable importance as a coaching inn.

In 1820 a coach left there for London each morning at half-past six and each evening for Worcester at seven. In 1825 a coach called the *Aurora* was calling at the inn and later the *Monarch* used to leave the Woolpack for London every evening, except Sundays, at seven but as it travelled at a slower rate than the Royal Mail which started from the Northwick Arms at the same hour the fare was less, 13 shillings single and 24 shillings return. The *Monarch* called at the inn at 5 am on the return journey to Worcester. In 1835 a coach called the *Wonder-to-many* left the Woolpack every

Monday afternoon at 4 pm. for Campden via Broadway. The villages of Toddington, Dumbleton and Sedgeberrow were served by Jackson the Carrier who departed from the Woolpack at half past three every Monday afternoon in 1873.

When the estate of the late George Day, of Prospect House, was disposed of by Messrs W. and J. Murrell by auction on Thursday, 10th June 1830, the Woolpack Inn was the scene of the sale. Lot 7 in the catalogue appeared thus:

> The Woolpack Inn being leasehold, with a capital range of stabling, yard, garden land and outbuildings, situate in Bengeworth, in the high road from London to Worcester and now in the occupation of Mrs Sarah Doyle, a yearly tenant, rent £35, chief rent £1 5s. Leasehold from Lord Northwick on 99 years lease determinable on three lives.

Prior to Mrs Doyle, William Smith had been tenant from 1818. Mrs Doyle was succeeded by James Pugh or Pew (1850), Richard Matthews (1863/73), Charles Evans (1894), Mrs Emily Evans (1904), Frederick Charles Evans (1909 to his retirement in 1950), Mr F.J. Smith (1951), and at the present time Mrs Marion Smith.

64: Woolpack, Port Street (c.1900)
In the doorway can be seen Mr and Mrs Charles Evans, with Frederick Wheeler the town crier. The Woolpack closed on Saturday 25th September 1971.

Last Word

So ends the last article in the series *Evesham Inns and signs*.

Mr Baylis, a master at Swan Lane School, Evesham, and the chairman of the Vale of Evesham Historical Society, began the series in March 1953, after carrying out a research project for the Historical Society.

The outcome is that the records of all the known inns of Evesham, past and present, are fully documented and preserved to an extent that one would not expect to find in any other town of England.

In the wide field of general affairs, it may appear to be of little consequence that this should be so. But records such as these, painstakingly compiled with the emphasis on proved facts rather than romance, are the raw materials of local history.

Looking Back on the History of Evesham Inns and Signs

In the fifty years or so since Tom Baylis wrote his series of articles on Evesham inns and signs for the *Evesham Journal*, there have been significant changes in the town as well as its inns.

From 1951 to 1991 the population of Evesham grew from 12,066 to 17,801. Huge new housing estates have appeared, including Four Pools, Eastwick Park and Cotswold Rise. Huge new industrial and trading estates have been developed, starting in 1962 with the industrial estates on the Worcester Road, and continuing through to Vale Park on the outside of the by-pass (itself another recent development). Out-of-town supermarkets have appeared together with a shopping centre in the heart of the town.

Curiously, at the same time as this unprecedented growth, certain key services have disappeared. The Briar-close cottage hospital, built by public subscription in 1879, was sold by the local Health Authority for housing. Avonside hospital no longer has a maternity ward. The closure of the Magistrates Court means that local justice is now administered from Worcester. On the positive side, the Town Hall was refurbished (the ugly grey stucco was stripped from some of its walls to reveal the original warm Cotswold stone), the fire station was moved to its own building in Merstow Green, and the Market Place and Bridge Street have been pedestrianised.

The inns, too, have changed. Perhaps the most significant change is that quite a number have closed down, notably the Cross Keys, Crown, Duke of York, Falcon, Old Anchor, Rose and Crown and Woolpack. Meanwhile the King Charles Bar has been transformed into an arcade of shops and offices, though mercifully including a bar (Chancers). Some new inns appeared, including Strawberry Field (just off the by-pass) and the Moon and Sixpence (tucked underneath the town hall), although the latter closed after only a handful of years and the site is now boarded-up.

There have been some name changes too. Soon after Tom Baylis finished writing his history of Evesham inns and signs, Mitchells and Butlers re-named the Plough, giving it back its old name of the Maiden's Head. This return to roots, however, did not last. The inn was later re-named Ducks Don't Float, then later re-named Mojo, then later still re-named Karma (I'm not sure what Tom Baylis would have thought of any of that). At the same time as this ancient name was being updated, the Star Hotel found its history and become the Old Swanne Inne.

The Golden Hart, whose name suggests an origin before the Dissolution, was until recently the only inn in Cowl Street (which, at different times, has been home to the Dun Cow, Why Not?, American Tavern, Hare and Hounds, Blue Bell, White Hart, and Pure Drop). Intriguingly, in 1997, pottery fragments from the 13th century were found in the foundation trench of a wall at the Golden Hart, which adds to the suspicion of this inn's antiquity. Just round the corner, the Green Dragon until recently boasted its own micro-brewery brewing the aptly-named Asum Ale. These two inns have now been linked together to create the Blue Maze.

Happily, though, many of the inns that Tom Baylis knew are still with us. The Talbot (which appeared in 1573 as the Bell), Trumpet (first mentioned in 1685), Royal Oak and Old Red Horse are still with us, fine reminders of the town's long history and how Evesham used to be.

65: Moon and Sixpence, Market Place (2003)
Throughout the 1970s there was a long-running campaign to open up the arches of the town hall to create an open market space, returning the building to its traditional appearance and function.

66: Strawberry Field, the Link (2003)

Appendices

Appendix A: Summary of Articles

Date of publication	No.	Title of article	Name of inn
14-02-1954	1	The last of the four Angels	
27-02-1954	2	The Vicar v. Mr Strayne	
13-03-1954	3	Brewing in the Mortuary	
25-03-1954	4	The Dolphin – A Loyal Snoek	
10-04-1954	5	And Wine for His Worship	
24-04-1954	6	Where the Council adjourned	
12-05-1954	7	Inspector Arton reports…	
26-05-1954	8	In praise of Evesham pubs	
09-06-1954	9	A Catalogue of Inns	
The following articles relate to obsolete inns and inn signs in Evesham			
23-06-1954	10	The American Tavern: Last of the Tiddleywinks	American Tavern
03-07-1954	11	The Bell	The Bell Blue Bell
17-07-1954	12	A Black Sheep at the Black Dog	Black Dog
31-07-1954	13	Black Horse	Black Horse Blue Boar
15-08-1954	14	The Versatile Thos Cull	Bridge Inn
28-08-1954	15	A Present for the Teacher	Butchers' Arms
11-09-1954	16	He was 'one of the Nobs'	Bug and Louse Coach Makers' Arms Cockatoo
25-09-1954	17	The Dolphin Inn	Dolphin
23-10-1954	18	Four Old Evesham Inns	Dun Cow Elm Eight Bells Evesham Arms
09-10-1954	19	At the Ewe and Lamb	Ewe and Lamb
06-11-1954		Sunday Mornings at Betty Tailers	Five Bells
27-11-1954		At the Golden Fleece Inn	Golden Fleece
11-12-1954		Police cleared the Fox	Fox
18-12-1954		Mr Smythe kept The George	George
01-01-1955		A Chapel in the Cellar?	George
15-01-1955		The Goat on the Green	Goat
29-01-1955		The Golden Cross	Golden Cross

Date of publication	No.	Title of article	Name of inn
19-02-1955		Murder planned in Market Place inn	Horse and Groom
19-03-1955		The Hop Pole Inn	Hop Pole
19-03-1955		The Jolly Gardeners	Jolly Gardeners
09-04-1955		Unlucky for some	Horse Shoe King's Arms
23-04-1955		Room for strange butchers	King's Head Butchers' Arms
07-05-1955		The last of the King's Head	King's Head
21-05-1955		The popular King of Prussia	King of Prussia
04-06-1955		The Nelson	Nelson Nag's Head
18-06-1955		'Snuffy' and the Quart Pot	Quart Pot
02-07-1955		The Prince of Wales	Prince of Wales
16-07-1955		Signs of the times	Maiden's Head
30-07-1955		The Old Red Lion	Red Lion (Market Place)
13-08-1955		Most conspicuous of Evesham inns	Round House
27-08-1955		'On the Box' – the rules	Shoe and Boot
10-09-1955		Glovers at the 'Shoulder of Mutton'	Shoulder of Mutton Three Tuns Three Crowns
24-09-1955		A fabulous beast in Port Street	Unicorn
08-10-1955		Old Evesham Penny	Unicorn
22-10-1955		Volunteers ready as Nelson fought Trafalgar	Volunteer
05-11-1955		The White Hart in Bridge Street	White Hart
19-11-1955		Keen politics at the White Hart	White Hart
17-12-1955		Six old inns – and now for the present	Star and Garter Vine White Hart White Horse William Why Not?
07-01-1956		And what did Mr Gladstone Say in…	Various
The following articles relate to present inns and inn signs in Evesham [1957]			
21-01-1956		How the Angel came to guard the gate of Evesham	Angel (Bridge Street) Angel (Waterside)
24-03-1956		Three Angels and their keepers	Angel (Bengeworth) Angel (Port Street) Angel Vaults

Date of publication	No.	Title of article	Name of inn
07-04-1956		The Bear in Port Street	Bear
21-04-1956		Surprises under the Roof of the Cross Keys	Cross Keys
05-05-1956		Survivor from Tudor times: The Crown Hotel	Crown
19-05-1956		The rise, decline and eventual fall of Mr Rowland Broadstock	Crown
09-06-1956		The Crown, Evesham: 19th Century	Crown
23-06-1956		The 'Navvy' or Navigation	Crown (aka Navigation)
20-07-1956		He had ten thousand men	Duke of York
04-08-1956		The Falcon Hotel – an old wine lodge in Vine Street	Falcon
18-08-1956		Two more old Evesham inns	Gardeners' Arms George and Dragon
31-08-1956		Landlord of Golden Hart and good old days	Golden Hart
14-09-1956		'King Charles' in Vine Street and the 'Green Dragon'	Farriers' Arms Green Dragon King Charles
28-09-1956		A Quaking Innkeeper	Red Lion (Waterside)
12-10-1956		Dinners at the Northwick Arms	Northwick Arms
20-10-1956		Now there is only one free house	Oddfellows' Arms Cider Mill
09-11-1956		The origin of the Old Anchor	Old Anchor
23-11-1956		Pistols under her counter	Plough
02-01-1957		How the Railways first came to Evesham	Railway Hotel
09-01-1957		The Old Red Horse Inn	Red Horse
18-01-1957		The Rose and Crown Inn	Rose and Crown
25-01-1957		Royal Oak 'sheltered a king'	Royal Oak
01-02-1957		The Star Hotel, Evesham – 1	Star
08-02-1957		The Star Hotel, Evesham – 2	Star
15-02-1957		The Star Hotel, Evesham – 3	Star
22-02-1957		The Swan Hotel, Bengeworth	Swan
01-03-1957		The Talbot, Bengeworth	Talbot
08-03-1957		The Trumpet Inn	Trumpet
15-03-1957		Vauxhall and Woolpack: last of the Evesham inns	Vauxhall Woolpack

Appendix B: Glossary

Area	Term	Notes
Trades	Mercer	A dealer in textiles.
	Cordwainer	A shoe-maker, although strictly speaking one who works in cordovan (that is, goatskin leather). The name derives from Cordova in Spain.
	Ostler	One who looks after horses. The name is a corruption of hostler.
	Boots	The man who cleaned the boots, the lowest-ranking adult male servant. Today the term is used figuratively for one who does very menial jobs such as cleaning boots.

Area	Term	Notes
Drinks	Holland	A type of gin imported, appropriately enough, from Holland.
	Negus	A composition of hot water and sweet wine (usually port or sherry), sweetened and flavoured, named after its 18th-century inventor, Colonel Francis Negus.
	Port	Wine made near the upper reaches of the River Douro some 50 miles inland from the sea (by the town of Oporto). The name derives from the Portuguese for 'wine of Oporto'. Before circa 1800 it was a low-strength wine similar to burgundy.
	Porter	About 1720 a certain Mr Harwood brewed a beer, which he called 'Entire', that united the flavours of ale, beer, and twopenny (a strong beer costing twopence a quart). Apparently it became known as 'Porters' Ale' or 'Porter' because of its popularity with the porters of the London street markets.
	Sack	White wine typically imported from Spain or the Canaries, but sometimes also imported from Malaga, Galicia and Portugal. The meaning of the name is obscure but may be related to 'sec'.
	Sherry	Blended high-strength wine made from wines mainly from the Jerez region in Spain. The name 'sherry' is a corruption of 'Jerez'.
	Stout	A very strong porter. The original term was 'Stout Porter' which was eventually shortened to 'Stout'

Area	Term	Notes
Capacity	Minim	Basic unit of capacity.
	Fluid drachm	60 minims
	Fluid ounce	8 fluid drachms
	Gill	5 fluid ounces
	Cup	2 gills
	Pint	4 gills or 2 cups or 20 fluid ounces
	Quart	2 pints
	Gallon	4 quarts or 8 pints

Area	Term	Notes
Dry measure	Peck	2 gallons (mentioned in *Piers Plowman*)
	Bushel	4 pecks or 8 gallons
	Sack	3 bushels
	Quarter	8 bushels
	Chaldron	12 sacks or 36 bushels

Area	Term	Notes
Liquid measure	Pin	4½ gallons
	Firkin	9 gallons or 2 pins
	Kilderkin	18 gallons or 2 firkins
	Barrel	36 gallons or 2 kilderkins
	Hogshead	54 gallons or 6 firkins
	Puncheon	70 gallons or 2 barrels
	Butt	108 gallons or 2 hogsheads
	Tun	216 gallons or 3 puncheons or 2 butts

Area	Term	Notes
Length	Inch	Traditionally, the distance across the thick of a thumb
	Foot	12 inches. Traditionally, the length of a foot.
	Yard	3 feet or 36 inches. Traditionally, the length of a stride
	Chain	22 yards
	Furlong	10 chains
	Mile	8 furlongs or 1,760 yards or 5,280 feet.

Area	Term	Notes
Area	Square foot	144 square inches
	Square yard	9 square feet
	Acre	4,840 square yards. Traditionally, the amount of land a team of oxen could plough in one full day.
	Square mile	640 acres

Area	Term	Notes
Currency	Penny	Denoted by 'd' (from 'denarius', a Roman silver coin and the name for the English silver penny)
	Shilling	12 pence (from the late 18th century a shilling was popularly called a 'bob'). Denoted by 's' (from 'solidus').
	Pound	20 shillings or 240 pence. Denoted by a crossed copper-plate L, now shown as '£' (from 'librum' meaning pound).
	Guinea	1 pound and 1 shilling. Denoted by 'g' or 'gn'. A third of a guinea is exactly 7 shillings.

Coins	Farthing	Coin worth ¼ penny
	Halfpenny	Coin worth ½ penny
	Penny	Coin made of bronze from 1860.
	Threepence	Coin worth 3 pence. Made of silver until 1944, and of nickel-brass from 1937.
	Groat	Coin worth four pence, and typically minted in silver. Sometimes called Joeys.
	Sixpence	Coin worth 6 pence. Known as a 'tanner'.
	Shilling	Coin worth 12 pence
	Florin	Coin worth 24 pence (or 2 shillings)
	Crown	Silver coin worth 5 shillings or 5 bob (from the early 19th century sometimes called a dollar). From 1965 onwards, a crown is worth 5 pounds.
	Sovereign	Gold coin worth 1 pound. From 1918 onwards it was replaced by the pound note.

Currency: Having a pound divisible into 240 equal parts means one pound is exactly divisible into halves, thirds, quarters, fifths, sixths, eighths, tenths, twelfths, fifteenths, sixteenths, twentieths, twenty-fourths, thirtieths, fortieths, forty-eighths, sixtieths, eightieths, and one-hundred-and-twentieths. A decimal system, on the other hand, means one pound is exactly divisible into halves, quarters, fifths, tenths, twentieths, twenty-fifths, and fiftieths.

Imperial: The Imperial system was originally defined by three standard measures – the yard, the pound and the gallon. Three major Weights and Measures Acts (1963, 1976 and 1985) gradually abolished various Imperial units and re-defined standards of measurement. Only metric units are now allowed with the following exceptions:

- miles, yards, feet and inches for road traffic signs and measurements of speed and distance
- pints for draught beer and cider, and for milk in returnable containers
- acres for land registration
- troy ounces for transactions in precious metals

Appendix C: Innkeepers and Inns

The following table lists the innkeepers and inns mentioned in the text. It is not intended to be exhaustive or comprehensive. For further details about named individuals please see *Index of Local People*.

Name	Inn	Date(s)
Adams, W.H.	Volunteer, Market Place	c.1880
Aldridge, William	American Tavern, 15, Cowl Street	1903
Allard, William	Fleece, Bridge Street	1820
Andrew, Harry	Plough, Vine Street	1956
Andrews, F.S.	Angel Vaults, 11, Port Street	to 1941
Andrews, James	Angel Vaults, 11, Port Street	1910
Ashmore, Mr	Crown, Bridge Street	1726
Atkins, John	2, Vine Street (later the Falcon)	1820
Attwood, Thomas R.	American Tavern, 15, Cowl Street	1897

Name	Inn	Date(s)
Badger, Charles	Duke of York, Bridge Street	1850
Bailey, James Spicer	Vauxhall Inn, Merstow Green	1925
Bailey, W.	Bear, Port Street	1898
Ballard, R.B.	Vine, 54, Port Street	1915
Bayley, Widow	Crown, Bridge Street	1678
Baylis, Charles	Talbot, Port Street	1854
Baylis, Isaac	Blue Bell, Cowl Street	c.1900
Baylis, Sarah Maria	Volunteer, Market Place	1850
Bayliss, J.B.	Duke of York, Bridge Street	1894
Bayzand, John	Golden Cross, Vine Street	1729 – c.1745
Beckitt, Robert	Fox, 39, Bridge Street	c.1769
Bedenham, Frederick	Swan Hotel, Port Street	1863
Bedenham, John	Swan Hotel, Port Street	1851
Bell, A.	Swan Hotel, Port Street	1956
Bell, C.H.	American Tavern, 15, Cowl Street	1900
	Royal Oak, Vine Street	1902
Bell, George	Royal Oak, Vine Street	1920
	Rose and Crown, High Street	c.1935 – 1949
Bell, W.	Swan Hotel, Port Street	1910
Bladon, Edward	Plough, Vine Street	1951 – 1956
Bomford, John	2, Vine Street (later the Falcon)	1850

Name	Inn	Date(s)
Booth, Charles	Angel, Bengeworth	1809
Booth, Mary Walker	Angel, Bengeworth	1820
Boswell, Henry	George and Dragon, Bewdley Street	1850
Bouts, Thomas	Ledden Post, 16 & 17 High Street	c.1685
Bouts, Thomas (son of Bouts, Thomas)	Ledden Post, 16 & 17 High Street	c.1688
Brearley, George	Royal Oak, Vine Street	1908
Broadstock, Rowland	George, High Street	c.1680?
Broadstock, Rowland (son of Broadstock, Rowland)	George, High Street	to c.1701
	Crown, Bridge Street	c.1702
Brooke, Anthony	Crown, Bridge Street	1682
Brotherton, A.	Old Red Horse, Vine Street	1913
Brotherton, C.	Royal Oak, Vine Street	1898
Brotherton, Charles	Eight Bells, Bewdley Street	1830 – 1850
Brotherton, Charles	Golden Hart, Cowl Street	1873
Brotherton, Charles	Volunteer, Market Place	1894
Brotherton, G.	Vauxhall Inn, Merstow Green	1941
Brotherton, G.J.	New Anchor, 1, Brick-kiln Street	to c.1895?
Brotherton, George	George and Dragon, Bewdley Street	1840
	Rose and Crown, High Street	1850
Brotherton, George James	Jolly Gardeners, 16, Bewdley Street	1934
Brotherton, James	Gardeners' Arms, Littleworth Street	1857
Brotherton, John	New Anchor, 1, Brick-kiln Street	c.1875?
Brotherton, William	Old Red Horse, Vine Street	1894
Brown, N.J.	Trumpet Inn, Merstow Green	1951
Brown, Stephen	Swan Inn, High Street	to 1724
Burlingham, Mrs	Red Lion, 6, Market Place	1766
Burton, J.A.	Rose and Crown, High Street	1949
Bushell, William	Star Hotel, High Street	1832
Butler, Samuel	Star Hotel, High Street	1863
Byrd, Charles	Fleece, Bridge Street	from 1871
Byrd, Elizabeth	Swan Hotel, Port Street	1807
Byrd, George	Red Lion, 6, Market Place	1894
Byrd, Harry	Green Dragon, Oat Street	1897
	Vine, 54, Port Street	1906
	Bear, Port Street	c.1910 – 1919
Byrd, J.	Swan Hotel, Port Street	1829

Name	Inn	Date(s)
Callow, James	New Anchor, 1, Brick-kiln Street	1865
Callow, Thomas	Angel, Bengeworth	from 1874
	Blue Anchor, Brick-kiln Street	to 1874
Camkin, John	George and Dragon, Bewdley Street	1903
Careless, Richard	Vauxhall Inn, Merstow Green	1863
Chamberlayne, John	Farriers' Arms, No. 1, Vine Street	1766
Churchley, David	Old Anchor, No. 3, Bewdley Street	1907
Clarke, F.J.	Bear, Port Street	1920
Clements, Samuel	Trumpet Inn, Merstow Green	1813
Cole, George	Vauxhall Inn, Merstow Green	1873
Cole, George F.	Vauxhall Inn, Merstow Green	1894 – 1898
Cole, John	Volunteer, Market Place	1840
Coles, Joseph	Fox, 39, Bridge Street	1830
Coles, Wilson Herbert	King's Head, 60, High Street	1886
Collins, John	Fleece, Bridge Street	1839 – 1859
Collins, William	Fleece, Bridge Street	1834
Cook, John	Nelson, Port Street	c.1815
Cook, Richard	Plough, Vine Street	1790
Cooke, W.	Jolly Gardeners, 16, Bewdley Street	1873
Cooke, William (son of Cooke, W.)	Jolly Gardeners, 16, Bewdley Street	1894
Cooke, William	Bear, Port Street	from 1904
Cooke, William	Trumpet Inn, Merstow Green	1866
Cowell, T.N.	Vauxhall Inn, Merstow Green	1950
Cox, William	Crown, Bridge Street	1744
Cox, William	Rose and Crown, High Street	1870
Cox, William	White Hart, 19, Bridge Street	1735
Cox, William (son of Cox, William)	White Hart, 19, Bridge Street	1758
Cull, J.	Plough, Vine Street	1820
Cull, James	Angel, Bengeworth	1809
	Plough and Harrow, 1, Vine Street	c.1812
Cull, Thomas	Bridge Inn, 34, Bridge Street	c.1845
	Angel Inn, Waterside	1855
	Talbot, Port Street	1856
Cuttridge, James	Duke of York, Bridge Street	c.1840

Name	Inn	Date(s)
Darby, John	Bear, Port Street	c.1860
Dawes, Thomas	Golden Hart, Cowl Street	1857
Day, Thomas	Bug and Louse, Rynal Street	c.1850
Deacon, Martin	Swan Inn, High Street	1711
Dentith, C.	Jolly Gardeners, 16, Bewdley Street	1908
Dingley, Frank	Old Anchor, No. 3, Bewdley Street	c.1940
Dobbins, Walter	Fox, 39, Bridge Street	1820
Doust, John E.	Railway Hotel, High Street	to 1956
Doyle, James	White Hart, 19, Bridge Street	1818
Doyle, Sarah	Woolpack, Port Street	1830
Doyle, W.C.	Cross Keys, High Street	1920
Doyle, W.J.	Cross Keys, High Street	1917
Drinkwater, William	Trumpet Inn, Merstow Green	1818
Dyke, F.J.A.	Star Hotel, High Street	1950

Name	Inn	Date(s)
Edwards, A.P.	Bear, Port Street	1925
Ellis, W.	Angel Vaults, 11, Port Street	1898
Elvins, Arthur	American Tavern, 15, Cowl Street	1906
Evans, Charles	Woolpack, Port Street	1894
Evans, Emily	Woolpack, Port Street	1904
Evans, Frederick Charles	Woolpack, Port Street	1909 – 1950

Name	Inn	Date(s)
Felton, Edwin	2, Vine Street (later the Falcon)	c.1860
Felton, J. Lloyd	King's Head, 60, High Street	1898
Fennel, E.	Angel Vaults, 11, Port Street	1897
Field, G.H.	Talbot, Port Street	1915/25
Field, Mrs	Three Tuns,	1741
Firth, W.	Cross Keys, High Street	1894
Fisher, Miss	Old Anchor, No. 3, Bewdley Street	c.1920
Fox, Mary Louise	Duke of York, Bridge Street	c.1955
Fox, Robert	Duke of York, Bridge Street	1913
Frankum, Raymond	Old Red Horse, Vine Street	1953
Freame, Edward	Swan Inn, High Street	1586

Name	Inn	Date(s)
Gardiner, John	Nag's Head, Vine Street	c.1750
Gardner, George	Swan Inn, High Street	1711

Name	Inn	Date(s)
Gardner, William	Plough, Vine Street	1684
George, Alfred	American Tavern, 15, Cowl Street	1870
George, W.	Royal Oak, Vine Street	1840
George, William	Old Red Horse, Vine Street	1873
Gilbert, A.H.	Old Red Horse, Vine Street	1945
Gladwin, William	Why Not? Cowl Street	1840
Glassbrook, Thomas	Vine, 54, Port Street	1898
Glover, Hannah	Duke of York, Bridge Street	c.1835
Gold, Nathaniel	Swan Inn, High Street	c.1670
Gold, William	Swan Inn, High Street	1659
Goodall, F.W.	Volunteer, Market Place	1873
Gould, Joseph	Golden Hart, Cowl Street	1850
Grove, George	Cider Mill, Hampton	c.1900
Grove, George	Royal Oak, Vine Street	c.1940
Grove, James	Masons' Arms, Pershore Road	?
Grove, Kate	Royal Oak, Vine Street	to 1956
Grove, W.	Old Red Horse, Vine Street	1920
Grove, William	Farriers' Arms, No. 1, Vine Street	c.1820
Grove, William	King's Head, 60, High Street	to 1846
Grove, William	Old Anchor, No. 3, Bewdley Street	1897
Grove, William	Royal Oak, Vine Street	1930
Groves, John	Old Red Horse, Vine Street	1863
Groves, Mrs	George and Dragon, Bewdley Street	1837
Guion, James	Angel, Bengeworth	1812
	White Hart, Cowl Street	1820 – 1842

Name	Inn	Date(s)
Haines, Alfred	George and Dragon, Bewdley Street	1873
Haines, Sarah	George and Dragon, Bewdley Street	1897
Haines, Thomas	Golden Hart, Cowl Street	1852
Halford, George	Old Anchor, No. 3, Bewdley Street	c.1956
Hands, James	Horse and Groom, Vine Street	c.1825
Harris, Mr	King's Arms, Bengeworth	1805
Harris, Thomas	Trumpet Inn, Merstow Green	1685
Hawkins, George	Goat, Merstow Green	1583
Haynes, Arthur	Vine, 54, Port Street	1919
Hazard, Thomas	Black Dog, 16 & 17 High Street	c.1702
Headley, John	Crown, Bridge Street	1791

Name	Inn	Date(s)
Hicken, Alfred	Swan Hotel, Port Street	1903 – 1910
Hickman, F.G.	Railway Hotel, High Street	c.1945
Hiles, G.S.	Railway Hotel, High Street	1930
Hill, C.E.	Vauxhall Inn, Merstow Green	1898
Hill, W.	Old Red Horse, Vine Street	1930
Hodges, Thomas	Fleece, Bridge Street	to 1751
	Crown, Bridge Street	from 1751
Hodgetts, Henry	Ewe and Lamb, 71, High Street	1840
Holder, F.A.	Swan Hotel, Port Street	1872 – 1903
Hook, William	Fleece, Bridge Street	to 1871
Houlle, John	Talbot, Port Street	c.1570
Huban, Mrs	Gardeners' Arms, Littleworth Street	to 1934
Huband, James	George and Dragon	c.1956
Hughes, George 'Bodger'	Trumpet Inn, Merstow Green	1880
Hughes, Mark	Cross Keys, High Street	1854
Hughes, Richard Hemming	Star Hotel, High Street	1842
Hughes, William	Bear, Port Street	1840 – 1850
Hunt, Mrs	George and Dragon, Bewdley Street	1836
Hunting, Thomas	Old Red Horse, Vine Street	1850
Huxley, George John	Jolly Gardeners, 16, Bewdley Street	1917

Iorns, John	Trumpet Inn, Merstow Green	1873

Jarrett, Thomas	Crown, Bridge Street	1801
Jaynes, A.W.	Star Hotel, High Street	1925
Jenks, H.J.	Green Dragon, Oat Street	1901
Johnson, Henry	Swan Inn, High Street	from 1724
Jones, F.	Star Hotel, High Street	1935
Joseland, Joseph	2, Vine Street (later the Falcon)	1842

Kean, Joseph	Duke of York, Bridge Street	c.1840
Keen, Hannah	Prince of Wales, Bridge Street	c.1850
Keen, Joseph	Prince of Wales, Bridge Street	1840
Kendrick, Bobby	Sheep's Head, New Street	c.1860
Kings, W.	Plough, Vine Street	1865
Knowles, Thomas	Golden Hart, Cowl Street	1787

Name	Inn	Date(s)
Langston, George	Gardeners' Arms, Littleworth Street	1869?
Laurence, George	Rose and Crown, High Street	1820
Lawrence, Edward	Rose and Crown, High Street	1873
Lawrence, Joseph	Vauxhall Inn, Merstow Green	1859
Leach, H.	Navigation, Avonside	1894
Lewis, John	King's Head, 60, High Street	c.1820
Lightborne, John	Navigation, Avonside	1840
Lucas, Charles	Farriers' Arms, No. 1, Vine Street	1923
Luxton, Benjamin	Blue Bell, 43, High Street	1842
	Cross Keys, High Street	1850
Luxton, Mrs	George and Dragon, Bewdley Street	1863

Name	Inn	Date(s)
Major, Herbert	Golden Hart, Cowl Street	1904
Major, James	Plough, Vine Street	1873
Major, Thomas Anthony	Duke of York, Bridge Street	1897
Maries, H.C.	Angel Vaults, 11, Port Street	from 1941
Matthews, J.	Talbot, Port Street	1940 – 1955
Matthews, Jemima	Fox, 39, Bridge Street	1840
Matthews, Richard	Angel, Bengeworth	1806
Matthews, Richard	Woolpack, Port Street	1863/73
Matthews, Samuel	Dun Cow, 3, Cowl Street	c.1820
Meadows, E.C.	King's Head, 60, High Street	1901
Meadows, U.C.	Cross Keys, High Street	1913
Meddings, John	Railway Hotel, High Street	1868
Melen, Elizabeth	Royal Oak, Vine Street	1873
Melen, Thomas	Royal Oak, Vine Street	1850
Memmory, Alfred James	King's Head, 60, High Street	c.1850?
Michell, James	George, 48 High Street	c.1685/1688
Millington, Mrs	Farriers' Arms, No. 1, Vine Street	c.1835
Millington, Richard	Angel, Waterside	1820
Millington, Thomas	Farriers' Arms, No. 1, Vine Street	c.1830
	Volunteer, Market Place	1854
Mills, John	Ewe and Lamb, 71, High Street	1818
	Angel, Waterside	c.1830 – 1855
Mills, Prudence	Angel, Bengeworth	1863
Milward, A.A.	Talbot, Port Street	1930
	Bear, Port Street	1935

Name	Inn	Date(s)
Morgan, E.F.	Star Hotel, High Street	1951
Morgan, H.W.	Star Hotel, High Street	1920
Morris, Hector C.	Plough, 1, Vine Street	c.1926 – 1951
	Cross Keys, High Street	from 1951
Morton, Harry	Golden Hart, Cowl Street	1904 – 1930
	Falcon, Vine Street	1930 – c.1950
Moulting, John	Blue Bell, 43, High Street	c.1830
Mustoe, George	George and Dragon, Bewdley Street	1901

Name	Inn	Date(s)
Nappin, Mrs (later Mrs Tooley)	George and Dragon, Bewdley Street	1911 to 1927
Nappin, Thomas	George and Dragon, Bewdley Street	1906
Nash, F.	American Tavern, 15, Cowl Street	1894
Nash, W.	Royal Oak, Vine Street	1894
New, James	Butchers' Arms, High Street	to c.1808
	King's Head, 60, High Street	from c.1808
New, Thomas	Golden Hart, Cowl Street	c.1835
New, William	Golden Hart, Cowl Street	1842
Newbury, Annie	Plough, Vine Street	c.1925
Newbury, Louis	Plough, Vine Street	1902
Nightingale, Jack	Old Anchor, No. 3, Bewdley Street	c.1950
Nobbs, Joseph	Cockatoo, 29 Greenhill	c.1840 – 1850

Name	Inn	Date(s)
O'Hara, J.	Gardeners' Arms, Littleworth Street	c.1954
Orton, T.	Cross Keys, High Street	1915
Osborne, Thomas	Talbot, Port Street	1910
Ovard, Frank	Green Dragon, Oat Street	1925

Name	Inn	Date(s)
Parr, Henry	Old Red Horse, Vine Street	1842
Partington, Thomas	Cross Keys, High Street	1862
	King's Head, 60, High Street	c.1880
Partridge, J.R.	Rose and Crown, High Street	c.1890 – 1935
Penny, Peter	Unicorn, Bengeworth	1724
Penny, William (son of Penny, Peter)	Unicorn, Bengeworth	c.1765
Penny, William	Royal Oak, Vine Street	1818
Petitt, H.	Trumpet Inn, Merstow Green	c.1925

Name	Inn	Date(s)
Pettit, Herbert	Jolly Gardeners, 16, Bewdley Street	1909
Phillips, Charles	Navigation, Avonside	1873
Phillips, Mrs A.M.	Bear, Port Street	1933
Phipps, H.J.	Red Lion, 6, Market Place	1897
Phipps, John	Plough, Vine Street	1894
Phipps, Mrs	Plough, Vine Street	1901
Phophet, Mr	Volunteer, Market Place	1864
Pitman, Charles	Talbot, Port Street	1895
Pitman, George	Talbot, Port Street	1873
Pitman, Mrs	Talbot, Port Street	1898
Pittway, Edward	Red Lion, Waterside	1655
Poole, William	Cider Mill, Hampton	to 1912
Porter, A.J.	Vauxhall Inn, Merstow Green	1920
Porter, J.G.	Vauxhall Inn, Merstow Green	1913
Porter, Joseph	Green Dragon, Oat Street	1907
Porter, Mrs	Green Dragon, Oat Street	1920
Powell, William	White Hart, 19, Bridge Street	1728?
Price, William	Golden Hart, Cowl Street	1880
Pritchard, Samuel	Cider Mill, Hampton	1912
Prosser, Lewis	Crown, Bridge Street	1803
Pugh, James	Woolpack, Port Street	1850

Robbins, Joseph	Trumpet Inn, Merstow Green	1863
Roberts, J.H.	Railway Hotel, High Street	1920
Roberts, John	White Hart, 19, Bridge Street	1684
Rodbourne, H.	Vauxhall Inn, Merstow Green	1935
Rogers, Charles	Old Anchor, No. 3, Bewdley Street	1863
Roper, Mary	Old Red Horse, Vine Street	1820
Roper, Thomas	Fox, 39, Bridge Street	c.1751
Russ, James	Butchers' Arms, 8 Market Place	1820

Sallis, Frederick William	Volunteer, Market Place	1928
Salmon, John	Evesham Arms, Great Hampton	c.1827
Salmon, William	Red Lion, 6, Market Place	1900 – 1908
	King's Head, 60, High Street	from 1909
Saunders, David	Railway Hotel, High Street	1880
Saunders, H.	Railway Hotel, High Street	1890

Name	Inn	Date(s)
Schofield, Mr	Talbot, Port Street	1861
Sears, Edward	Blue Bell, 43, High Street	1835
Sears, J.	Rose and Crown, High Street	1840
Sears, John	Ewe and Lamb, 71, High Street	1835
Shakles, Percy	Talbot, Port Street	1935
Shenton, Frederick Shakespeare	King's Head, 60, High Street	c.1860?
Sheppard, S.	Old Red Horse, Vine Street	1835
Short, Frank	Old Anchor, No. 3, Bewdley Street	c.1930
Simpson, John	Old Anchor, No. 3, Bewdley Street	1857
Slatter, John	Ledden Post, 16 & 17 High Street	c.1692
Smith, Arthur	Old Anchor, No. 3, Bewdley Street	1906
Smith, Enoch	Old Anchor, No. 3, Bewdley Street	1820 – 1854
Smith, F.J.	Woolpack, Port Street	1951
Smith, George	George and Dragon, Bewdley Street	1902
Smith, H.	Old Anchor, No. 3, Bewdley Street	c.1910
Smith, John	Railway Hotel, High Street	1901
Smith, Joseph	Red Lion, 6, Market Place	1835 - 1850
Smith, Marion	Woolpack, Port Street	1957
Smith, S.	Trumpet Inn, Merstow Green	c.1930
Smith, William	White Hart, 19, Bridge Street	1838
Smith, William	Woolpack, Port Street	1818
Smythe, John	Le George	c.1577
Souch, Mr	Green Dragon, Oat Street	1817
Spiers, Annie	Oddfellows' Arm, Briar-close	to 1956
Spiers, Joseph	Oddfellows' Arm, Briar-close	1929
Spiers, R.E.	Vauxhall Inn, Merstow Green	1952
Sprosen, Louis	Duke of York, Bridge Street	1911
Sprosen, Louis	Jolly Gardeners, 16, Bewdley Street	1904
Sprosen, Louis	New Anchor, 1, Brick-kiln Street	from c.1895?
Stafford, Frederick William	Red Lion, 6, Market Place	1908 – 1910
Stanbra, S.	Cross Keys, High Street	1935
Stanley, G.	Green Dragon, Oat Street	1898
Stanley, J.	Railway Hotel, High Street	1956
Stanley, James	Green Dragon, Oat Street	c.1950
Stanley, T.	Red Lion, 6, Market Place	1898
Stanley, Walter	Golden Hart, Cowl Street	1897

Name	Inn	Date(s)
Stephens, John	Green Dragon, Oat Street	c.1850
Stephens, William	Green Dragon, Oat Street	1835
Stickley, Moses	Fleece, Bridge Street	1761
Stratton, Anthony	2, Vine Street (later the Falcon)	1764
Stratton, Charles Frederick	Plough, Vine Street	1835
Streatfield, Mr	Royal Oak, Vine Street	from 1956
Swinbourne, Leonard	Green Dragon, Oat Street	1935
Symonds, Benjamin	Three Crowns, Bridge Street	c.1750
Syms, Miss	Bear, Port Street	1930

Name	Inn	Date(s)
Talbot, Thomas	Vine, 54, Port Street	1858
Taylor, H.	Star Hotel, High Street	1906
Taylor, Thomas	King's Head, 60, High Street	c.1870?
Taylor, Thomas	Talbot, Port Street	1908
Taylor, Thomas	Volunteer, Market Place	1909
Teague, R.A.	Gardeners' Arms, Littleworth Street	c.1953
Teague, R.A.	Talbot, Port Street	1956
Thorp, Jonathan	King's Head, 60, High Street	from 1846
Tigwell, H.L.	Railway Hotel, High Street	1935
Timms, Elizabeth	Duke of York, Bridge Street	to c.1873
Timms, George	Duke of York, Bridge Street	1854
Tomes, Charles	Farriers' Arms, No. 1, Vine Street	c.1840
Tomkins, John	George and Dragon, Bewdley Street	1835
Tooley, Emily	Gardeners' Arms, Littleworth Street	1934 – 1952
Tovey, Joseph	Farriers' Arms, No. 1, Vine Street	from 1724
Tovey, Mrs	Red Lion, 6, Market Place	1760
Tovy, Mary	Farriers' Arms, No. 1, Vine Street	c.1768
Trotman, Susannah	Cross Keys, High Street	1842
Trotman, William	Cross Keys, High Street	1820 – 1840
Turberville, John	Fox, 39, Bridge Street	1842
Twist, C.H.	Vine, 54, Port Street	1916
Tymbs, Samuel	Horse and Groom, Vine Street	c.1775

Name	Inn	Date(s)
Vant, Richard C.	Angel Vaults, 11, Port Street	1906
Vince, Robert	Angel, Bengeworth	1836
Vines, G.	Vauxhall Inn, Merstow Green	1943
Vivian, G.S.	Green Dragon, Oat Street	1904

Name	Inn	Date(s)
Walker, John	Shoe and Boot, Bengeworth	1785
Walker, Margaret	Angel, Bengeworth	1835
	Bear, Port Street	1835
Walker, Stephen	Bear, Port Street	1820
Walker, Thomas	Plough, Vine Street	1837
Walker, Thomas	Red Lion, 6, Market Place	1865
Walter-Candy, William	Angel, Bengeworth	c.1900
Waring, Thomas	Farriers' Arms, No. 1, Vine Street	to 1724
Waring, William	Farriers' Arms, No. 1, Vine Street	1688
Warran, Hannah	Rose and Crown, High Street	1762
Watkins, George	Old Anchor, No. 3, Bewdley Street	1894
Watkins, John	Old Anchor, No. 3, Bewdley Street	1873
Watkins, Joseph	Horse Shoe, Bengeworth	1820
Watson, Mrs	Blue Bell, 43, High Street	c.1750
Weightman, George	Plough, Vine Street	c.1850
Welsborne, Charles	Butchers' Arms, 8, Market Place	c.1750
Welsborne, Charles (son of Welsborne, Charles)	George, High Street	to c.1775
	Butchers' Arms, 8, Market Place	from c.1775
Welsh, John	Crown, Bridge Street	to c.1724
Wheatley, Josiah	Blue Bell, 43, High Street	1837
Wheeler, William	Quart Pot, Bengeworth	1820
White, Mr	White Hart, 19, Bridge Street	c.1795
White, William	Cider Mill, Hampton	c.1900
Whitford, Henry	Ewe and Lamb, 71, High Street	1820
Williams, Charles	Hop Pole, 1, Vine Street	1850
Williams, George	Angel Vaults, 11, Port Street	1901
Williams, James	Ewe and Lamb, 71, High Street	1844 – c.1850
Williams, Thomas	Coach Makers' Arms	c.1850 – 1875
Williams, William	Rose and Crown, High Street	1842
Wilmot, Ernest S.	Golden Hart, Cowl Street	from 1930
Wood, J.L.	Cross Keys, High Street	1898
Wood, John Levi	Railway Hotel, High Street	1912
Woods, F.	Old Red Horse, Vine Street	1935
Woodward, William	Unicorn, Bengeworth	1658

Appendix D: Inns and Innkeepers

The following table alphabetically lists inns with their innkeepers over the years.

Inn	Date(s)	Name
American Tavern, Cowl Street	1870	George, Alfred
	1894	Nash, F.
	1897	Attwood, Thomas R.
	1900	Bell, C.H.
	1903	Aldridge, William
	1906	Elvins, Arthur

Inn	Date(s)	Name
Angel, Waterside	1820	Millington, Richard
	c.1830 – 1855	Mills, John
	1855	Cull, Thomas

Inn	Date(s)	Name
Angel Vaults, Port Street	1897	Fennel, E.
	1898	Ellis, W.
	1901	Williams, George
	1906	Vant, Richard C.
	1910	Andrews, James
	c.1941	Andrews, F.S.
	c.1941	Maries, H.C.

Inn	Date(s)	Name
Angel, Bengeworth	1806	Matthews, Richard
	1809	Booth, Charles
	1809	Cull, James
	1812	Guion, James
	1820	Booth, Mary Walker
	1835	Walker, Margaret
	1836	Vince, Robert
	1863	Mills, Prudence
	c.1874	Callow, Thomas
	c.1900	Walter-Candy, William

Inn	Date(s)	Name
Bear, Port Street	1820	Walker, Stephen
	1835	Walker, Margaret
	1840 – 1850	Hughes, William
	c.1860	Darby, John
	1898	Bailey, W.

Inn	Date(s)	Name
	c.1904	Cooke, William
	c.1910 – 1919	Byrd, Harry
	1920	Clarke, F.J.
	1925	Edwards, A.P.
	1930	Syms, Miss
	1933	Phillips, Mrs A.M.
	1935	Milward, A.A.

Black Dog, 16 & 17 High Street	c.1702	Hazard, Thomas

Blue Anchor, Brick-kiln Street	c.1874	Callow, Thomas

Blue Bell, 43 High Street	c.1750	Watson, Mrs
	c.1830	Moulting, John
	1835	Sears, Edward
	1837	Wheatley, Josiah
	1842	Luxton, Benjamin

Blue Bell, Cowl Street	c.1900	Baylis, Isaac

Bridge Inn, 34 Bridge Street	c.1845	Cull, Thomas

Bug and Louse, Rynal Street	c.1850	Day, Thomas

Butchers' Arms, 8 Market Place	c.1750	Welsborne, Charles
	c.1775	Welsborne, Charles (son)
	1820	Russ, James

Butchers' Arms, High Street	c.1808	New, James

Cider Mill, Hampton	c.1900	Grove, George
	c.1900	White, William
	c.1912	Poole, William
	1912	Pritchard, Samuel

Coach Makers' Arms	c.1850 – 1875	Williams, Thomas

Cockatoo, 29 Greenhill	c.1840 – 1850	Nobbs, Joseph

Inn	Date(s)	Name
Cross Keys, High Street	1820 – 1840	Trotman, William
	1842	Trotman, Susannah
	1850	Luxton, Benjamin
	1854	Hughes, Mark
	1862	Partington, Thomas
	1894	Firth, W.
	1898	Wood, J.L.
	1913	Meadows, U.C.
	1915	Orton, T.
	1917	Doyle, W.J.
	1920	Doyle, W.C.
	1935	Stanbra, S.
	c.1951	Morris, Hector

Inn	Date(s)	Name
Crown, Bridge Street	1678	Bayley, Widow
	1682	Brooke, Anthony
	c.1702	Broadstock, Rowland (son)
	c.1751	Hodges, Thomas
	c.1724	Welsh, John
	1726	Ashmore, Mr
	1744	Cox, William
	1751	Hodges, Thomas
	1791	Headley, John
	1801	Jarrett, Thomas
	1803	Prosser, Lewis

Inn	Date(s)	Name
Duke of York, Bridge Street	c.1835	Glover, Hannah
	c.1840	Cuttridge, James
	c.1840	Kean, Joseph
	1850	Badger, Charles
	1854	Timms, George
	c.1873	Timms, Elizabeth
	1894	Bayliss, J.B.
	1897	Major, Thomas Anthony
	1911	Sprosen, Louis
	1913	Fox, Robert
	c.1955	Fox, Mary Louise

Inn	Date(s)	Name
Dun Cow, 3 Cowl Street	c.1820	Matthews, Samuel

Inn	Date(s)	Name
Eight Bells, Bewdley Street	1830 – 1850	Brotherton, Charles

Inn	Date(s)	Name
Evesham Arms, Great Hampton	c.1827	Salmon, John

Inn	Date(s)	Name
Ewe and Lamb, 71 High Street	1818	Mills, John
	1820	Whitford, Henry
	1835	Sears, John
	1840	Hodgetts, Henry
	1844 – c.1850	Williams, James

Inn	Date(s)	Name
Falcon, 2 Vine Street	1764	Stratton, Anthony
	1820	Atkins, John
	1842	Joseland, Joseph
	1850	Bomford, John
	c.1860	Felton, Edwin
	1930 – c.1950	Morton, Harry

Inn	Date(s)	Name
Farriers' Arms, 1 Vine Street	1688	Waring, William
	c.1724	Tovey, Joseph
	c.1724	Waring, Thomas
	1766	Chamberlayne, John
	c.1768	Tovy, Mary
	c.1820	Grove, William
	c.1830	Millington, Thomas
	c.1835	Millington, Mrs
	c.1840	Tomes, Charles
	1923	Lucas, Charles

Inn	Date(s)	Name
Fleece, Bridge Street	1751	Hodges, Thomas
	1761	Stickley, Moses
	1820	Allard, William
	1834	Collins, William
	1839 – 1859	Collins, John
	c.1871	Byrd, Charles
	c.1871	Hook, William

Inn	Date(s)	Name
Fox, 39 Bridge Street	c.1751	Roper, Thomas
	c.1769	Beckitt, Robert
	1820	Dobbins, Walter
	1830	Coles, Joseph
	1840	Matthews, Jemima
	1842	Turberville, John
Gardeners' Arms, Littleworth Street	1857	Brotherton, James
	c.1869	Langston, George
	c.1934	Huban, Mrs
	1934 – 1952	Tooley, Emily
	c.1953	Teague, R.A.
	c.1954	O'Hara, J.
George, 48 High Street	c.1577	Smythe, John
	c.1680	Broadstock, Rowland
	c.1685/1688	Michell, James
	to c.1701	Broadstock, Rowland (son)
	to c.1775	Welsborne, Charles (son)
George & Dragon, Bewdley Street	1835	Tomkins, John
	1836	Hunt, Mrs
	1837	Groves, Mrs
	1840	Brotherton, George
	1850	Boswell, Henry
	1863	Luxton, Mrs
	1873	Haines, Alfred
	1897	Haines, Sarah
	1901	Mustoe, George
	1902	Smith, George
	1903	Camkin, John
	1906	Nappin, Thomas
	1911 to 1927	Nappin, Mrs (later Mrs Tooley)
	c.1956	Huband, James
Goat, Merstow Green	1583	Hawkins, George

Inn	Date(s)	Name
Golden Cross, Vine Street	1729 – c.1745	Bayzand, John

Inn	Date(s)	Name
Golden Hart, Cowl Street	1787	Knowles, Thomas
	c.1835	New, Thomas
	1842	New, William
	1850	Gould, Joseph
	1852	Haines, Thomas
	1857	Dawes, Thomas
	1873	Brotherton, Charles
	1880	Price, William
	1897	Stanley, Walter
	1904	Major, Herbert
	1904 – 1930	Morton, Harry
	c.1930	Wilmot, Ernest S.

Inn	Date(s)	Name
Green Dragon, Oat Street	1817	Souch, Mr
	1835	Stephens, William
	c.1850	Stephens, John
	1897	Byrd, Harry
	1898	Stanley, G.
	1901	Jenks, H.J.
	1904	Vivian, G.S.
	1907	Porter, Joseph
	1920	Porter, Mrs
	1925	Ovard, Frank
	1935	Swinbourne, Leonard
	c.1950	Stanley, James

Inn	Date(s)	Name
Hop Pole, 1 Vine Street	1850	Williams, Charles

Inn	Date(s)	Name
Horse and Groom, Vine Street	c.1775	Tymbs, Samuel
	c.1825	Hands, James

Inn	Date(s)	Name
Horse Shoe, Bengeworth	1820	Watkins, Joseph

Inn	Date(s)	Name
Jolly Gardeners, 16 Bewdley Street	1873	Cooke, W.
	1894	Cooke, William (son)

Inn	Date(s)	Name
	1904	Sprosen, Louis
	1908	Dentith, C.
	1909	Pettit, Herbert
	1917	Huxley, George John
	1934	Brotherton, George James

Inn	Date(s)	Name
King's Arms, Bengeworth	1805	Harris, Mr

Inn	Date(s)	Name
King's Head, 60 High Street	1807	New, James
	c.1820	Lewis, John
	c.1846	Grove, William
	c.1846	Thorp, Jonathan
	c.1850	Memmory, Alfred James
	c.1860	Shenton, Frederick Shakespeare
	c.1870	Taylor, Thomas
	c.1880	Partington, Thomas
	1886	Coles, Wilson Herbert
	1898	Felton, J. Lloyd
	1901	Meadows, E.C.
	c.1909	Salmon, William

Inn	Date(s)	Name
Ledden Post, 16 and 17 High Street	c.1685	Bouts, Thomas
	c.1688	Bouts, Thomas (son)
	c.1692	Slatter, John

Inn	Date(s)	Name
Masons' Arms, Pershore Road	?	Grove, James

Inn	Date(s)	Name
Nag's Head, Vine Street	c.1750	Gardiner, John

Inn	Date(s)	Name
Navigation, Avonside	1840	Lightborne, John
	1873	Phillips, Charles
	1894	Leach, H.

Inn	Date(s)	Name
Nelson, Port Street	c.1815	Cook, John

Inn	Date(s)	Name
New Anchor, 1 Brick-kiln Street	1865	Callow, James
	c.1875	Brotherton, John

Inn	Date(s)	Name
	c.1895	Brotherton, G.J.
	c.1895	Sprosen, Louis
Oddfellows' Arm, Briar-close	1929	Spiers, Joseph
	to 1956	Spiers, Annie
Old Anchor, 3 Bewdley Street	1820 – 1854	Smith, Enoch
	1857	Simpson, John
	1863	Rogers, Charles
	1873	Watkins, John
	1894	Watkins, George
	1897	Grove, William
	1906	Smith, Arthur
	1907	Churchley, David
	c.1910	Smith, H.
	c.1920	Fisher, Miss
	c.1930	Short, Frank
	c.1940	Dingley, Frank
	c.1950	Nightingale, Jack
	c.1956	Halford, George
Old Red Horse, Vine Street	1820	Roper, Mary
	1835	Sheppard, S.
	1842	Parr, Henry
	1850	Hunting, Thomas
	1863	Groves, John
	1873	George, William
	1894	Brotherton, William
	1913	Brotherton, A.
	1920	Grove, W.
	1930	Hill, W.
	1935	Woods, F.
	1945	Gilbert, A.H.
	1953	Frankum, Raymond
Plough, Vine Street	1684	Gardner, William
	1790	Cook, Richard
	1820	Cull, J.

Inn	Date(s)	Name
	1835	Stratton, Charles Frederick
	1837	Walker, Thomas
	c.1850	Weightman, George
	1865	Kings, W.
	1873	Major, James
	1894	Phipps, John
	1901	Phipps, Mrs
	1902	Newbury, Louis
	c.1925	Newbury, Annie
	c.1926 – 1951	Morris, Hector C.
	1951 – 1956	Bladon, Edward
	1956	Andrew, Harry

Inn	Date(s)	Name
Plough and Harrow, 1 Vine Street	c.1812	Cull, James

Inn	Date(s)	Name
Prince of Wales, Bridge Street	1840	Keen, Joseph
	c.1850	Keen, Hannah

Inn	Date(s)	Name
Quart Pot, Bengeworth	1820	Wheeler, William

Inn	Date(s)	Name
Railway Hotel, High Street	1868	Meddings, John
	1880	Saunders, David
	1890	Saunders, H.
	1901	Smith, John
	1912	Wood, John Levi
	1920	Roberts, J.H.
	1930	Hiles, G.S.
	1935	Tigwell, H.L.
	c.1945	Hickman, F.G.
	c.1956	Doust, John E.
	1956	Stanley, J.

Inn	Date(s)	Name
Red Lion, 6 Market Place	1760	Tovey, Mrs
	1766	Burlingham, Mrs
	1835 - 1850	Smith, Joseph
	1865	Walker, Thomas
	1894	Byrd, George
	1897	Phipps, H.J.

Inn	Date(s)	Name
	1898	Stanley, T.
	1900 – 1908	Salmon, William
	1908 – 1910	Stafford, Frederick William

Inn	Date(s)	Name
Red Lion, Waterside	1655	Pittway, Edward

Inn	Date(s)	Name
Rose and Crown, High Street	1762	Warran, Hannah
	1820	Laurence, George
	1840	Sears, J.
	1842	Williams, William
	1850	Brotherton, George
	1870	Cox, William
	1873	Lawrence, Edward
	c.1890 – 1935	Partridge, J.R.
	c.1935 – 1949	Bell, George
	1949	Burton, J.A.

Inn	Date(s)	Name
Royal Oak, Vine Street	1818	Penny, William
	1840	George, W.
	1850	Melen, Thomas
	1873	Melen, Elizabeth
	1894	Nash, W.
	1898	Brotherton, C.
	1902	Bell, C.H.
	1908	Brearley, George
	1920	Bell, George
	1930	Grove, William
	c.1940	Grove, George
	c.1956	Grove, Kate
	c.1956	Streatfield, Mr

Inn	Date(s)	Name
Sheep's Head, New Street	c.1860	Kendrick, Bobby

Inn	Date(s)	Name
Shoe and Boot, Bengeworth	1785	Walker, John

Inn	Date(s)	Name
Star Hotel, High Street	1832	Bushell, William
	1842	Hughes, Richard Hemming
	1863	Butler, Samuel

Inn	Date(s)	Name
	1906	Taylor, H.
	1920	Morgan, H.W.
	1925	Jaynes, A.W.
	1935	Jones, F.
	1950	Dyke, F.J.A.
	1951	Morgan, E.F.

Inn	Date(s)	Name
Swan Hotel, Port Street	1807	Byrd, Elizabeth
	1829	Byrd, J.
	1851	Bedenham, John
	1863	Bedenham, Frederick
	1872 – 1903	Holder, F.A.
	1903 – 1910	Hicken, Alfred
	1910	Bell, W.
	1956	Bell, A.

Inn	Date(s)	Name
Swan Inn, High Street	1586	Freame, Edward
	1659	Gold, William
	c.1670	Gold, Nathaniel
	1711	Deacon, Martin
	1711	Gardner, George
	c.1724	Brown, Stephen
	c.1724	Johnson, Henry

Inn	Date(s)	Name
Talbot, Port Street	c.1570	Houlle, John
	1854	Baylis, Charles
	1856	Cull, Thomas
	1861	Schofield, Mr
	1873	Pitman, George
	1895	Pitman, Charles
	1898	Pitman, Mrs
	1908	Taylor, Thomas
	1910	Osborne, Thomas
	1915/25	Field, G.H.
	1930	Milward, A.A.
	1935	Shakles, Percy
	1940 – 1955	Matthews, J.
	1956	Teague, R.A.

Inn	Date(s)	Name
Three Crowns, Bridge Street	c.1750	Symonds, Benjamin

Inn	Date(s)	Name
Three Tuns,	1741	Field, Mrs

Inn	Date(s)	Name
Trumpet Inn, Merstow Green	1685	Harris, Thomas
	1813	Clements, Samuel
	1818	Drinkwater, William
	1863	Robbins, Joseph
	1866	Cooke, William
	1873	Iorns, John
	1880	Hughes, George 'Bodger'
	c.1925	Petitt, H.
	c.1930	Smith, S.
	1951	Brown, N.J.

Inn	Date(s)	Name
Unicorn, Port Street	1658	Woodward, William
	1724	Penny, Peter
	c.1765	Penny, William (son)

Inn	Date(s)	Name
Vauxhall Inn, Merstow Green	1859	Lawrence, Joseph
	1863	Careless, Richard
	1873	Cole, George
	1894 – 1898	Cole, George F.
	1898	Hill, C.E.
	1913	Porter, J.G.
	1920	Porter, A.J.
	1925	Bailey, James Spicer
	1935	Rodbourne, H.
	1941	Brotherton, G.
	1943	Vines, G.
	1950	Cowell, T.N.
	1952	Spiers, R.E.

Inn	Date(s)	Name
Vine, 54 Port Street	1858	Talbot, Thomas
	1898	Glassbrook, Thomas
	1906	Byrd, Harry
	1915	Ballard, R.B.

Inn	Date(s)	Name
	1916	Twist, C.H.
	1919	Haynes, Arthur

Inn	Date(s)	Name
Volunteer, Market Place	1840	Cole, John
	1850	Baylis, Sarah Maria
	1854	Millington, Thomas
	1864	Phophet, Mr
	1873	Goodall, F.W.
	c.1880	Adams, W.H.
	1894	Brotherton, Charles
	1909	Taylor, Thomas
	1928	Sallis, Frederick William

Inn	Date(s)	Name
White Hart, 19 Bridge Street	1684	Roberts, John
	c.1728	Powell, William
	1735	Cox, William
	1758	Cox, William (son)
	c.1795	White, Mr
	1818	Doyle, James
	1838	Smith, William

Inn	Date(s)	Name
White Hart, Cowl Street	1820 – 1842	Guion, James

Inn	Date(s)	Name
Why Not?, Cowl Street	1840	Gladwin, William

Inn	Date(s)	Name
Woolpack, Port Street	1818	Smith, William
	1830	Doyle, Sarah
	1850	Pugh, James
	1863/73	Matthews, Richard
	1894	Evans, Charles
	1904	Evans, Emily
	1909 – 1950	Evans, Frederick Charles
	1951	Smith, F.J.
	1957	Smith, Marion

Indexes

Index of Inns

Numbers in bold denote main articles. If an entry does not have a number in bold, the inn name is an alternative or previous name. Also see the article *A Catalogue of Inns*.

Index of Local People

The following index is based upon the occurrence of names closely connected with Evesham (excluding Emperors, Kings, Abbots, Saints, Prime Ministers, etc., but including mayors and M.P.s).

Mayors and M.P.s are also included in the General Index.

Different people sharing the same name may be included under one entry.

Kinsey, Mr 58

Kitchner, Thomas 58

Knight, Ann 136

Knowles, Ann 90

Knowles, John 90

Knowles, Thomas 101, 102

Koush, John 18

Kyte, G.V. 47

L

Langston, George 85

Langston, Sam 85

Langstone, Anthony 12

Langstone, Mr 171

Laurence, George 150

Lavender, Mr 174

Lawford, Mary 97

Lawrence, Edward 150

Lawrence, Joseph 178

Leach, H. 120

Leech, Samuel 80

Legitt, K.H. 120

Lehmann, Frederick 144

Leigh, Theophilus 153

Leslie, Dr. 129

Lewis, John 115

Lightborne, John 120

Liley, Mr 100

Lloyd, Mrs 129

Long, Colonel 129

Lucas, Charles 81

Lunn, Mr 174

Luxton, Benjamin 44, 58

Luxton, Mrs 91

Lydeat, Richard 89

Lygon, Mrs 182

Lynal, Michael 102

Lysons, Daniel 153

M

Machin, F.J. 129

Major, Herbert 103

Major, James 138

Major, Thomas Anthony 72

Mann, Sergeant 131

Manning, William 140

Maries, Edith 31

Maries, H.C. 125

Marshall, Arthur 40

Martin, Jane 153

Martin, Robert 148, 149

Martin, Thomas 60

Master, H. 112

Masters, Henry 158

Masters, Joseph 164

Matthews, George 191

Matthews, J. 169

Matthews, J.H. 129

Matthews, Jemima 84

Matthews, Joshua 44

Matthews, Mrs 169

Matthews, Richard 35, 36, 194

Matthews, Samuel 73

Matthews, William 36

Mayer, H.W. 69

Mayfield, John 129

Mayo, Richard 84

Mayor, J. 129

McHugh, Mr. 70

Meadows, E.C. 116

Meadows, U.C. 58

Meddings, John 143

Melen, Elizabeth 155

Melen, Thomas 154

Memmory, Alfred James 116

Michell, James 40, 41, 86, 88, 90

Michell, Margaret 41

Michell, Matthew 13

Index of Local Places

This index does not include well-known places such as the High Street or All Saints.

A

Abbey Gardens..........................46, 134
Abbey Gate..............................61, 151
Abbey Manor...................................64
Alley, The..........................76, 99, 183
Almonry.................69, 133, 151, 167
Almswood.....................................191
Avonside Turnpike Road...............175

B

Badsey Lane..................................141
Baptist Chapel, Cowl Street.....61, 164
Battleton Bridge.................33, 47, 120
Battlewell..4
Bell Tower.....17, 49, 65, 72, 114, 130, 139
Bench Hill.....................................112
Benge Hill....................................175
Bengeworth Bridge........122, 175, 193
Bengeworth Castle............37, 93, 168
Berryfield.....................................119
Bewdley Stile Lane........................152
Bishop's Corner.............................141
Black Lane....................................152
Blaney's Lane..................................62
Borthwick Street..............................45
Borthwick Terrace...........................45
Brick-kiln Street..............................87
Bridge Foot...................................100
Britain Street (footnote)...................87
Brittayne Street................................87
Bug Alley..48
Burford Road...........................38, 124
Burlingham's wharf..........................47
Butcher Row....................................48

C

Cambria Road..................................47
Capon Lane......................................86
Caponpot Lane.................................87
Charnel House....................................9
Cheltenham Road.............47, 120, 193
Church Bank....................................74
Church of the Blessed Trinity........168
Clark's Hill......................................78
Clarke's Hill..................................179
Clarke's Hill Farm........................100
Cotswold House.............................191
Cross Churchyard.............................60
Cross Keys Lane.............................191

D

Donneybrook..................................166
Dresden House...42, 43, 114, 169, 192
Drury Lane (footnote)......................25

E

Elm, The..73
Evesham Turnpike..........................112

F

Fairfield Cottages.....................36, 125
Fairwater......................................129
Fairways.......................................112
Falcon Hotel and Hydro...................54
Farmers' Hall................................120
Fleece Meadow..............................101
Four Corners....................................76
Four Corners of Hell........................30

G

Gallows Hill..................................113

Index of Local Businesses

This index includes local companies and businesses mentioned in the book.

Index of References

The following index includes general works (but excluding the *Evesham Journal*) mentioned in the main body of the book.

General Index

This index includes people, events and places mentioned in the book but not included in previous indexes.

Lightning Source UK Ltd.
Milton Keynes UK
16 September 2009

143752UK00001B/38/P

9 780955 848728